Explor...

NELLES

KENYA

Authors:
Eva Ambros, Angela Anchieng, Zdenka Bondzio, Michie Gitau,
Eric Hanna, Jean Hartley, Brigitte Henninges, Clive Mutiso,
Clement Obare, Osaga Odak, Philip Okwaro, Mourine Wambugu,
Rupert Watson

*An Up-to-date travel guide with 153 color photos
and 14 maps*

**Second Revised Edition
1996**

Dear Reader,

Being up-to-date is the main goal of the Nelles series. To achieve it, we have a net-work of far-flung correspondents who keep us abreast of the latest developments in the travel scene, and our cartographers always make sure that maps and texts are adjusted to each other.

Each travel chapter ends with its own list of useful tips, accommodations, restaur-ants, tourist offices, sights. At the end of the book you will find practical information from A to Z. But the travel world is fast moving, and we cannot guarantee that all the contents are always valid. Should you come across a discrepancy, please write us at:

Nelles Verlag GmbH, Schleissheimer Str. 371 b, D-80935 München, Germany.

LEGEND

						National Border
✈	Place of Interest	🏖	Beach			Expressway
▪	Public or Significant Building	Kilaguni	Place Mentioned in Text			Principal Highway (mainly asphalt)
■ ⌂ ⋀	Hotel, Lodge, Camp	🐘	National Park			Highway (unpaved)
●	Restaurant, Casino	✈	International Airport			Provincial Road (partly paved)
○	Market	✈	National Airport			Secondary Road, Track, Path
✝ ☪	Church, Mosque	✈	Landing Strip			Railway
✡	Synagogue	A14	Route number			
৬	Hindu Temple	Kitumbeine 2865	Mountain Summit (Height in Meters)	\18/		Distance in Kilometers
◡	Water source					

KENYA
© Nelles Verlag GmbH, 80935 München
   All rights reserved

Second Revised Edition 1996
ISBN 3-88618-052-2
Printed in Slovenia

Publisher:	Günter Nelles	**Editor in Charge:**	M. Radkai
			G. Theato
Editor in Chief:	Berthold Schwarz	**Cartography:**	Nelles Verlag GmbH,
Project Editor:	Clive Mutiso		München
Project		**Color Separation:**	Scannerstudio
Coordination:	Hans H. Koschany		Schaller, München
Translation:	Roger Rosko	**Printed by:**	Gorenjski Tisk

   - X03 -

TABLE OF CONTENTS

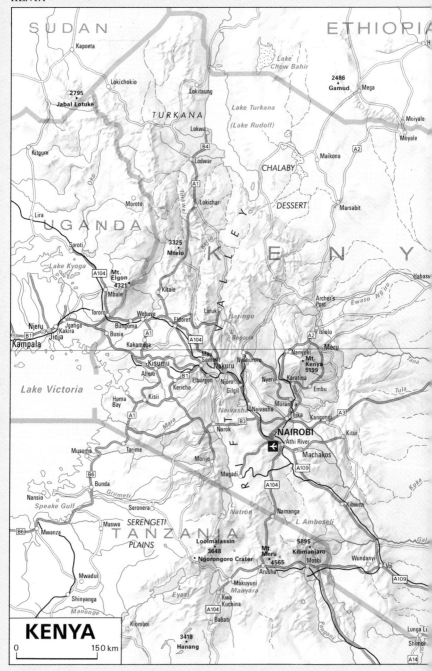

KENYA

0 |_____| 150 km

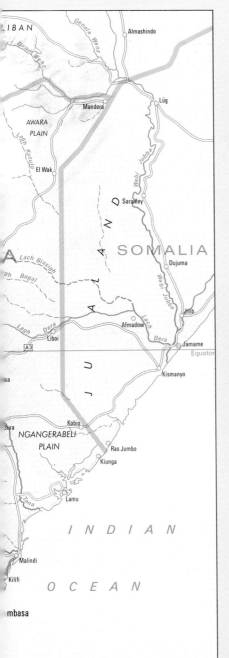

LIST OF MAPS

HISTORY OF

KENYA

Kenya's history is just as diverse as its landscape. The original population of this section of East Africa now called Kenya played as much a role in the course of its history as the various waves of immigrants from Europe, Asia and other African countries.

Kenya's history and culture begins all the way back in prehistoric times. Archeological and paleoanthropological finds from Rusinga Island in Lake Victoria, at Fort Ternan and at Lake Turkana are evidence that the much-discussed "cradle of humanity" was indeed in East Africa. The excavators have discovered all of the significant evolutionary stages of humanity, from primitive man to *homo sapiens*. One of the most important sites for such finds is the Lake Turkana region, where stone tools and skeletal remains with ages of over two million years have been discovered. The prehistoric development of humanity and its culture in East Africa can be subdivided into three major epochs: the Stone Age, Neolithic Age and Iron Age.

Earliest Discoveries in Koobi Fora

The Stone Age began in the area of today's Kenya roughly two million years ago and was succeeded by the Neolithic Age about 10,000 years ago. The Iron Age commenced some 2000 years ago, and only came to an end with the colonization of East Africa.

The Stone Age itself is subdivided into the Paleolithic and Middle Stone Age;

Preceding pages: Elephants dwarfed by the Kilimanjaro. Sundown on the steppes. Herd of gnus. Left: Defending Fort Jesus, Mombasa.

these in turn are made up of various individual periods. The earliest phase of the Paleolithic Period, the Old Paleolithic, is characterized by tools made of fist-sized stones and chips of rock. The oldest pieces of evidence from this period were found in Koobi Fora, to the east of Lake Turkana; they are around two million years old. The second phase, the so-called Neopaleolithic, began approximately one million years ago. Typical for this period are tools honed on two sides, such as the ones excavated at Olorgesailie (near Lake Magadi) and in Kariandusi on Lake Elementaita. The archeologists have left their discoveries in the places they were originally found, so that today the excavation sites, which are accessible to everybody, have become an interesting open-air museum.

The Middle Stone Age is typified by the appearance of improved methods in the production of stone tools. These allowed for the creation of smaller, better shaped and refined pieces. Roughly 15,000 years ago, even more advanced techniques in the production of tools were commonplace, indicating the commencement of the final phase of the Stone Age. Prevalent during this period were various types of very small tools, called microliths in the vernacular. The leading fossil is a small sickle with a sharp cutting edge. In addition there are awls for sewing as well as specialized tools for scraping and carving.

The Neolithic Age is the period of greatest significance for the history of humanity. Namely, in the course of this period the old hunter-gatherer cultures started cultivating crops and domesticating animals. This meant the revolutionary step from a life hunting and gathering to tending to herds and farming the land. There is in fact no direct evidence of the existence of agricultural peoples in Kenya during the earliest phase of the Neolithic Age, although that much more for the presence of tribes living from

15

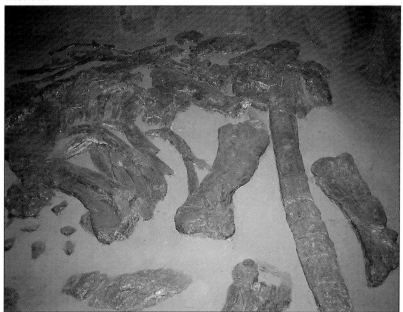

herding. Discoveries of animal bones indicate that cattle, sheep and goats were already among the domesticated species. Tools and utensils used included polished stone blades for axes of various design, microliths and other stone tools, millstones, bowls and plates of stone, pottery, wooden vessels and beads of bone, pebbles and seeds. The ceramics also exhibit a diversity in size and form, and the types of decoration applied on them are also highly variable, with a preference for grooves and simple stamping techniques.

The Iron Age

The Iron Age is the period which was first and foremost marked by the impact of the new material iron and its manifold possible applications in toolmaking and arms technology. Since in the course of time iron corrodes, the archeologists rela-

Above: A skeleton and tools, remains from prehistory in the Nairobi Museum. Right: Prehistoric murals.

tively seldom find any well-preserved articles made of it. However, deposits of iron slag and the discovery of special tubes used as bellows nozzles offer enough significant evidence of iron working and its related techniques. Alongside these, isolated iron tools have also been brought to light, although much more common from this period are artifacts of stone, ceramic and beads as well as sheep, goat and cattle bone. Ceramic articles are the most significant group of discoveries in that they permit the archeologist to perform a fine chronological dating of this era.

The early Iron Age is characterized by pottery, decorated with fine grooves and fluting, that form indentations and reliefs with rounded off triangles at the bottom. A second group of Iron Age ceramics originates from the end of the first millenium A.D., and is apparently limited to the area of the Turkwell Basin, where the individual vessels were decorated with grooves in varying graduations. There is a third group from central Kenya the dis-

tinguishing features of which are that the vessels are worked with a simple stamping technique for the most part.

The Immigrants

Kenya's non-African ethnic groups made their first appearance with the Arabians of the 7th century, at first only as a consequence of the developing trade connections between the East African coast and the Orient. However, the rise of Islam and tumult taking place in countries including Oman, Iran and Syria ultimately led to a great wave of immigration into the coastal areas of East Africa. The immigration of Moslem Arabs can be established as early as the 8th century A.D. The ancestors of the present-day Swahili ethnic group were the product of interbreeding between the Moslem immigrants and the indigenous population. The trade between East Africa and the Middle East – in fact, even the Far East – experienced a huge upswing in the following centuries. When early European explorers landed on the coast in the 15th century (the first to come were the Portuguese), the wealthy urban cultures already had three centuries of a blossoming period behind them, whose legacy is still in evidence today in the mosques and the ancient buildings and cities constructed of stone on the East African coast.

Very much later, during the course of the European exploration of Africa and the establishment of missions and colonial settlements, great numbers of Europeans and other nationalities arrived, predominantly Englishmen, Indians and Pakistanis.

Swahili and Azani Cultures

The trading relations of the coastal inhabitants with the Islamic world and other oriental peoples like the Chinese, Indians or Indonesians branded the indigenous civilization with some very special features. The result was Swahili culture, whose intellectual fulcrum is the Islamic world-view. Swahili architecture in

Kenya is typified by buildings of coral limestone with unique *makuti* roofs of palm fronds.

The trading centers of the Swahilis lay scattered along the entire coastline, where they developed into regular city-states. These altogether more than 20 coastal cities existed independently of each other, even if they were repeatedly entering into new alliances, in which one city would dominate one day, and another the next. Thus, for example, in the course of history Pate, Lamu and Faza alternated in their role of most powerful city on the east coast.

The inhabitants of these city-states manufactured ceramics and iron-mongeries, and created masterpieces of architectural engineering such as are seen in Manda, where a wall was erected using monolithic coral blocks, each of which weighed more than a ton.

Above: The ruins of the town of Gedi, one of the significant excavation sites. Right: The veil is part of the Islamic heritage on Lamu.

During the 11th century there was a flourishing iron works in the Lamu Archipelago, and indeed iron was one of the most important trade commodities. During this period new Arabic settlements were continuously popping up, and consequently Swahili culture increasingly got caught up in the Islamic sphere of influence.

Parallel to the blossoming of the Swahili culture, the so-called Azani culture developed in Kenya. It went in a completely different direction, in that its characteristic features were African through and through. Among the legacies left by the Azanis are stone palaces and monumental fortifications. Archeologists have found traces of stone walls, cavities in the ground, the so-called sirikwa holes, in addition to ruins of stone buildings, ancient irrigation systems and indications of terrace agriculture.

The Azani culture's area of dissemination included great portions of the Kenyan interior, in particular the Rift Valley and the western highlands. Several traces

of its later features can be found in the South Nyanza District and among the Bukusu in the more remote regions of western Kenya. Found in this area are the so-called Bukusu forts, which so very clearly display signs of the influence of the Azani culture.

The Portuguese Hegemony

The first Europeans to land on the Kenyan coast were the Portuguese, who ultimately brought about the downfall of Swahili rule. The famous explorer and mariner Vasco da Gama landed in Malindi with his fleet in 1498 on his search for a sea route to India. He was followed by many more of his countrymen. Allured by the riches of the East African coast, they sailed around the southern tip of Africa, plundered the affluent city-states and ultimately took over political control for some 200 years.

One of the most successful Portuguese was Francisco d'Almeida, who moved against Mombasa in 1505 with 23 ships and subjugated the city after a grisly battle. The city of Malindi conducted itself diplomatically, and true to its motto: "The enemies of Mombasa are the friends of Malindi" gave the Portuguese a very friendly reception. Economically, things went downhill for the coastal cities under Portuguese hegemony. The previously flourishing trade with the Arab countries was taken over by the Portuguese for themselves and channeled to Europe via Portugal. Any resistance from the natives was ruthlessly suppressed. Mombasa, where Fort Jesus had defied enemy attacks since 1593, became the most important stronghold of the Portuguese on the coast of East Africa.

The New Masters of the Coast

The position of the Portuguese was weakened by repeated armed insurgencies by the native population as well as by epidemics and difficulties resulting from their overextended supply lines. In 1696, the Sultanate of Oman, which was

also under Portuguese domination, made an alliance with the local rulers of Mombasa to stage a rebellion. Fort Jesus fell in 1698 after a fifteen-month long siege. Then it was the victorious party from Oman who called the tune on the East African coast.

However, the Omanis, though Moslems like the Swahili, were soon suppressing the coastal inhabitants just as unscrupulously as their predecessors. Following a brief phase of cooperation, antipathy towards them increased very rapidly, and the population reacted once again with rebellions. Omanis held onto power nonetheless. In 1828 they relocated their capital to Zanzibar and gradually established domestic trade as their domain. Whereas ivory was the most important commodity at the beginning, the slave trade soon developed into the most lucrative source of revenue. In 1836, dealers from Zanzibar had already ad-

Above: Waiters in the Hunter's Bar, dressed in old-fashioned fashions.

vanced as far as the Wakikuyu region, and by 1854 had even left the borders of Kenya behind them and begun establishing contacts in Uganda. Bribed with weapons and glass beads, the chiefs cast their fellow tribal members into slavery. By the end of the 19th century, several million African slaves, coming primarily from West Africa, had been deported to the southern states of the USA, Brazil and the Carribean as well as to Zanzibar.

The influence of the Omanis continued to increase as the French and British occupied the Réunion Islands, Mauritius and the Seychelles, thus opening up new markets for slaves. Great Britain's commitment in the battle against the slave trade which followed was certainly not based on purely humanistic grounds, but served as a convenient pretext to establish themselves on the East African coast and seize control of the Omani Empires' trade routes. Slavery was officially forbidden in 1873, though it took almost another two decades before the flourishing trade finally came to a standstill.

As tumultuous as the history along the coast was in the 19th century, for centuries the course of inland events was quite unsensational. Ethnic or tribal interaction only took place between African peoples who either subsisted from agriculture and livestock breeding or roved across the land as nomads.

Exploratory Voyages

In the 19th century, the "unexplored" regions of the African interior lured German and British missionaries, explorers, traders and scientists to East Africa. The Germans Krapf and Rebmann reported of the snow-capped Mount Kilimanjaro; the Englishmen Burton and Speke forged ahead to Lake Tanganyika, after which Speke made it as far as Lake Victoria without his partner, who had fallen ill; the Scotsman Thomson travelled the Masai regions and Count Teleki reached a huge lake in the north which he then named Lake Rudolf (now Lake Turkana) for the then-crown prince of Austria.

The knowledge these explorers assembled about Kenya laid the foundations for its later colonization. The missionaries didn't bring exclusively positive things to the so-called Dark Continent either. They destroyed the existing social fabric, convinced of the notion that the only right forms of religion and lifestyle were European. Parallel to this, British and German trade corporations concluded contracts locally with the tribal chiefs. These later formed the basis for the territorial claims of their respective home countries. In this manner, Carl Peters founded the German-East African Company and forced the chiefs to conclude so-called "protective contracts" by applying more or less brutal methods.

The Colonial Powers' Plaything

The territorial claims of Great Britain and Germany brought about considerable diplomatic activity. Under the terms of the Helgoland Treaty, Great Britain secured its dominion over Zanzibar, Kenya and Uganda. In exchange, Germany received the theretofore British Helgoland and Tanganyika. Still, the rulers of both European countries could take pleasure in the fact that each possessed one of Africa's snow-capped mountains: Kilimanjaro for Kaiser Wilhelm and Mount Kenya for Queen Victoria. The borders that were established at that time still exist in large part today.

At first, the British governed their new protectorate, British East Africa, from Zanzibar. However, in reality they more or less left the administrative functions to the *Imperial British East African Company*, which had, for example, to concern itself with the imposition and collection of taxes. Trading posts were established that were to make the exploitation of the economic resources more feasible. Furthermore, in Uganda there were profits in store from the ivory trade; the problem, however, was transporting it from the interior to the coasts.

To begin with, a railroad route was to connect Mombasa with Port Florence, the present-day Kisumu. The work began in 1896. This railroad line, which was later extended to Uganda, was primarily intended to reduce transportation costs and thus contribute to the development of plantation agriculture. The railroad was accompanied into the country by the telephone and telegraph as well. Its construction through the wild regions of East Africa brought many challenges and hardships with it, whether it was the steep slopes of the Rift Valley, man-eating lions or epidemics and surprise attacks by natives. The majority of the over 30,000 laborers came from India, whereas the local population derived precious little benefit from the gigantic project.

The extremely high costs of the railroad had to be amortized, so the previously inaccessible highland was pub-

licized as a farming and settlement region. As a result, innumerable immigrants flooded into Kenya, hailing primarily from Great Britain, but also from other European countries. The majority of them were farmers who then appropriated huge landed estates for themselves in the "White Highlands", the name they coined for this fertile region, which was supposed to remain in the clutches of the white settlers.

The European colonists did not limit their land grabbing to those uninhabited regions between the tribal lands. The African population was ruthlessly driven away, and for many of them the only alternative left was to enter into the service of the white farmers. The military superiority of the Europeans also left the indigenous population scarcely a prayer of putting up resistance. An additional act of suppression was the compulsory registra-

tion of Africans, with the stipulation that they were to carry an identification card, the *kipande*.

The white colonial rulers played their role with tremendous success. A lot more than sufficient cheap labor stood at their disposal, the colonial government was always ready to help out with subsidies, and the timid grumbling from Europe concerning the exploitation of the African population hardly reached any important ears.

The political ringleader of the settlers was the legendary Lord Delamere, who, however, was consistently in the front line of his "Kenya cowboys" when it came to riotous debaucheries as well.

But not only farmers came to East Africa in those days. The country also attracted hunters and adventurers, who had heard tell of its immeasurable hunting grounds, as well as some rather prominent tourists, among them personalities from major league – politics like US President Theodore Roosevelt and Sir Winston Churchill.

Above: The first railroad in Kenya dates from 1896. Right: Woodcarving is one of the major handicrafts practised in Kenya.

In the meanwhile, Great Britain had relocated the administration from Zanzibar to Mombasa, and, in 1907, yet again, to the former railroad base of Nairobi. When the First World War broke out it didn't remain without its consequences in East Africa either. Indeed, the British and Germans had a common border in this area, rendering a confrontation virtually unavoidable.

The patriotism of the British caused a large part of the settlers to hurry to arms. They advanced together with African recruits against the Germans, who stood under the command of Paul von Lettow-Vorbeck, on ponies disguised as zebras. Ultimately, their campaign failed, since Lettow-Vorbeck managed to stand his ground against his superior opponents with subterfuge and cunning until the end of the war.

After the war's end the white settlers consolidated their positions yet further. For example they prolonged their claims to the landed estates from a previous 99 years to 999 years. An additional influx

of British immigrants intensified these developments. Ever increasing amounts of the Kikuyu's lands in particular were occupied by the farmers.

In 1920, Kenya officially became a British crown colony – with the exception of the coastal strip, which had remained in the possession of the Sultan of Zanzibar, although this was considered a British area of tenancy.

In response to drastic economic crises, in 1921 the wages of Africans were cut. In addition, they were forbidden to cultivate lucrative export fruits in order to increase their dependence. Besides the natives, other people of color, including the Indian population, were forbidden to settle in the White Highlands. However, the white settlers failed to achieve their goal, the transformation of the colony into a self-governed "White Kenya". In 1923, the British government decreed that Kenya was an African country and that therefore the interests of the African were to be put first. But the reality was to remain otherwise for a long while yet.

23

The Road to Independence

Now the Africans reacted with an organized political protest for the first time. One of its outcomes was the foundation of the Young Wakikuyu Association was founded, from which sprang the East African Association. The organization was soon forbidden, though, and its leader, Harry Thuku, was arrested. The fact that the Kikuyu were the first to put up resistance against the policies of colonialism was primarily because they were suffering most from the land expropriations. Other political groups and parties followed, especially in West Kenya. They were also organized along lines of tribal membership.

Between 1932 and 1938, a multitude of anti-colonialist movements fighting for the return of expropriated lands was established throughout the country. The call for independence, *uhuru* in Swahili, could no longer be silenced. Jomo Kenyatta, one of the leaders of the whole independence movement from the very beginning, headed a delegation that went to London in 1929 in order to discuss the interests of the Africans.

One thing that contributed to the intensification of the struggle for independence was that in 1914, the British had recruited Africans into their army, a measure which they repeated in 1939. The black soldiers, who had served in Kenya, Ethiopia, India and Burma, were experienced fighting men upon their return, and they knew that the time had come to assert their rights. Ultimately, the systematic political battle of the Africans forced a number of concessions from the colonial rulers. In 1944, Eliud Mathu became the first African appointee to the legislative chamber. In 1946,

Right: The future Queen Elizabeth II stayed at the Treetop Lodge in 1952. Far right: A Mau Mau warrior depiction, symbolizing Kenyatta.

Mathu established the first political movement to be effective beyond tribal boundaries, the Kenya African Association, later renamed the Kenya Africa Union, or KAU. The organization demanded of the colonial government the abrogation of the *kipande* system, the establishment of tuition-free schooling and permission to settle in the White Highlands. However, London simply turned a deaf ear to them. In the same year, Jomo Kenyatta, after having lived almost 16 years in England, returned to Kenya and was elected president of the KAU.

The social and economic situation embittered increasing numbers of young Kikuyus, who joined together in secret associations. They started a guerilla war against the government which has gone down in history by the name "Mau Mau Rebellion". Although the Kenya Africa Union didn't participate in the armed struggle, it was certainly the intention of the government, to discredit it and its rapidly increasing following by saying of the Union that it had a connection to the guerilla murders of white settlers.

On October 20, 1952, the government declared a state of national emergency and had various KAU leaders thrown in jail. In 1953, the prisoners, including Jomo Kenyatta, were put on trial in Kapenguria and sentenced to seven years forced labor. There followed years of desperate revolt against the colonial government. Grisly reports of the atrocities committed by the Mau Mau rebels were beamed around the world.

The facts, however, speak against these stories. Indeed, more than 10,000 Kikuyu and Mau-Mau rebels paid with their lives in comparison to 95 people of European heritage who died in the course of the rebellion. Furthermore, tens of thousands of African were interned in detention camps. In this manner, the British managed to contain the revolt, but only at great cost and with extreme brutality.

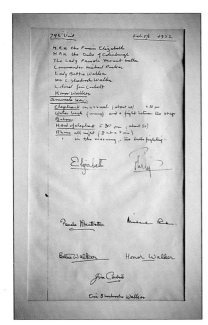

The turning point came in 1956: From that time on the British were ready to talk with the Africans. The political battle assumed diplomatic guise. A series of meetings were held with representatives of all concerned groups. In the course of the discussions it became clear that the real point was to create a suitable climate for a declaration of independence under a popularly elected government.

The Littleton Plan certainly had all the earmarks of racism, nonetheless it was a decisive step toward proportional African representation in the legislative chamber. Thus, following the 1957 election, eight additional Africans were entitled to represent their respective people in parliament, among them a young activist by the name of Daniel Arap Moi, who had been looking after the KAU leaders.

The Littleton Plan was soon dropped by the wayside, and replaced in 1958 by the Lennox-Boyd Constitution, which increased the number of African seats in the chamber to 16. As a result, in 1959, a number of new African parties were formed that demanded independence and the release of Jomo Kenyatta and the other KAU leaders.

In April 1960, the government suspended its emergency powers, opening up the possibility of beginning negotiations for independence. This round of discussions earned the Africans the right to send 33 representatives to the legislative chamber, and entitled them to four of thirteen ministerial posts.

In 1960, the Kenya African National Union, or KANU, was established under the leadership of James Gichuru, followed shortly thereafter by the competing Kenya African Democratic Union, or KADU. The ascent of the KADU was helped by the fact that the smaller tribes were worried that the KANU – dominated by the stronger tribal groups of the Wakikuyu and Luo – would fail to represent the interests of the minorities. Finally the two parties reached an agreement, whereby after the election a coalition government would be formed and the ministerial posts distributed proportionally.

In May 1963, the first general elections were held. The KANU was victorious, and Jomo Kenyatta became the first prime minister. The country was granted sovereignty over all domestic affairs with the exception of the military budget and foreign policy, which remained in the hands of the British government. Kenya didn't receive full independence until December 12, 1963. Kenyatta remained president until his death in 1978.

Uhuru and Harambee

Uhuru and *harambee*, independence and cooperation, have been the catchwords for the development of present-day Kenya. Freedom from the grips of British colonialism had been yearned for long enough, but the difficulties posed in forming a single state out of the many ethnic groups were not to be easily overcome. A period of Africanization began.

Above: Kenya's coat of arms. Right: Jomo Kenyatta, Kenya's first president.

Nor was the redistribution of settlement land without its problems. It's true that in the framework of a land reform package 600,000 hectares were apportioned to some 50,000 farmers, but additional allocations which had been announced failed to materialize. Furthermore, the larger farms went primarily to rich Kikuyus. The Europeans' holdings were not expropriated, although they were forbidden to acquire any new land, and Asians were unable to get any new business licenses unless they took Kenyan citizenship. The replacement of the Europeans in the leading positions of the economy and government has been carried out only slowly. Even today their central role in important sectors of the economy bears no relationship to their proportion of the population. Rivalries between parties' capitalist and socialist wings were just as much a part of the agenda as tribal feuds in the parliamentary assemblies of the young republic.

A civil war that was fought in the northeastern section of the country caused heavy losses; it was brought about because the Somalis of the *Shifta* movement, supported by Somalia, had demanded their independence.

In 1969, bloody conflicts arose between the Luo and Kikuyu following the assassination by a Kikuyu of the Luo politician Tom Mboya.

Kenya's political problems were not solved with the achievement of independence. Critics even from within the government were relieved of their posts, and demonstrations stifled while still in the germination phase. New elections were repeatedly announced, then postponed.

When Jomo Kenyatta, Kenya's first president, died at the mighty age of eighty years, he was succeeded by Daniel Arap Moi. The new president declared war on corruption and nepotism, and declared an amnesty for political prisoners.

Nonetheless, things didn't change substantially. The army stepped back onto the scene when riots broke out in the country's north as a consequence of a severe famine. An attempted coup by the air force (supported by students at Nairobi University) was quashed, and when his powerful rival Charles Njonjo was accused and sentenced for corruption, Moi granted him a reprieve anyway.

Establishing a genuine democracy in Kenya poses just as many problems now as ever, and the East African state is still being charged with violating human rights. Since the elections of 1993, however, the nation is under a multi-party system. But the president is still Daniel Arap Moi and the ruling party the KANU.

A Troubled Future?

Despite these difficulties, Kenya comes out quite well in comparison with its African neighbors and is still considered one of the most politically and economically stable countries on the con-

tinent. Be this as it may, Kenya's social contradictions can hardly be overlooked either.

Admittedly there are no race problems of the sort found in South Africa – the strictest lines of racial segregation run between Africans and Indians. However, as ever, the contrasts between economic classes are momentous. Even today there are practically no poor white people. The black plutocracy is more concerned with expanding its holdings than caring for the general prosperity. This becomes only too apparent in the fancy residential areas of Nairobi, which stand in blatant contrast to the city's slums, out of which advancement on the stratified social ladder is scarcely possible.

The legacy of the past millenia, the wealth of the animal world and its grandiose landscape make of Kenya a fascinating country; one can only express the hope that the future will be kind on its hospitable inhabitants and lead them out of their manifold social and economic predicaments.

27

KENYA'S PEOPLE
AND CULTURES

As manifold as its landscape is, so are the inhabitants of Kenya, within whose national territory some 25 million people coexist divided up into over 40 different ethnic groups. Modern Kenya is a country of contrasts, not only with a view to its geographic and climatic conditions, but also as concerns the ethnic diversity of its population. Africans from every region of the continent are living here together with the descendants of immigrants from Europe and Asia.

The Kenyan people of our days are the product of a variety of waves of immigration that have taken place in the past centuries, and to a certain extent during modern times as well. In the millenia past, it was tribes from throughout Africa that migrated into this fertile region in the continent's eastern reaches. They can therefore be viewed as the ancestors of all the African ethnic groups in modern Kenya.

Among the largest of the African immigrant groups were the Bantu, who came from the west and southwest to East Africa in several waves. The Kikuyu are also among the Bantu-speaking peoples; today they form the largest tribe in Kenya with over three million members. On the other hand, speakers of Nilotic and Cushitic languages came in from the north and northeast of the continent.

The Cushitic groups forced their way south from their homelands on the Somalian peninsula, waging numerous battles in the process, and ultimately driving out the Bantu and Arabs of their hereditary coastal settlements. Having achieved

Preceding pages: Mount Kilimanjaro, Africa's highest mountain, lies in Tanzania, but overshadows Kenya. Left: Kikuyu woman.

this, they swerved westward toward Kenya's interior.

The Cushitic language group is clearly divided into two subgroups. To the larger of these belong the Somalis, nomadic shepherds who settled in the eastern portion of Kenya's northeastern arid region. The tribes of the second subgroup live in the western portion of the region just mentioned; among the most important of these are the Rendille and the Orma. The speakers of the Cushitic languages inhabit a region unsuitable for farming, therefore their existence as herdsmen is an adaptation to the difficult environmental conditions they face. In recent years they have had to step up their efforts in their struggle against a marked deterioration of their living conditions. The increasing exploitation of the soil by both humans and livestock has had very adverse effects on the fragile surface vegetation that serves as a vital, protective cover. The net result has been an increase in desertification.

Even today, the Bantus, whose languages belong to the Niger-Congo linguistic stock, still represent the largest African population group in Kenya. According to the 1989 census, the Bantu peoples compose more than 60 percent of the aggregate population, and all indications are that this figure will continue to increase yet further in the coming years, due to their relatively high birth rate and a simultaneously low mortality rate. The Bantu peoples are presently concentrated south of an imaginary line between Mount Elgon and the city of Lamu on the Indian Ocean. They primarily appear in three geographic regions within this area: the Lake Victoria basin, the East Rift Highlands and in the coastal belt.

Among the main Bantu groups alongside the Kikuyu are the Embu, the Meru, the Mbere, the Wakamba and the Thakara. These tribes primarily inhabit the fertile central highlands, which extend from the Nyambene Hills in the Meru

31

District and along the northern and southern slopes of Mount Kenya to the first foothills of the impressive Nyandarua Mountains.

Roughly speaking, the remaining Kenyans of African heritage can be classified into two further linguistic groups – the Nilotic and Cushitic. The Nilotic groups include the Luo, Kalenjin, Maasai and related tribes. The Kalenjin and related Maasai groups were originally pastoral folk who traversed almost the entire land in a series of north-south migrations. In the course of these, they came in contact with the Cushitic groups living in the northern arid regions. Later these migrations were stopped, for the most part, by the large-scale agriculture of the whites. Nowadays these former herdsmen are mostly occupied with farming.

It is worth noting that no single tribe in Kenya can claim dominance over the

Above: Turkana woman with child. Right: The huts framing Lake Turkana are still built in the traditional manner.

others. The Bantu group is indeed the largest in terms of numbers, however, due to their cultural and geographical fragmentation they play virtually no role as a political force. The Kikuyu are the single largest tribe, but they make up only 20 percent of the total population. The seven largest tribes – the Kikuyu, Luhya, Luo, Wakamba, Kalenjin, Kisii and Meru – have altogether an 81.3 percent share of the population. With their 60 percent, the Bantu-speaking tribes fare rather well when compared to the representation of the Nilotic linguistic groups.

The borders of the young state of Kenya are a product of the colonial period, when English and Germans divided up East Africa according to their own ideas and for their own purposes. In doing so they paid no attention to the ancestral land rights of the local inhabitants. Nor, as a result, do the national frontiers of Kenya correspond to the settlement areas of the tribes. For example, the migration roads of the Masai – which they have crossed as nomads for generations – extend far into neighboring Tanzania.

Ethnic Migrations

The first inhabitants of Kenya were hunter-gatherers who lived in the open savannahs and dryer forested regions. These groups can scarcely be fit into ethnic classifications. It can be maintained that the Cushitic groups that migrated to the south from the Ethiopian highlands had already reached the region of present-day northern Tanzania by the beginning of the Christian Era, and were then driven away by Nilotic groups and the Bantus. It has also been established that, as early as the period around 6000 B.C., a perceptible change had begun in the means of subsistence, from the hunter-gatherer culture to the cultivation of crops. Furthermore, around 1000 B.C., pastoral tribes were scattered over Kenya and throughout the whole of East Africa.

These developments promoted a tendency toward a sedentary existence, which in turn brought about an increase in population growth and a corresponding spatial expansion of the various groups. Thus, around 1000 B.C. agriculture and animal husbandry had become the predominant way of life, whereas the hunter-gatherer communities that had flourished until this time were pushed aside into marginal areas.

The Cushites managed to fend off complete subjugation and absorption by other tribes. Their descendants, among them the Somalis, the Galla or Oromo, the Rendille and the Boni, inhabit the northern and eastern sections of Kenya today. The ancestors of the Omo-Tana Cushites started out in the lands lying between Lakes Abaya and Turkana. In 500 A.D. the region between Lake Turkana and the Indian Ocean was settled by the ancestors of the Jabarti, Boni and Somalis, who were predominantly camel breeders. The Galla (Oromo) came down from the Ethiopian highlands in several waves and had reached the Juba River by the mid-16th century. Their ensuing displacement by the Somalis continued on into the 20th century.

The **Bantu**, whose languages form Kenya's largest linguistic stock by a good margin, penetrated into the country from the south and west. They have been spreading out from the region of present-day Cameroon to central and southern Africa since the beginning of the Christian Era. The waves of Bantu migration and subsequent settlement in Kenya lasted into the second millenium. At one point they advanced so far to the north along the coast that they ran up against the Galla and Somali, who apparently forced them to retreat back southward. According to the Mijikenda, this is how they ultimately reached Shungwaya, the mysterious empire somewhere in northern Kenya.

The second Bantu wave went from the coast into the highlands, a fact whose corroboration rests on information orally handed down through the centuries

33

among the Meru and Wakamba. Thus, roughly between 1450 and 1550, the Wakamba moved step-by-step from the Kilimanjaro region to Ukambani.

At about the same time, prior to the beginning of the 15th century the remaining Mount Kenya tribes – the Chuka, Mbeere, Embu, Ndia, Gicugu and Wakikiyu went on the move, migrating from Tiggania and Igembe to the northeastern tip of Meru. They bypassed the Meru Hills, and then proceeded southwards through the Ntugi Forest by way of Igambangombe, Kiambere and Ithanga before they finally advanced into what are today Wakikuyu lands toward the close of the 16th century.

In the following three centuries, these communities consolidated themselves and continued to expand. The Wakikuyu, for example, spread out to Murang'a, Nyeri and Kiambu.

Above: It is common practice for men as well as women to wear jewelry. Right: The Masai and Luo belong to the Nilotic tribes.

Great sections of western Kenya were originally (until the end of the 16th century) settled by the Nilotic Kalenjin groups, while the ancestors of the Bantu Luyia tribe inhabited only small pockets of the southern Baluyia region. However, toward the end of the 16th century and at the beginning of the 17th, further Bantu tribes, some of which had been driven off by the Nilotic Luo, came streaming in from Uganda. These were the predecessors of the present-day Tiriki, Wanga, Bukhoya, Maragoli and Marachi. Simultaneously, the Masai and Nandi groups were absorbed by the Bantus, as indicated by the relinquishment of their own language and culture. Further waves of immigration swept over the region, and by 1870 the Baluyia region was almost completely settled. During the same period the Gusii advanced into their present living areas.

The Nilotic peoples, who inhabit considerable portions of East Africa, can be classified into three groups: the river-lake Nilots, the flatland and the highland Ni-

lotis. Unlike the river-lake tribes, we do not have as complete a picture of the flatland Nilots' history. Nonetheless, more recent research indicates that their original homeland must have been in the region of Lake Turkana.

During the first century A.D., the highland Nilots came into closer contact with their neighbors, the eastern and southern Cushites. Thus, for example, the ancestors of the Kalenjin migrated south into the Uasin Gishu Plain. In the course of the second century, these groups divided into the Elgon, Pokot, Nandi and Southern Kalenjin. The Southern Kalenjin continued their expansion to the south, arriving in northern Tanzania in the process. By 1600, these demographic transformations seemed to have come to a close.

The Masai also played a significant role in the development of the ultimate form of Kalenjin society. In the 18th century, the Masai, who had also settled in the Uasin Gishu Plain, split the Nandi-speaking Kalenjin into two major groups. On the one hand there was an eastern group, the ancestral wellspring of the present-day Tugen, Marakwet and Keiyo; and on the other a western group, which includes the Nandi and Kipsigi. By 1850 the Masai, who were particularly renowned for their military prowess, had established themselves as one of the most powerful Nilotic tribes in East Africa.

Among the exponents of the Nilotic language group is one of Kenya's smallest ethnic communities, the El-Molo, who numbered a mere 538 remaining tribal members in the 1979 census. Since that time their numbers have decreased further, so that not long ago the government ordered special measures be taken to prevent them from dying out altogether. The El-Molo are a side-branch of the Turkana and live as fishermen on Lake Turkana. That they are now classified in the Nilotic language group is a living example of how rapidly cultures and languages succumb to changing times or merge into one another. Namely, until quite recently the El-Molo still spoke their ancestral Cushitic language, how-

35

ever, their mingling with the neighboring Samburu brought them a new Nilotic tongue as well as a number of new cultural elements.

One can understand the various Kenyan tribes and subgroups better when keeping clearly in mind what influence the location of their settlement areas exerts upon their development. Thus, the well-watered landscape of central Kenya, with its valleys and mountain ranges, has left its imprint on the social and political institutions of the Wakikuyu, just as the fishing peoples of the river-lake Nilots' lives and traditions have developed to harmonize with a habitat of rivers and lakes. On the other hand, the Cushites, whose native regions have extreme climatic conditions, are dependent on the breeding of camels, sheep and goats as well as cattle. The resistant camel has traditionally played a major role as a sup-

plier of milk, meat and leather (which is also used for making tents), in addition to being the most important means of transport for the nomadic Cushites.

According to the most recent population census, there are 38 tribes in the country, not counting non-Kenyan Africans and other groups. This figure also neglects those tribes which constitute parts of other linguistic communities, such as the Kalenjin, the Mijikenda or the Luyia. Kalenjin, for example, is actually a generic term for a variety of ethnic communities that have grown together for a number of reasons including the kinship of their languages and geographic locations, as well as political considerations.

The Nandi, Kipsigi, Tugen, Marakwet and Keiyo are considered members of the Kalenjin. They all inhabit neighboring districts in the Great Rift Valley.

In contrast, the nine tribes or subgroups belonging to the Mijikenda have languages that resemble each other so closely that they could be construed as

Above: Babies are usually wrapped in cloth and carried around by their mothers.

dialects of one and the same language. To name them individually: Digo, Rabai, Giriama, Kauma, Ribe, Kambe, Jibana, Chonyi and Duruma.

This is also true, to a greater extent, of the Luyia who do not infact consist of a single tribe, but rather of a grouping of 16 distinct tribes that probably combined forces for the sake of improving their defenses. Their idioms are also very similar, a situation which is also not unusual among the Bantu groups. The Luyia belong to the Marigoli; at the moment they are the leading group in matters of size and level of development. In addition, there are the Bunyore, Isukha, Idakho, Tachoni, Kabras, Wanga, Bukhayo, Samia, Abanyala ba Ndombi, Marama, Kisa and Bukusu.

Differing living conditions have resulted in differing customs and ways of life among the various ethnic groups. The following sketches of several Kenyan peoples should provide a bit of insight in the traditional life of the whole African population.

The Kikuyu

The main areas of settlement for the Kikuyu, the largest of Kenya's ethnic groups, are the districts of Murang'a, Kiambu and Nyeri in central Kenya. The fertile land has promoted their development as successful farmers, and landed property has traditionally had a high social importance among the Kikuyu. However, they are not only thought of as good agriculturalists, they are also known as gifted traders and entrepreneurs.

Today many Kikuyu live in Nairobi, occupying quite a number of important positions in business and politics. Jomo Kenyatta, the first president of independent Kenya, was also a Kikuyu.

The myths of the Kikuyu tell of a progenitor couple by the name of Gikuyu and Mumbi. Their god, Ngai, created the mountain Kirinyaga and allocated to the man Gikuyu a portion of its valleys and animals. From the summit of the mountain, the god showed Gikuyu the beauty of the land, in particular a place under a huge fig tree where Gikuyu was to build his home. There he found Mumbi, whom he took as his wife, and with whom he had nine daughters. The daughters had grown up, and nowhere was there a man whom they could marry. Gikuyu beseeched Ngai for help and offered up a lamb and a kid as sacrifices to him. And, the next time he went to the sacrificial place, there were nine men waiting there for him, whom he delightedly brought to his family.

However, Gikuyu would only give his approval to the marraige under two conditions: That the men promise him not to move away with their wives after the wedding, and that they acknowledge the matriarchate. So, they all continued to live together as a group, which they named "Mbari ya Mumbi" in honor of their clan-mother.

Not until the parents had died did each daughter found her own familial group with her offspring, although the sense of fellowship between the individual clans continued. For many generations the women ruled the families, as had been agreed. However, in the course of time the men became displeased with the increasinly overbearing behavior of the women as well as their polyandry. Finally, they got together and conspired against the women.

They had no intention of using force to achieve their goals, instead they relied on cunning and deceit. They courted and seduced the women, and when all of them were pregnant the men took command. From then on, everything was turned around: Now the men were the chiefs of the communities, and, in turn, they also practiced polygamy. The only privilege which they left the women was that they could remain the patronesses *in nomine* of the nine most important Kikuyu clans.

The Luo

The Luo constitute Kenya's second-largest tribe. They settled primarily in the neighborhood of Lake Victoria and in the districts of South and North Nyanza, where they live from fishing and agriculture. Many important politicians have emerged from their ranks.

In earlier times, the Luo lived as semi-nomadic herdmen, but because of strong increases in their populations they migrated into the highlands and settled there as farmers and fishermen. Whereas they had originally placed no particular value on land ownership, that changed with sedentary existence. Land was the common property of the people and secured the social position of each individual. The allotment of fields was decided by the council of elders, according to the requirements and the size of each family.

Above and right: Temperature in the mountains can drop considerably – hats and scarves are normal for tribes living there.

The intensive missionary activities in western Kenya, which were also responsible for the establishment of numerous schools and training centers during the colonial period, also had the effect that the educational level of the Luo was very high in comparison with other population groups. One consequence of this was that in earlier times a major portion of the political leadership was recruited from the ranks of the Luo. This included such renowned personalities as Tom Mboya and Oginga Odinga. Odinga, a leader of the opposition and an adamant supporter of democracy, died in January 1993.

Nonetheless, in addition their political activities, the Luo are known first and foremost as skilled fishermen. In the Winam Gulf and along the shores of Lake Victoria they catch the coveted tilapia with hooks and floating nets.

The Masai

Kenya's most famous tribe are the Masai, who live today in the country's

southern region. A portion of this people, which combines warlike and pastoral traits, still rejects every innovation of the modern age and is proud of its time-honored ancestral traditions.

Linguists classify the Masai among the groups of East Nilots, whose language, *maa*, is at any rate strongly influenced by the Cushitic. The Samburu and Njemps also belong to the Maa-speaking ethnic groups.

At present, the history of the Masai has still evaded the careful scrutiny of all the ethnographers and anthropologists. Merely one thing is certain: Until the 15th century, they lived in the areas surrounding Lake Turkana. Only slowly did they move from there further to the south mostly in small groups. For a long period of time they were the unchallenged rulers of the broad savannahs of central Kenya and of the south of the land, a piece of territory extending well into present-day Tanzania.

During the 19th century, confrontations occurred between the various tribes of the Masai over livestock thievery and grazing rights. The conflicts had their primary origins in the fact that one group of Masai was permanently settled, while the others wanted to continue their nomadic life. The disputes culminated in a desperate battle near Nakuru, in which members of the Laikipia tribe were thrown to their deaths into the crater of the Menegai crater by their opponents. The few survivors of the Laikipia were scattered in every direction and absorbed by other ethnic groups.

In contrast with many other ethnic groups, the Masai cooperated with the British in the beginning of the colonial period. They offered scarcely any resistance, even when increasing numbers of immigrants pushed into the country and disputed the Masais' rights to their ancestral pasturelands. Nor did they do much to stop the construction of the railroad, which went right through the middle of their lands. One of the reasons for this was a devastating cattle plague which claimed 90 percent of their herds, simul-

taneously breaking the strength of the proud Masai warriors. Against their will, the Masai were resettled in the unfertile savannah region of the country's south in the area which was later to become the Masai Mara Reserve. And, in the following decades pasturelands grew even more scarce for the Masai.

The establishment of the Masai Mara and Amboseli National Parks as well as the Serengeti on the Tanzanian side of the border have seriously constricted the agrarian strivings of the Masai by depriving them of vital grazing lands. On top of that, the Kikuyu bought a lot of property and transformed it into farmland. These were enormous curtailments for a nomadic people who since time immemorial, had lived without having to contend with state or property lines.

According to the oral traditions of the Masai, just as for the Somalis, Maa was

Above: Jewelry and make-up play an important role for Masai warriors. Right: Clay huts are small for a large family.

the progenitor of both tribes. The legendary ancestors of the Maasai are called the Parakwo. They were the chosen people of their god, and received their cattle directly from heaven. To this day, the Masai still claim that other peoples only have cattle because they stole them from the tribe in the mists of prehistory. So the current law in Kenya which prohibits them from retrieving their "stolen" property from their neighbors must seem all the more incomprehensible.

There is hardly another ethnic group which has held on to its traditional practices and customs as firmly as the Masai. Their most important asset is livestock, whereas the possession of land is completely irrelevant for this nomadic people. The number of their cattle is of greatest importance, not how much meat or milk they yield. The diet of the Masai consists primarily of milk, millet, maize and blood, which they draw from their cattle. They live in huts which are arranged in the round, so-called *bomas*; these they leave behind when setting off to new lands. When the clans have reached their next stop they build new huts of branches with a layer of mud bound with cow-dung. A fence of thorns provides protection from wild animals. Donkeys serve as pack animals for their household articles.

A Masai man's sense of membership within his age-group is every bit as important as membership in his clan. All male Masai pass through three main stages during their lives: Following childhood, their circumcision between 14 and 18 years of age signifies the transition into the age-group of the warriors, who are called *moran* in the Masai language. There is a series of taboos that apply to this age-group, including a prohibition on alcohol. The moran live together in huts with their peers and girls of the same age. Among the usual tests (particularly in earlier times) of courage facing a warrior is the killing of a lion with nothing more than a spear. Within the community he has no other duties than keeping watch over the livestock and defending the clan against enemies.

The moran can be recognized by their long, elaborately braided hairdos. In fact, it would seem that appearance to the young Masai is just as important as it is to people of the same age in Europe or America. Only here it's not stylish clothing, but rather their hairstyles and jewelry that are especially valued.

After seven or eight years the next phase of life begins, with marriage and the cutting of their long hair. Now the young men are members of the community of elders, which gathers to make decisions for the clan. And when not performing this civic duty, they lead a relatively quiet family life.

The Mijikenda

The Mijikenda claim that their place of origin is Shungwaya, a mythical city that is supposed to have been located some-

where north of the island of Pate. Today they inhabit the Kwale and Kilifi districts. The Mijikenda call themselves the *Makaya Chenda*. They are the people who repeatedly turn up in the chronicles of the 18th century Europeans under the names *Wanyika* or *Monika* – "People of the Wilderness". Back then, the Mijikenda were in close contact with the city of Mombasa as intermediary traders, especially in timber and ivory bought from the peoples of the interior.

The Mijikenda are divided into nine ethnic groups: the Digo, Rabai, Giriama, Kauma, Ribe, Kambe, Jibana, Chonyi and Duruma. The most famous tribe among them nowadays is certainly the Giriama, which boasts a long and interesting culture, especially where music and dance are concerned. Vacationers visiting the coast will soon become familiar with their dance performances. Their most important musical instruments (and popular souvenirs) are the *kayamba*, made of reeds filled with grain; and the *chivoli*, a type of flute.

The Turkana

As regards their ethnic background, the Turkana of northwestern Kenya are nomadic Nilo-Hamites, still wandering through the vast region between Lake Turkana and the Great Rift Valley on the border of Uganda. The city of Lodwar is the seat of this region's district administration. The Turkana tribe consists of the Nimonia, an sylvan people, and the Nocuro, who live in the savannah. In turn, both of these are subdivided into some twenty clans, the so-called *ategerin*. These clans are loosely associated with each other in an umbrella union, the *adakar*. All Turkana men belong to one of two generational groups: the Stones (*nimur*) or the Leopards (*neisai*).

The British colonial administration, which entertained only the slightest interest on the Turkanas' tribal life, knew

Above: Woman from the Turkana tribe in northern Kenya. Right: Samburus dancing. Far right: El Molo girl near Turkana Lake.

merely that these people were supposedly "of gigantic height and extremely savage". It is historically established that the Turkana drove out the Maasai during the 1850s, and that they were themselves often ambushed and enslaved by the Ethiopians. German explorers noted that the Turkanas were "lanky, slender and imposing, with high cheekbones and very non-negroid thin lips. They wear head decorations of ostrich feathers, beads and metal bands as bracelets around their biceps, and, exclusively for ceremonies, capes of leopard skin."

The Turkana mainly nourish themselves with meat and blood from their cattle. Camels are an important status symbol, while donkeys serve strictly as pack animals. Sheep and goats end their lives as meals for guests, sacrifices at rituals, or as dried meat. Huge amounts of milk are boiled, dried on leather skins and used later in powdered form. Camels' milk, which has a low fat content and is easily digested, is used for feeding infants. Berries are either dried and pul-

verized, or mixed with blood and formed into cakes. During the rainy seasons millet is cultivated near watercourses. Despite the huge supply of fish in Lake Turkana, which is named after the tribe, they resign themselves to fishing only during droughts or periods of famine. The traditional dwellings of the polygamous Turkana are occupied by the head of the family, his favorite wife and their children, while his various secondary wives, together with their children and married sons live in their own demarcated areas. The main entrance of a dwelling is always oriented towards the east. Just as other of Kenya's ethnic groups have done, the Turkanas have also transformed their articles of everyday use into works of art. For example, they ornament their carved wooden water troughs by engraving them with fire, and decorate oil and milk containers of camel hide with beads and cowrie shells.

The Turkana man, who is traditionally a herdsman and hunter, is rarely seen outside of his home without his spear, his knife and his shield of buffalo, giraffe or hippopotamus hide. The women beautify themselves with bracelets and neck rings of brass or aluminium and improbable masses of stringed beads.

Modern civilization is also slowly making inroads into the world of the Turkana. Transistor radios have rendered the bush-drum superfluous, improved communications are bringing not only more contact with neighbors, but foreign influences from the western hemisphere as well. Governmental projects such as irrigated farming along the Turkwell and Kerio Rivers, and fishing cooperatives on the western shores of Lake Turkana are supposed to turn the nomadic Turkana into a stationary tribe; and the Turkwell Gorge Plan envisions irrigated agricultural settlements with electricity for thousands of hectares of land.

The Samburu

The Samburu tribe lives in northern Kenya on a region of roughly 28,490

other. One primary component of their nutrition is a yogurt-like curdled milk which is mixed with blood now and then. Meat is only served on special occasions. The wealth of each Samburu family is measured by the number of camels, cattle and goats it possesses.

The Samburu embellish themselves with beads and metal circlets around their arms and neck. The face and body of the warriors are usually emblazoned with ochre-colored clay, and their hair is elaborately styled with clay as well. The ochre-painted girls with their exposed breasts and sensuous movements are the very essence of a seductive ideal of beauty for the warriors – and in that the warriors are certainly not alone.

The Rendille

The southeast side of Lake Turkana is home to the Rendille tribe, which is related to the Somalis. Their legends tell of how, hundreds of years ago, nine Somali warriors lost their way as they were driving their camel herds. After many days of wandering through unknown territory, they came upon the region of the Samburu. Before the Samburu elders allowed them to marry women from their tribe, the Somalis had to give up their old traditions and renounce Islam. They agreed, and, as a result of this union, the Rendille people came into being.

Their men, women and children live in semi-permanent settlements where there are only a few milk-camels kept for nourishment. In the search for good pasturelands for their huge herds of camels, the boys and young men together with their mobile camps are in constant motion, while the girls care for the herds of sheep and goats.

Today, as in times past, the nomadic Rendille still drive their herds over the thorny brush of the desert. Recently built schools are intended to prepare coming generations for life in the modern world.

square kilometers that includes the Lerogi Plain with its cedar forests, and the arid bushlands of the north. The city of Maralal is the district administrative seat for the Samburu region. Both culturally and linguistically, the Samburu are closely related to the Masai. In the 16th century, during the period of migration along the Nile, they split away from the main group and headed south. The Samburu way of life hasn't changed much over the years either. This pastoral folk still lives in low huts made of woven branches, coated with mud and cow-dung for better insulation. Roof mats of sisal are added for extra protection. Each of these huts is furnished with two beds of woven twigs covered with goatskin or cowhide. The mother sleeps in the larger bed, the children in the smaller.

The Samburu also live polygamously, and the men visit their wives one after the

Above: Everything can be used in the production of jewelry. Right: Business and pleasure, a cattle market in western Kenya.

The Boran

The Boran are another pastoral tribe inhabiting the Turkana region. They are related to the Cushitic tribes of southern Ethiopia. The Boran believe in a higher deity, with whom they are able to communicate through their shamans and by prayer and sacrifices.

Just as in the majority of other African tribes, the children of the Boran are firmly bound into the traditional life of the tribe. Rituals and celebrations accompany their birth and naming. Whereas the initial ceremonies take place exclusively within the circle of relatives and closest friends, at a public celebration the supreme deity is thanked and beseeched for blessings.

The father shears off the hair of his male child before giving it a name following additional ceremonies. On the next morning, a previously consecrated bull is sacrificed. Slender armbands are made from its hide for the child and his relatives. A priest foretells the boy's des-tiny and the meat is consumed communally. Since girls born to a tribe are viewed as being of less importance, the naming ceremonies for them are, accordingly, much simpler.

Before a boy is allowed to let his hair grow again he must in advance prove his masculinity. He can either kill a lion, elephant or a man from another tribe, or else marry, found his own household and beget a child.

Every Boran tribe is divided into five generational strata; every eight years a Boran moves from one stratum to the next with an initiation ritual, and after 40 years he has reached the final level, that of the tribal elders. The Boran's culture has changed only slightly in the course of time, despite the establishment of schools and a modern agricultural project on the Uaso Nyiro River.

Arabic Descendants

As the first non-African group, Arabs began settling along the Kenyan coast in the beginning of the 7th century. The intermingling of the moslemic Arabs with the indigenous Bantu population brought forth the Swahili culture, which, organized into city-states, flourished along the entire coastline of East Africa.

The Swahili – the name quite simply means "coastal inhabitant" – still make up a considerable portion of the coastal population. Now as ever, it is of decisive importance to be descended from an old established family, since political power and even permission to settle in certain sections of a city are traditionally based on family membership. The residential area, or *mtaa*, is of central importance for the social life of the Swahili. Imprinted with a strong sense of fellowship and solidarity, life within the *mtaa* runs its course with total orientation toward the community. Its members celebrate, work and trade with each other, and go together to the mosque to perform their religious duties.

Kenya's ethnic groups of Arabic descent can be distinguished according to their lineage and religious confession. Not a few of the immigrants, who once sailed in their dhows from the Arabian Peninsula to East Africa, came from the Sultanate of Oman. Included among these are also the members of the Mazrui clans, which ruled in Mombasa after the Portuguese departed, and still play a significant role today. The majority of the over four million Moslems in Kenya are Sunnites. Nowadays they no longer live exclusively on the coast, having moved to cities in the entire country.

Asians and Europeans

Kenya's citizens of Asian extraction compose only four percent of the total population, while the descendants of the

Right: Freshly-felled mangroves have to be wetted before being transported to protect from woodworm and drying out.

European immigrants only make up a disappearingly small 0.2 percent. Today these population groups are primarily employed in trade and industry (the Europeans have almost nothing to do with agriculture anymore!), and they are therefore found mainly in the larger cities, such as Mombasa, Nairobi, Kisumu and Nakuru.

Kenya's coast has practically always been the front entrance for invaders from various countries, though with the onset of the British colonial period, the influx of Europeans (and Asians too) increased markedly. In the meantime, many of them have become Kenyan citizens, whether through naturalization, marriage, or by the simple fact of being born in Kenya. The Kenyans of European extraction are descendants of European settlers and missionaries, most of whom entered the country during the 19th century. There were British on the one hand, but alongside them came numerous Germans and Netherlanders.

The ancestors of Kenyans with Asian backgrounds came for the most part from India to Kenya at the close of the 19th century for the construction of the Mombasa-Kisumu railroad line. They were initially hired by the British as "coolies", and after their tedious work was completed – and if they survived the hardships, irate natives and hungry animals – many of them went back to India again. A fair number, however, remained in Kenya. In particular, small businessmen saw a promising future in this up-and-coming African land. They were not the first Indian immigrants to the country, though. Already in ages past, Indian seafarers and especially traders had established themselves on the East African coast. Today wholesale and retail trade still represent the economic fulcrum for the population of Indian ancestry.

When the Asian population was offered Kenyan citizenship in the course of the "Africanization" which followed the

country's independence, many Indians declined it and emigrated. The social role of those who stayed in Kenya is difficult, as it always has been. This is not least because the majority of Indians live in the self-contained unit of their caste, and tend to close themselves off from the lives of other ethnic groups. In addition to the Indians, there is also a smaller Japanese and a Chinese population group.

Ethnic Encounters

The majority of foreigners come to Kenya as tourists in search of relaxation and adventure. They are lured by the exotic dream of a faraway land, its abundance of wildlife, the enchanting landscape and gorgeous beaches. Almost all of them stay in comfortable hotels on the coast, or in the lodges and camps of the animal reserves. Unfortunately, by and large their contact with the native population is limited to placing their orders at restaurants or brief conversations with taxi drivers and safari guides. This is all

the more regrettable in that experiences of incalculable value are being passed by, namely, to become familiar with customs and traditions, behavior patterns and the ways of life of a different people, and, in the process, to break down prejudices and misunderstanding on both sides of the fence. Of course, it's not always easy to come in contact with another culture. The prerequisites most certainly include tolerance as well as respectful behavior.

There are definitely several factors that prevent encounters between a visitor to a country and its inhabitants. Without a doubt, one of the main difficulties is posed by the language problem. However, with a bit of good will from both sides this barrier can often be more easily overcome than one might expect.

For example, a large part of the Kenyan population speaks English. Indeed, frequently it's the tourists' way of expressing themselves that makes communication more difficult. Now and then one even hears the word "nigger" pass visitors' lips, which brings to mind the

47

discriminating mindset of colonialism or, worse yet, the slavery period. Another case in point is the summoning of waiters by using the term "boy": Hardly anyone would even think of such a thing in America or England, but it seems that many consider this normal in Africa.

The colonial past is still having aftereffects in African countries today, and racism, unfortunately, is still a reality, specifically in connection with tourists, some of who are all too easily prepared to attribute inadequacies in service at the airport or in shops to the "laziness, clumsiness or stupidity of Africans".

Above and beyond the basically questionable nature of such prejudices for a moment, one consistently encounters a completely different reality: Almost every Kenyan who works in tourism speaks, as a rule, several languages. (One of the basic prerequisites for a position in

Above: Spiritual business of sorts. Right: Handicrafts are among Kenya's bestselling souvenirs.

a hotel is a good knowledge of English). Furthermore, an African hotel manager is in no way inferior to his colleagues in other parts of the world. Indeed they should even be not a bit surprised when they notice that besides English he has a solid working knowledge of French, German, or Italian – and quite possibly possesses a diploma from a Swiss school of hotel management. The preponderance of the hotel personnel usually boast outstanding training in one of Kenya's own hotel trade schools.

Open-mindedness for novelty, for unusual and strange customs and ways of life in another country should be among the basic attitudes of each and every traveler. Furthermore, a bit of information about the social and economic situation is also useful for a better understanding of one's travel destination. The sad fact, though, is that many tourists don't want to be confronted with the problems of another country during their vacation; poverty and disease shouldn't exist in their vicinity. However, those

who give some thought, for example, to the fact that a developing country like Kenya is unable to finance a smoothly functioning social system might not treat the numerous beggars they may encounter with disdain. In addition, certain behavior patterns will be easier to understand if one is aware that the monthly income of a waiter or driver roughly corresponds to the budget of many westerners for a single vacation day.

A typical example of thoughtlessness among tourists is swimming in the nude. Whereas it was primarily Christian missionaries who managed to convince the Africans that their nakedness was a lack of culture and didn't correspond to the usual conceptions of clothing, it is precisely the European tourists who are filled with indignation by the fact that today it's the Africans who forbid swimming *au naturel* on their beaches.

There are many reasons why, up to now, tourism hasn't contributed more to understanding between peoples. But it's up to each individual to improve this.

The Languages

Two official languages exist side by side with equal claims in Kenya: English and Swahili, also called *Kiswahili*, or "language of the Swahili". Swaheli is not, as was long assumed, a young language, rather it has its origins in the period of the Arabic immigrations to the East African coast. As they mingled with the indigenous population a new, independent language arose, with Bantu as the basic stock and an abundance of Arabic words and characteristics. Even if Swahili is the second national language in Kenya today, it is the mother tongue for only a few people. The first language every African learns, is that of his or her ethnic group, in other words a dialect of the Cushitic or Nilotic language group or a Bantu language. In all of East Africa about 50 million people speak Swahili today. Nonetheless, is still hasn't achieved the societal rank of English, which is part and parcel of the school curriculum for every Kenyan.

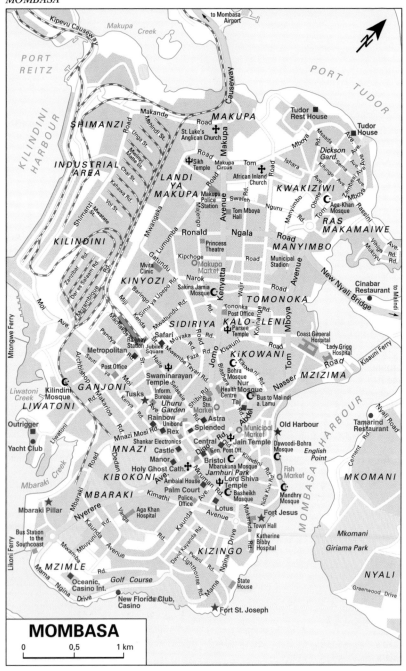

MOMBASA

0   0,5   1 km

THE GATE TO EAST AFRICA

MOMBASA
THE COAST

MOMBASA

The Port city of Mombasa, which was constructed on a coral island, is a jewel of the East African coast. Extolled by poets and travellers alike, heatedly fought over by seafarers and one of the most important gates to East Africa for hundreds of years, today Mombasa is a popular destination for sun-hungry vacationers from around the world. In the last few decades the floods of tourists have very nearly influenced the life and look of the city as much as the conquerers of the last century. Despite this, however, the "Beautiful", as Mombasa is also named, still hangs onto its own special flair.

Mombasa is Kenya's oldest city, with a history extending back more than two thousand years. As early as 150 A.D., the great geographer Ptolemy indicated it on his map of the world. Roman, Persian, Indian and Arabic mariners called at the port while on their trade missions. Some of them settled on the island of Mombasa and drank in its incomparable beauty.

Mombasa owes its founding to its opportune location in a bay, with a passage to the sea through the offshore reef. This

Preceding pages: Hot-air balloons give a bird's eye view of the expanses of the Masai Mara. Giraffes at dusk.

safe, natural harbor provides sailing ships with the necessary protection, and gave Mombasa the basis for its economic development. By the 16th century, it had developed into the most powerful city on the East African coast, with a population of some 10,000. Even its wealth, however, attracted booty-hungry conquerers over and over again.

The Portugueses repeatedly tried hard to capture it, but Mombasa was able to defend its independence up to the end of the 16th century. Only then, weakened by a number of battles with the Zimba warriors and the attacks of the rival Malinidis, was it forced to submit to the Portugueses. In order to protect themselves from soon being the next vanquished party, the new rulers of Mombasa constructed Fort Jesus, which held them in good stead up until the arrival of the Arabs from Oman a century later. Only after a lengthy seige the Omanis assumed power and retained it until they, in turn, were forced to cede the island to the British in 1873.

The English finally brought an end to the Arabs' flourishing slave trade and installed an effective administrative apparatus. In 1896 they furthermore began construction on the Uganda Railroad to Lake Victoria, and Mombasa became the "gateway to British East Africa". From

1895 to 1907, it remained the main seat of the British protectorate. Nairobi, the current capital, then usurped the dominant position.

Until 1896, Mombasa could only be reached by boat, but the railroad made a bridge to the mainland necessary; it was replaced later by a dam. Even today the connection with the south coast consists exclusively of one ferry boat, the **Likoni**, which shuttles back and forth, day and night between the southwest shore of the island and the mainland. The broad **New Nyali Bridge** was built several years ago as a direct route to the north coast (as with all larger bridges, it costs a toll to use). It replaced the old Nyali Bridge, which was once the longest pontoon bridge in the world.

Modern-day Mombasa seems to have effortlessly united past and present, tradi-

Above: The city of Mombasa was built on a coral island. Right: Busses are a popular and therefore crowded means of public transportation.

tion and novelty. Rising up alongside the medieval old town with its straggling ancient *dhow* harbor is a modern highrise quarter; churches from the European missionary days are harmoniously lined up in a row with several mosques and Indian temples.

Up until the turn of the century, this coastal city was inhabited almost exclusively by Arabs, Indians and Swahilis. Africans and Europeans didn't settle in Mombasa until well into this century. After Kenya's independence in 1963, many business people established themselves in Mombasa, and made the city what it is today: A banking, trade and tourist center that also plays, thanks to the **Bamburi Cement Factory,** an important industrial role.

Mombasa's lively history has made it into a melting pot of the most differing cultures. Today African, Asian, Arabic and European elements set the scene of this city, which, with its roughly one-half million inhabitants is Kenya's second-largest metropolitan area.

Touring the City

The best starting point for a stroll through Mombasa's inner city is **Digo Road**, one of the city's main streets. Starting from the south coast, it prolongs **Nyerere Avenue**; coming from the **New Nyali Bridge**, on the other hand, it's reached via **Tom Mboya Avenue** and the **Abdel Nasser Road**.

Along Digo Road the first things that catch the eye are the big market halls. Exotic fruits, vegetables and spices are piled up on the stands, between which the buyers and sellers jostle each other. However, a shopping trip amidst the lively bustle is only recommended for those who, having said *no*, are able to hold their ground resolutely. The indigenous traders crowd all-too-gladly around the tourists looking helpless, in order to tout the virtues of their generally overpriced mangos, lemons and cashews so emphatically that the only escape begins to look like taking the bull by its horns – in other words, buying. At any rate, bar-

gaining is the first commandment! A basket of fresh fruit is, after all, certainly worth a turbulent shopping trip, and added to that it makes a pretty souvenir for those who are soon to head home. Those seeking peace and quiet for their shopping trips yet will be better served at the street stands in the outlying districts or at the shops in the **Nyali** district.

Surrounding the market are numerous shops with a huge assortment of teas, coffees, spices and basketware. Some businesses are nevertheless so much tourist-oriented that they even display price lists in several languages. In addition, the numerous hawkers working for them are thoroughly polyglot and are able to guess – with great accuracy – the nationality of a potential buyer ambling by, without even having heard a peep from him.

The market just across the way in **Biashara Street** consists primarily of one Indian textile shop after another. They sell the colorfully printed cotton fabric for the traditional shawl-wraps, the *kikois* and *kangas*. Tailors sit right outside these

shops, on the street, with their old sewing machines, ready to prepair new articles for a few shillings or repair used item. Communicating with them, however, is not always so simple, since in contrast to the far too cosmopolitan shop owners, these older craftsmen frequently speak only Swahili.

Located on the road running parallel to Biashara Street, **Jomo Kenyatta Avenue**, was once the largest market in the city, the **Mwembe Tayari**. Nowadays it's merely a jumble of snack stands, and the terminal for busses and group taxis (*matatus*) departing for every corner of the country. Only the busses to Lamu and Malindi depart from the stop at Abdel Nasser / Digo Road. There, right next to the bus stop, stands Mombasa's great Friday mosque, the **Nur Mosque**, which was reconstructed in the modern Indian style.

Above: The Great Tusks, hallmark of Mombasa. Right: In the Old Town. Far right: The Swaminarajan temple in the religious melting pot of Mombasa.

Ambling again down Digo Road, one crosses **Haile Selassie Road**, which leads at the train station, and soon afterwards arrives to the turbulent traffic-circle between **Nkrumah Road** and **Moi Avenue**, an Eldorado for souvenir shops. Stand after little stand line Moi Avenue all the way to the **Elephant Tusks**, four giant aluminium tusks that span the street and serve as Mombasa's hallmark. Everything a tourist's heart desires can be had here, from wooden carvings of elephants and lions to attractive chess sets and ash trays of soapstone. Along with numerous banks, travel agencies and car rental agencies, the **Tourist Information Bureau** is also located on this commercial strip. The terrace of the tradition-steeped **New Castle Hotel** is nearby, an important meeting place for the exchange of news among both tourists and Kenyan natives, as well as a popular meeting-place for lonely people of every nationality. This charming hotel from the colonial period is just the right place for a little snack or a refreshing drink.

Legacy of the Past

One hasn't really gotten to know Mombasa without having made a foray through the narrow roads and alleyways of the **Old Town**. The original appearance of the town is still preserved between **Digo Road** and the **Old Harbor**: buildings constructed of coral limestone, enchanting little gardens, carved doors and balconies. Of course, they are sometimes a bit dilapidated, but they do radiate the charm of past splendor. Along the East African coast, this type of beautifully carved door is found not only in Mombasa, but also in Lamu and Zanzibar. Made of precious mahogany and teak woods, for centuries they were the most important status symbols of Swahili houses. The doors are ornamented with a variety of symbols and signs, depending in the first place on the origins of the owner. The Indian style features ornamentation are consisting primarily of leaves, flowers, fish and birds, while the Arabic craftsmen showed a religion-based preference for geometric patterns and sayings from the Koran.

Most these houses once were erected on the foundations of earlier clay buildings. As a rule, the people who settled in this quarter were Indian traders or gold and silversmiths. Behind the latticework of their windows and doors they still ply their crafts to this day.

The **Old Harbor**, which for centuries was a port-of-call for trading fleets, is located on the eastern edge of the old town. Its former significance has, however, already been lost for a long while, not least since the construction of the new deepsea harbor **Kilindini** in the city's west side. Even so, the Arabic dhows still drop anchor at the Old Harbor. These nimble sailing ships haven't changed their appearance since the days of the *One-Thousand-and-One Nights* (only the diesel motor has in the meantime become almost always a part of the standard equipment). For centuries they transported spices and carpets over the Indian Ocean to Kenya during the winter monsoon season (from December to April), and after the wind had turned they loaded their boats with slaves and ivory for the return trip. In our day as well, these great sailing ships cover thousands of kilometers on the high seas, and frequently without the use of modern navigational aids such as radio and radar. During the winter, when the *dhows* arrive from Iran, Arabia and India, it is possible to ride out on a rented boat to visit them. It's also interesting to take a morning walk through the fish market next to the Old Harbor, where something interesting is always happening during the auctioning of various seafood delicacies.

The coexistence of mosques, temples and churches in the Old Town plainly demonstrates the multitude of religious communities living alongside each other in Mombasa. Many Moslems, Hindus and Christians have found common ground in this residential section. The **Mandhry Mosque**, originating in the year 1570, is Mombasa's oldest functioning Islamic temple. The **Basheikh** or **Tangana Mosque** also dates from the 16th century, while the **Baluchi Mosque** on Makadara Road is a new building replacing the old 1875 Mosque.

The Indian temples can also be numbered among Mombasa's most beautiful sights. On **Langoni Road** the white marble of the **Jain Temple** rises up like something out of a fairy-tale. The entrance of this religious shrine, built in 1963, is flanked by two elephants, while displayed in the interior are three figures of the *Tirthankaras*, or mythical founders of the Jain religion, of which there are 24 altogether.

The **Lord Shiva Temple**, the religious center of the Hindus, is located on the edge of the Old Town. Continuing from there via Nkrumah Road you arrive back to Digo Road.

Right: For 400 years Mombasa was pro-
tected by the mighty walls of Fort Jesus.

The **Holy Ghost Cathedral** stands at the intersection of the two streets. In 1891, the missionary le Roy acquired this plot of land for the original church. The present structure, dating from 1918, was built of coral limestone and sandstone in Neo-Romanesque style.

Fort Jesus

Fort Jesus, situated on the south end of the Old City, is without doubt one of the most interesting sights in Mombasa. Located on a coral ledge, it towers majestically over the harbor entrance, beckoning visitors both on land and at sea.

It was founded in 1593, when the Portuguese determined to protect their position on the East African coast with stout fortifications. Roughly 100 years later, in 1696, the Omanis laid siege to the fortress. The fighting went on for two years, but, despite the alternating battle successes on both sides, the Omanis finally achieved victory and marched triumphantly into both the city and the fortress in 1698. The once-proud fortress was degraded into a prison when the British established their hegemony. This humiliating epoch of its glorious history came to an end in 1958, when the Gulbenkian Foundation provided 30,000 pounds sterling for its restoration and the establishment of a museum.

Six cannons from British and German ships guard the main gate today. At their base the walls are 15 meters tall and 2.5 meters thick, and visitors are often astonished that this imposing fortress could ever have been taken at all. In the interior courtyard of the fortress, signs indicate the most noteworthy sights, among them Portuguese wall drawings, and the house of the former captain. There is also a gorgeous view of the sea from the fortification walls.

Any chance to view the museum shouldn't be passed up either. Drawings and maps of old Mombasa, precious

jewelry and pieces of furniture, yellowed photographs and models of dhows weave a fascinating tale of earlier days.

Kilindini Harbor

The southern and western sections of this island-city are best reached by automobile. In the last few decades the harbor at **Kilindini Creek** has developed into one of the most important on the East African coast. Goods from Kenya as well as from Uganda, Zaire and the Sudan are loaded on its docks.

Mombasa's modern harbor was made necessary by the construction of the railroad lines, which helped strengthen trade with the hinterland. The crowded, narrow Old Town could no longer cope with the resulting traffic. Today tens of thousands find employment in and around the harbor and have made it into one of the most important economic factors of the city and the surrounding area.

Also located in the western part of the city are the ruins of the 17th-century **Ki-lindini** or **Three-Tribe Mosque**, which has decayed right down to its foundation walls. Rising up right next to it stands the 16-meter-high **Mbakari Pillar** dating presumably from the 17th or 18th century. It may have served to mark the tomb of a sheikh of one of the three tribes, after which the mosque was named.

Nocturnal Meeting-places

Driving along Nyerere Avenue toward the **Likoni Ferry**, head through the traffic-circle, taking the **Mama Ngina Drive** which branches off to the left and continue around the southern tip of the island up to the ruins of **Fort St. Joseph**. The popular promenade, which is an evening rendezvous spot particularly for the Asian population, is named after the wife of Jomo Kenyatta.

For those interested in lightening (or filling!?) their vacation purse, there are two equally stylish gambling institutions on Mama Ngina Drive: The **Casino** in the luxurious **Hotel Oceanic** and the

Florida Nightclub, which has a hot discotheque with plenty of titillating atmosphere in addition to roulette and blackjack.

There are numerous bars, nightclubs, gambling casinos and cinemas to keep the visitor entertained in Mombasa. In addition, there is a copious selection of restaurants: One can dine here not only on Arabic, Chinese, Indian, Pakistani and European cuisine, but of course sample local African dishes as well.

Quite probably the most famous restaurant on the coast, the **Tamarind**, is located in the elegant upper-crust suburban district of **Nyali**. It is reached via the New Nyali Bridge, after which you turn off to the right at the next intersection. After driving a bit further there are signs pointing the way. Constructed in a moorish style, from its terrace the guests have a romantic view of the Old Harbor. The

Above: The coast of Kenya offers luxuriant vegetation, including succulent banana trees and palms.

stylish ambience here, with a band performing nostalgic music, is a fitting counterpart in the restaurant's cuisine. Far simpler, but almost as romantic, the **Joli Coin** is located in the neighborhood of the Severin Sea Lodge. It provides the best opprtunity to sit near the beach in all of Mombasa.

THE COAST

The majority of visitors to Mombasa do not stay in the city itself, but rather in one of the numerous beach-hotels on the north and south coasts (see next chapter). Altogether, Kenya's coastline extends over 480 kilometers, from Somalia in the north down to Tanzania in the south. The white, palm-lined beach, which is protected along almost its entire length by a tremendous coral reef, attracts vacationers from around the world. The reef, which follows the coast at a distance of about one kilometer, has only a few passages like the one at Mombasa. Its natural pools form a chain of blue lagoons in which one can swim and dive in complete safety. Just about all forms of watersport can be practiced here.

The coastal vegetation indeed is luxuriant: Palms and oleanders grow rank here, just as do frangipani and casuarina bushes, cashew and mango trees. The greater part of the hotel and bungalow complexes are situated in the midst of this blooming paradise.

However beautiful it may be on the coast, one should certainly plan in some time for a sight-seeing tour or a shopping excursion to Mombasa. Most hotels offer tours or at least bus transportation to the city. Those wishing to make a trip to Mombasa on their own have a choice between taking a taxi, the public bus or the *matatus*. However, the public transportation system is hopelessly overloaded, especially during the high tourist season. It's also popular with rather skilled pickpockets.

MOMBASA
Accommodation

LUXURY: **Castle Hotel**, Moi Avenue, PO Box 84231, Tel: 223403. **New Outrigger Hotel**, Ras Liwatoni (on the outskirts of Mombasa), PO Box 84851, Tel: 220822. **Oceanic Beach Hotel**, Mama Ngina Drive, PO Box 90371, Tel: 314199. **Paradise Beach Hotel**, PO Box 81443, Tel: 486104/5.

MODERATE: **Hotel Manor**, Nyerere Avenue, PO Box 84851, Tel:314643. **Hotel Splendid**, Msanifu Kombo Street, PO Box 90482, Tel: 220967. **Oyster Bay Beach Hotel**, PO Box 10252, Tel: 485061/2.

BUDGET: **Hydro Hotel**, Digo/Langoni Road, PO Box 85360, Tel: 23784. **New Peoples Hotel**, Abdel Nasser Road, PO Box 85342, Tel: 312831. **Manson Hotel**, PO Box 83565, Tel: 222356.

Restaurants

AFRICAN: **Recoda Hotel**, Nyeri Street.

CHINESE: **Chinese Overseas**, Moi Avenue, Tel: 21585. **Hong Kong**, Moi Avenue, Tel: 226707.

ITALIAN: **Cinabar**, New Nyali Bridge, Tel: 472373. **Capri Restaurant**, Ampala House, 3rd floor, Tel: 311156, PO Box 90574. **La Terrazza**, at the Oceanic Beach Hotel, Mama Ngina Drive, Tel: 312838. **Pistacchio**, Chembe Road, Tel: 219 89.

INDIAN: **Hermes**, Msanifu Kombo Road, Tel: 313599. **Indo Africa**, Haile Selassie Road, Tel: 21430. **Shehnai**, Fatemi House, Maungano Street, Tel: 312482. **Singh**, Mwembe Tayari Road, Tel: 493283. **Nawab**, Moi Avenue, Tel: 207 54.

FISH: **Tamarind**, Nyali, Tel: 471747.

Museums

Fort Jesus, Nkrumah Road, Tel: 312839. Open daily (including Sun and public holidays) from 8 a.m.–6.30 p.m. Historical fort (16th century) with an interesting museum.

Nightlife

New Florida (with casino), Mama Ngina Drive. **Rainbows** (bargain-price bar), Mnazi Moja Road. **Shunshine**, Moi Avenue. **Toyz**, Baluchi Street. **Tiffany's**, Ambalal House. **International Casino**, at the Oceanic Hotel, Lighthouse Road, Tel. 312 838.

Pharmacies

Coast Medical Stores Ltd, Digo Road, Tel: 25600, 26435. Open 8 a.m.–12.30 p.m., 2–6 p.m. **Digo Chemist Ltd**, Meru Road, Tel: 316065. Open Mon–Fri 8 a.m.–7 p.m., Sat 8 a.m.–3 p.m., Sun 9 a.m.–1 p.m.

Medical Service and Hospitals

Most hotels employ contractual doctors who will visit and treat hotel guests in case of sickness. In addition, there are two hospitals: **The Mombasa Hospital**, Mama Ngina Drive, Tel: 312190, 312099, 24-hour emergency service. **The Aga Khan Hospital**, Vanga Road, Tel: 312953.

Post

The **Main Post Office** on Digo Road is open Mon–Fri 8 a.m.–12.30 p.m. and 2–4.30 p.m.

Banks

All banks in Mombasa are open from 9 a.m. – 2 p.m. **Barclays Bank** on Moi Avenue has a foreign exchange counter, opening times Mon–Fri 9 a.m.–4.30 p.m. and Sat from 9 a.m.–2 p.m.

Shopping

Countless shops in the city center, selling wood carvings, T-shirts, baskets, curios and souvenirs, try their best to compete with the multitude of street stalls offering their wares at rock-bottom prices.

Biashara Street is the best place to buy local textiles such as *khangas, kikois, kitenge*, as well as tie-dyed materials.

Crossing Digo Road brings you to **Mackinnon Market**; the **Ebrahim Stores** next to the market specialize in woven textiles and basketry. Several shops behind the market offer spices, batiks and wood carvings, tea and coffee, jewellery and gems. For a special treat try the **Bhagwanji Hansraj & Sons** store with its wide variety of delicious Indian snacks and sweets.

In the Old Town, near Fort Jesus, you can discover some fascinating shops selling antiques, curios and perfume. Interesting too are the streets around Mbarak Hinaway Road and Ndia Kuu.

Most stores open from 8 a.m.–6 p.m. with a lunch break from noon/12.30–2 p.m.

Police

The police headquarters are on Makadara Road, near the Lotus Cinema, Tel: 311401.

Rail

Daily trains to Nairobi depart at 5 and 7 p.m.; trains from Nairobi arrive every morning at 8 and 8.30 a.m. Please note: tickets must be confirmed before departure.

Air

The **Moi International Airport** is situated on the mainland near Changamwe. Transport to the city can be arranged through Kenya Airways. If you take a taxi into town, make sure to negotiate the fare into town beforehand.

Car

The new Nyali Bridge, a continuation of Ronald Ngala Road, runs to the north coast.

For a trip to the south coast take the Digo Road and the Likoni Ferry.

Car Rental: **Avis**: Moi Avenue, Tel: 230 48. Moi Airport, Tel: 433 211. **Coast Car Hire**: Ambalal House, Nkrumah Road, Tel: 311 752.

Tourist Information

Moi Avenue, Tel: 25428. The information office is open Monday–Friday 8 a.m.–noon and 2–4.30 p.m., Saturday 8 a.m.–noon.

COCONUTS AND SILVERY BEACHES

THE SOUTH COAST
SHIMBA HILLS

Kenya's 60-kilometer long south coast consists of a virtually uninterrupted chain of broad, gleaming beaches alternating with charming villages and numerous hotels of varying price classes, all located directly on the beach. They are among the prime destinations of vacationers hungering for relaxation, who go swimming in the protected lagoons and sunbathe in the fine-grained sand that reaches right up to the hotels and bungalows.

The majority of hotels and tourist establishments on the south coast are concentrated on **Diani Beach**, approximately 40 kilometers from Mombasa. There are also many hotels in **Likoni** (across from the Likoni ferry harbor in Mombasa). Likoni, however, is not a well-tended town, and a side-trip there is not recommendable. The entire south coast is easily accessible from a well-built highway that runs parallel to the coast about one kilometer inland. In addition, there is a landing strip for small aircraft at **Ukunda** (Diani Beach), which serves primarily as a point of departure for air-safaris over the animal reserves.

The Likoni ferry dock is the main starting point for a drive along the south

Preceding pages: Diani Beach is one of Kenya's most beautiful swimming spots. Left: The easy life can be paid for in a hotel.

coast. Shortly after leaving the ferry a street branches off from the main road to **Shelly Beach**, an attractive stretch with camping grounds and hotels, though from time to time there is also a lot of seaweed. Back again on the main road, a trail another kilometer further on leads to a coconut palm plantation, near which the ruins of an Arabian mosque are located.

The dazzling, white **Tiwi Beach** extends south from the plantation to the mouth of the **Mwachema River**. This perhaps cleanest and most original of all the beaches on the entire coast offers lodging in bungalows and camping grounds. The **Congo Mosque** rises up on an outcropping along the southern bank of the river. This structure from the 18th century is now classified as a national monument and is still being used by its religious community. This mosque, picturesquely surrounded by baobab trees (also called monkey bread trees), is located only a few minutes by foot from the beach and the river's estuary.

Diani Beach, at Ukunda, is Kenya's longest. One hotel after another is lined up along the beach, and everything here rotates around the desires of the numerous vacationers. Most of the hotels offer a broad selection of sport and recreational activities. In the town of **Ukunda** a shopping center was completed a short

67

while ago, and in Diani there is also a shopping center with banks, supermarkets, drugstores, pharmacies and various boutiques catering to the tourists.

Behind the hotel strip lies a minute piece of this area's original landscape, the **Diani Forest**, which is a habitat for the Kolobus monkeys, among others. In addition the forest is home to several species of bird, exotic butterflies and small mammals which have survived only here, separated from the development of their West African ancestors. Thousands of years ago a rain forest stretched without interruption from West Africa all the way to the Kenyan coast. Today however, only a few small islands of it remain. The gigantic 500-year-old baobob tree near the Trade Winds Hotel is also well deserving of admiration.

Toward the south, Diani Beach extends down to **Gazu**, where it runs

Above: Wind surfing is one of many water sports people traveling to Kenya can practice in the Indian Ocean.

around a small bay and comes to an end at **Chale Island**. This little islet is a popular destination for boat excursions from Diani. They start in the mornings with swimming and snorkeling and ring out the day with barbecue parties on Chale Island.

Gazu was once this district's administrative center. Today its significance is derived primarily from its huge coconut plantations. On the other side of the main road the **House of Sheik Mbaruk bin Rashid** is a reminder of the period when, in the beginning of the 19th century, the Omani Mazrui clan lived here. The house's ornately carved door is one of its most interesting features.

When driving further to the south on the main road you come upon the village of **Msambweni**, located 48 kilometers past Likoni. Its name means "town of the sabre antelope", although nowadays this animal lives for the most part in the Shimba Hills Reserve. Msambweni is known for its well-equipped hospital, the best on the south coast. Turn off at the

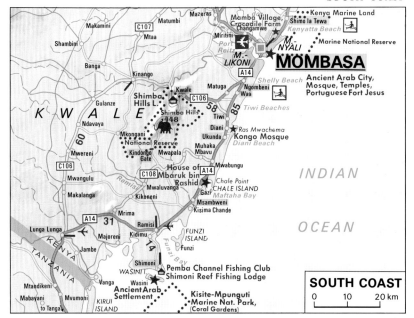

SOUTH COAST

0   10   20 km

sign pointing to the hospital, and drive through the village towards the beach. This area was developed for tourists only a short while ago, although in the meantime numerous bungalows and vacation cottages have already been constructed as well as a hotel with Italian management and an exclusive clientele. These accomodations are located on the highest crest of the coral reef; getting to the untouched beaches involves a steep climb down narrow paths. The handful of ruins in the north of the area are thought to have once been a slave detention camp.

South of Msambweni the road cuts through seemingly endless fields of sugar cane and through the village of **Ramisi**. At the end of the sugar cane plantation, a road branching off to the left leads to **Shimoni**, the "Place of the Hole". This sleepy little fishing village owes its name to a broadly ramified system of caves on the west side of town. There – or so it is said – slaves were once held captive before being shipped to the several overseas markets. In Shimoni proper there is a fish market, a station of the Marine National Park and two hotels for sport fishermen. The older of the two hotels, the **Pemba Channel Fishing Club**, is a traditional meeting-place for deep-sea fishermen and is known for its record catches, although the **Shimoni Reef Fishing Lodge** also has its fans. This area is especially popular for marlin fishing, and quite a few "big fish stories" are also spun about the size of the specimen someone may have sighted (or even caught!). Both of the hotels are located on the **Wasini Channel** and have a beautiful view of **Wasini Island**.

The new village pier is used by the boats of the national park patrol, which is responsible for supervising the **Kisite Marine National Park** and the adjacent **Mpunguti Marine Reservation**. Snorkeling enthusiasts can arrange trips to Kisite through the national park administration as well as at the hotels on Diani Beach. Word has been going around about the *dhow* excursions arranged by Thorn Tree Safaris, which start in the

69

mornings, as usual, with snorkeling and swimming. In the afternoons the dhow lays up at **Wasini Island**, where the seafood restaurant **Ras Mondini** serves its guests delectable meals. A little stroll to aid digestion leads under the shadow of baobob trees into the village of Wasini. The women of this village, which was once an Arab settlement, offer homemade handicrafts for sale.

Wasini Island, measuring about three square kilometers, is called to this day the "forgotten island". Indeed, it wasn't inhabited until about 300 years ago. This certainly comes as no surprise when one realizes that there is practically no fresh water here: even the well-water is salty.

There are several additional smaller coral islands located off the coast further to the south that can be reached from Shimoni on fishing boats. They are wonderfully suited for a diving or snorkeling outing. A full-day dhow safari is avail-

able to the island of **Kisite**. It travels first through the Wasini Channel out to the island for sun-bathing or diving, and then passes the **Coral Gardens** of Wasini Island on the return trip.

The last town before the Tanzanian frontier is **Lunga Lunga**, 95 kilometers from Mombasa and still 5 kilometers away from the border crossing.

SHIMBA HILLS NATIONAL RESERVE

With a size of 192 square kilometers, the **Shimba Hills National Reserve** is among the smallest animal reserves in the country. Starting from Mombasa, the Likoni ferry crosses over to the south coast; from there the main road goes for a few kilometers to **Ngombeni**. It then turns to the right inland toward **Kwale** (16 km). From there the route is indicated with signs and leads over partially forested hills into the reserve. About one-half day should be allowed for a tour. The wildlife reserve is well-known for the primeval

Above: The Shimba Hills – a peaceful, pristine landscape in which to admire nature.

70

landscape of the Shimba Hills and for its unique stock of horse and rappen antelope. In addition, it is home to buffalo, bushbucks, leopards and a few shy families of elephants. In the **Mwele Mdogo Forest** the visitor is greeted by impenetrable jungle with lianas as thick as an arm and huge tree-limbs between which colorful butterfly flutter about.

Alongside the rare plants and butterflies there are also many bird species in the dense tropical rain forest such as the turaco. The spurfowl, which makes its home here, is called the "kwale" in Swahili, and is the heraldic animal of the eponymous district.

In places the reserve is situated as much as 400 meters above sea-level, so that the entire lengths of the Tiwi and Diani beaches can be viewed from its observation points.

The three-leveled **Shimba Hills Lodge** was constructed following the example of the famed Treetops Lounge in the Aberdares. Opened only a few years ago, the lodge is a masterpiece of wooden construction and characteristic of the Kenyan tree-hotel. The connecting walkways at the level of the tree crowns make it easy to observe the animals from close up, especially the vicinity's fascinating ornithological world. The watering-hole not far from the lodge, which draws elephants, buffalos and antelopes, is surrounded by trees, which, unfortunately, hampers watching the animals coming to it. There is, however, some compensation in the nearby clearing and the artificial salt licks, which also attract wildlife. Since the Shimba Hills Lodge has yet developed into a popular destination for weekend excursionists from Mombasa, it's definitely recommended to make reservations ahead of time.

If you would prefer not to use the same road for the return journey, it is possible to leave from the other side of the reserve at the **Kidongo Gate** and drive back to Mombasa over the coastal route.

SOUTH COAST
Accommodation

LUXURY: **Golden Beach Hotel**, PO Box 31 Ukunda, Tel: (Diani Beach) 01261/2625. **Diani Reef Grand Hotel**, PO Box 35, Ukunda, Tel: 01261/2723. **Leisure Lodge Club Hotel**, PO Box 84383, Mombasa, Tel: 01261/2011. **Africana Sea Lodge**, PO Box 84616, Mombasa, Tel: 01261/2052. **Jadini Beach Hotel**, PO Box 84616, Mombasa, Tel: 01261/2622. **Robinson Baobab Club Hotel**, PO Box 32, Ukunda, Tel: 01261/2623. **Safari Beach Hotel**, PO Box 90690, Tel: 01261/2726. **Leopard Beach Hotel**, PO Box 34, Ukunda, Tel: 01261/3422/2110-2. **Indian Ocean Beach Club**, PO Box 73, Ukunda, Tel: 3556/3730.
MODERATE: **Two Fishes Beach Hotel**, PO Ukunda, Tel: 01261/2101. **Ocean Village**, PO Box 88, Ukunda, Tel: 01261/2188. **Club Green Oasis**, PO Box 80, Ukunda, Tel: 105, Msambweni. **Diani Sea Resort**, PO Box 37, Tel: 3081/3. **Falcon Bay Beach Lodge**, PO Box 2084, Ukunda, Tel: 2502.
BUDGET: **Trade Winds Hotel**, PO Box 8, Ukunda, Tel: 01261/2016. **Shelly Beach Hotel**, Likoni, PO Box 96030, Mombasa, Tel: 451001. **Pemba Channel Fishing Club**, PO Box 44, Msambweni, Tel: 471349. **Shimoni Reef Lodge**, PO Box 82234, Mombasa, Tel: 471349. **Twiga Lodge** with camping ground and bandas, PO Box 80820, Tel: Kwale 4061.

Restaurants
Ali Barbour's (an absolute must, French food in a gigantic stalagtite cavern), Tel: 01261/2033. **Nomads**, Tel: 01261/2155. **Wasini Island Restaurant**, Tel: 01261/ 2331. **Cheers**, Diani Shopping Center. **Maharani**, opposite Trade Winds Hotel. **Nomads**, Diani Beach South. **Vulcano Italian Restaurant**, PO Box 291, Ukunda, Tel: 2004. **Boko Boko**, in the south of Diani Beach – Galu.

Nightclubs
Ngoma, Diani Reef Grand Hotel. **Banda**, Africana Sea Lodge, Diani Beach. **Safari Sands Club**, Hotel Safari Beach, Diani Beach. **Leisure Lodge**, Hotel Leisure Lodge, Diani Beach.

Crossing the border into Tanzania
The checkpoint near the village of Lunga-Lunga can be reached either by bus from Mombasa to Tanga or Dar es Salaam, or by car. Bear in mind that the elaborate border formalities may take up to several hours; a visa – and patience – is absolutely essential.

SHIMBA HILLS NATIONAL RESERVE
Accommodation
Shimba Hills Lodge, reservations through Nyali Beach Hotel, Mombasa, Tel: 471551.

A TOUCH OF ARABY

THE NORTH COAST

KILIFI

GEDI

MALINDI

LAMU AND VICINITY

THE NORTH COAST OF MOMBASA

The island city of Mombasa divides the Kenyan coast along the Indian ocean into the "north" and "south" coasts. The north coast extends from Mombasa past the coastal towns of **Kilifi** and **Malindi** to the islands of the **Lamu Archipelago** and comes to an end at the village of **Shakani** on the Somalian border. Whereas the narrow coastal strip north of Mombasa and in the vicinity of Malindi is among the most densely settled areas in the country, the northern administrative district of Lamu is still developed for tourism.

Situated just beyond the New Nyali Bridge, which connects Mombasa with the mainland, is the high-priced suburban district of **Nyali**, where Mombasa's upper class resides in elegant homes amidst lots of well-maintained gardens. The **Bahari Club**, a center for watersports and deep-seas sport fishermen, is located off of the road to Nyali.

The promontory known as **English Point** was named by the first slaves freed by the British who settled here. A monument also recalls the renowned German

Preceding pages: Entertainment is one thing that the coastal hotels are not lacking. Left: There is always time for a little flirt.

missionary Johann Ludwig Krapf (1810-1881), who came with his wife to Mombasa in 1844. Located nearby is the **Moi Park**, where the exhibition of the *Mombasa Agricultural Society of Kenya* has taken place annually since 1963 – an event to which Kenyan President Daniel Arap Moi usually travels as well. On these occasions the roads approaching Mombasa and the city itself are decorated everywhere with large banners welcoming the President to town. If you should by chance find yourself standing on a street through which the presidential convoy is driving you would be well advised to not pull out your camera under any circumstances. This could entail becoming an unwilling guest of President Moi himself; and Kenyan jails are not known for their comfort.

The feudally sumptuous, exclusive **Nyali Grounds** includes a twelve-hole golf course as well as squash and tennis courts. Located right beside it are several of the best hotels in the area. The oldest of these is the **Nyali Beach Hotel**, which was erected in 1946.

The **Mamba Village**, opposite the golf club, boasts of being the largest crocodile farm in Africa. Over 10,000 crocodiles, ranging from enormous man-eaters down to the tiny freshly-hatched young live here in natural surroundings.

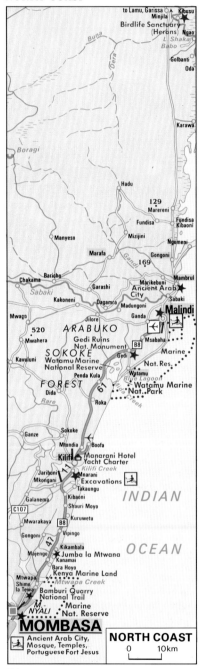

to Lamu, Garissa
Kibusu
Minjila
Birdlife Sanctuary
(Herons) Ngao
L. Shaka
Babo
Buna
Dera
Golbanti
Oda
Karawa
Boragi
Hadu
129
Marereni
Fundisa
Fundisa Kibaoni
Mizijini
Manyeso
Ngomeni
Marafa
Gongoni
169
Gandi
Chakama
Baricho
Marikebuni
Mambrul
Garashi
Ancient Arab City
Sabaki
Kakoneni
Dagamra
Madungoni
Sabaki
Mwago
Jilore
Ganda
Malindi
520
A R A B U K O
Mwahera
Gedi Ruins
Msabaha
Nat. Monument
88
Marine
S O K O K E
Gedi
Kaviluni
Watamu Marine
Nat. Res.
National Reserve
Penda Kula
Watamu
F O R E S T
Blue Lagoon
Dida
Watamu Marine
Nat. Park
Rare
Roka
Creek
Ganze
Sokoke
Mtondia
Boofa
Kilifi
Manarani Hotel
Yacht Charter
Kilifi Creek
Jaribuni
Mnarani
Mkongani
Excavations
Takaungu
Galanema
Kibaoni
C107
Shauri Moyo
I N D I A N
Mwarakaya
88
Kuruwetu
Gongoni
Vipingo
Kikambala
Majengo
Jumba la Mtwana
O C E A N
Kanamai
Bara Hoyo
Mtwapa
Kenya Marine Land
Shimo
Mtwapa Creek
la Tewa
Bamburi Quarry
M.
National Trail
NYALI
Marine
Nat. Reserve
MOMBASA
Ancient Arab City,
Mosque, Temples,
Portuguese Fort Jesus
NORTH COAST
0   10km

Nyali extends all the way to **Freretown**, which is reached by following the main road past the New Nyali Bridge on toward Malindi. In 1874, Sir Bartle Frere founded a missionary station for freed and runaway slaves, who are still commemorated at the **Emanuel Church**.

Signs along the road point the way to the **Bombolulu Workshops** for the physically handicapped, where African jewelry, wood carvings and bags are sold at very reasonable prices.

A few kilometers further the main road bypasses the private forest and animal preserve of the **Bamburi Cement Company**. Here the Swiss agronomist René Haller helped to eliminate the ugly scars which decades of coral limestone mining left on the landscape with a remarkable program of reforestation. The Bamburi Quarry Nature Trail is open to visitors the whole week through. The feeding of the animals takes place around four o'clock in the afternoon. A wide variety of birds and mammal species, as well as crocodiles and hippopotami live on this 24 hectare tract. An extensive fish-farming outfit, whose output is sold to restaurants and hotels in the vicinity, contributes to the financing of this noteworthy environmental project.

Located on the other side of the road, in the neighborhood of the **German Biergarten**, is the **Kipepeo Aquatic Zoo** which features 17 large-scale aquariums accomodating 150 different fish species from tropical waters.

The north coast of Mombasa up to **Shimo la Tewa** at the **Mtwapa Creek** is the most highly developed tourist area in Kenya. Dozens of hotels are lined up one after the other along the beaches of **Nyali**, **Bamburi** and **Shanzu**. Nonetheless, the beaches are not overcrowded, and those who want to can still find a quiet little spot for sunbathing and swimming.

The tourism boom has also brought about the establishment of many new restaurants; in addition, discotheques and

gambling casinos belong to the scenery just as much as the car rental agencies, shopping centers and sporting complexes. The **Discotheque Bora Bora** is well-known, it also features special midnight shows. Fortunately, the majority of hotel installations here are quite different from the gigantic, sterile, bed-stuffed highrises that are so much a part of the tourist scenery in other countries. The buildings, covered with attractive Makuti roofs, are at most two levels high and are usually cleverly hidden amidst palms and blooming gardens.

FROM SHIMO LA TEWA TO KILIFI

The **Mtwapa Creek**, actually a sea-inlet which cuts deep into the mainland, separates Mombasa's northern coast from the next section of coastline, ex-

Above: Deep see divers and fishermen should be able to test their skills in the bountiful waters of the Kenyan coast.

tending to Kilifi. Years ago the bay still had to be crossed with an old chain-ferry pulled by hand, and the black boatmen knew how to delight their passengers with improvised sea-shanties. Today, however, the modern age has also slithered into this part of the land, and now a slick bridge spans the creek.

Past the bridge the road branching off to the right goes to the **Kenya Marine Land**, a marine park with huge aquariums, in which sharks, turtles, barracudas, thorn-backs, and other sea-creatures lively swim about. Feeding is done once daily by a diver; visitors are also allowed to look on.

In addition, this is a great place to go water skiing or deep sea fishing. One alternative for a jolly excursion is a dhow ride from the dock at the marine park into the creek. Up to three dhows cruise together along the mangrove-overgrown banks, through the ramified arms of the inlet. For on-board entertainment there are Giriama dances, drumming recitals and acrobatic performances.

77

Among the other attractions at Kenya Marine Land are a snake zoo with mambas, cobras and other serpents as well as a reconstructed Masai village where jewelry and carvings are produced and traditional dances are presented. The restaurant **Le Pichet** is the place to go for gourmets.

Located on the coast not far from here is one of Kenya's national monuments, a 400-year-old slave-traders' outpost. Today the ruins of the city **Jumba la Mtwana**, "Home of the Slave-holder", is an interesting open air museum. If you should happen to drive through here at meal-time, stop at **Claudio's** for a romantic Italian dinner with a view of the sea.

Kikambala, located further to the north, is the last clean swimming spot on the north coast. Beyond it, on up to Kilifi, 40 kilometers away, the main road is hemmed with one sisal plantation after

the other. The sisal hemp, the price of which undergoes extreme fluctuations on the world market is produced from the fibrous leaves of the sisal agave. The people here create many attractive articles from sisal, particularly mats and *kiondos*, the typical African baskets.

Beyond the plantations the road winds up to Kilifi Creek one of the most beautiful inlets on the coast. On the other side of the bay, which has eaten its way eight kilometers in land, is the town of **Kilifi,** located roughly half-way between the cities of Mombasa and Malindi. Where the road branches shortly before reaching the creek, the right-hand way leads to the **Mnarani Hotel**, one of Kenya's oldest and at the same time a center for deep sea sport fishermen and divers. The new bridge from Kilifi recently took the place of the ferry.

Due to its protected location, **Kilifi Creek** is ideal for wind-surfing and water skiing enthusiasts. Furthermore, it has especially picturesque scenery, particularly in the evenings, when it is common to

Above: Fishing is Kenya's second most important source of income. Right: Sisal plantation near Kilifi.

take a boat out on the bay to watch the breathtaking sunset. At this time of day, dense clouds of carmine-red bee-eaters gather so that the air practically vibrates from the flapping of their wings as the last sunlight glows on their luminous red plumage.

Kilifi, the capital of the Kilifi District, can also be reached by driving over the bumpy road that goes around the creek. The town itself, however, has no interesting sights to speak of.

A CITY OF RUINS

Extending north of Kilifi before the junction to Watamu is the **Arabuko Sokoke Forest**, a seriously endangered forest region that is rather famous among ornithologists for its extraordinarily rare bird species. At present new boundaries are being discussed for the reserve in order to save this precious ecological zone from the charcoal-making and forest products industries. Of course, as is so frequently the case, a compromise between industry and nature conservation is difficult to achieve. The area is accessible to visitors.

Further to the north toward Watamu a marked road branches off to the ruins of **Gedi**, one of Kenya's most significant archeological excavation sites. Here, in the midst of primeval forest, a flourishing Islamic city of more than 2500 inhabitants extended over an area of 18 hectares. It was abandoned at the beginning of the 17th century. Rediscovered in 1884, the ruins site was declared a national monument in 1948, and scientifically excavated. Nowadays visitors can stroll through the well-preserved ruins of the city on groomed paths with informative signs. It is at times difficult to pull oneself away from this atmosphere of brooding calm. Sometimes the hot midday sun suddenly lights up the darker recesses of the jungle, a bird unexpectedly takes flight, or a monkey breaks out in strange laughter. It can even seem eerie at times, and some people are quite happy when they have left the area before sundown.

fairly good appraisal of their wealth in view of such precious finds as Chinese porcelain from the Ming Dynasty, glazed stoneware from Persia and rose-hued beads from India. And finally, nothing is known of the reasons which lead this city to be suddenly abandoned after some 300 years of existence. Perhaps raids by neighboring peoples were the cause? The small **museum** at the entrance displays the most interesting finds. Those wishing to learn more details about Gedi should purchase the brochure simply titled *Gedi* authored by James Kirkman.

It isn't far from Gedi to the sea-side resort **Watamu** with its gorgeous crescent-shaped **Watamu Bay**, **Turtle Bay** and **Blue Lagoon**. From the beach one can see small islands in the sea, and behind the beach are idyillic little woods which are enticing places to take a stroll. Located in the protection of the offshore reef is the interesting **Watamu Marine Park**. The first-class hotels here have everything one could even dream of.

Near the dunes of the Blue Lagoon, the ruins of two mosques and some tombs serve to remind us that Watamu was founded all of 500 years ago.

Gedi was built at the end of the 13th or at the beginning of the 14th centuries. The well-preserved buildings of coral limestone, numerous fountains and a water system (pipes), various mosques including the Great Mosque with its 17 columns, several gigantic pillar tombs and a prison building bear mute witness to the city's once highly developed culture. The vast palace of the sultan is also impressive; in the front courtyards containers embedded into the earth for catching rainwater can be seen. A find of particular archeological significance is the "Date Grave" on which is engraved the Islamic year 802, corresponding to 1399 A.D.

To this day it remains unclear who the founders of the city were, and why they built here and not on the sea, which would have been better for trade and shipping. One can, however, make a

MALINDI

Malindi is further to the north. It is the second most important tourist center on the coast after Mombasa, although in contrast to the latter the hotels here are grouped around the core of the city, so that the entire community completely geared up for tourism.

Malindi is reputed to be a millenium old, although its existence has only been established as early as the 13th century, as evidenced by Arabic reports and ceramic finds. In 1498, Vasco Da Gama put in at Malindi's harbor on his journey to India and made the city into a stalwart ally of Portugal. Today, this historic event is commemorated by the Vasco da Gama Cross, located on a spit of land in

Above: The ghost city of Gedi, near the vacation resort of Watamu. Right: Dance performances are often organized for tourists.

the south of the city. For centuries it remained a popular port of call for all ships that were following the route around the Cape of Good Hope toward India. Starting in the mid-17th century Malindi lost much of its power and significance as a result of numerous raids and attacks. An upswing brought about by the slave trade in the mid-19th century was only of short duration. The rise of tourism in the 1930s resuscitated the sleepy backwater. The first hotels, the **Blue Marlin** and **Lawfords** were constructed and sheltered such prominent guests as Ernest Hemingway, who pursued his passion for deep sea fishing. He was followed by many emulators.

Many of the hotels are located directly on the beach, which abruptly metamorphoses into a Mecca for surfers when, during the months of July and August, the monsoon pushes giant waves through the openings in the reef.

Casinos and night-clubs, a colorful market and the **Malindi Marine National Park** are what make this town so appealing to vacationers. Some further attractions include the fish market and the sailing club, from which quite a number of sport fishing enthusiasts have set out to bring home the biggest fish of all time. Incidentally, Kenya holds various world records in sport fishing. Since fishing is forbidden within the Malindi-Watamu Marine Park, to do so one must go far enough out to sea. The same applies to the exploitation of shells and corals.

In the Inhospitable North

Leaving northward from Malindi the road continues up to Somalia. Depending on the road conditions, the weather and water level of the **Tana River,** the trip by automobile can take from one-half up to two days. Busses also travel this route from Mombasa and Malindi; they are able to manage it in six hours providing they suffer no mechanical failure, flats or other incidents. Nonetheless, only a few travelers to Kenya are willing to bother with the fatiguing overland drive, par-

ticularly since there are air connections to Lamu and Kiwaiyu.

Beyond Malindi the asphalt road becomes unpaved. After ten kilometers you cross the **Sabaki River**, which inundates the bay at Malindi with brown mud from time to time during the rainy season. Somewhat further to the north you come to **Mambrui**, a fishing village that the Portuguese discovered as early as the 15th century. A pillared tomb decorated with porcelain globes from the Ming dynasty reminds of those days as well as a mosque with domed roof which is ornamented with sayings from the Koran.

Not far past Mambrui a trail branches off towards **Marafa**. In the area of the village is an interesting landscape formation called **Hell's Kitchen** by the locals. With its hills and mountains eaten away by erosion and precipitous gorges up to 30 meters in height the area resembles a sort of bizarre moonscape.

Above: Many of Kenya's hotel complexes have been built amid flourishing vegetation.

The next leg of the journey, through **Gongoni**, passes by the Italian space exploration center **San Marco.** Its satellite launching platform, some kilometers further on in the middle of **Formosa Bay**, looks rather exotic when elephants go swimming on the beach. In the north of Formosa Bay the road runs further inland around the delta of the Tana River. On the southern banks of the delta is the city of **Garsen**, where an ancient ferry crosses Kenya's longest river. It frequently runs late, and often, during high water, the ferry doesn't run for days at a time. On the other shore, a wild scramble breaks out to catch a bus or taxi to **Witu**, where at the beginning of this century attempts were made to grow rubber trees. To the east of Witu lies **Kenyatta** on the shores of an eponymous lake. This settlement on the largest lake along the coast was created for Kenians which were expelled from Tanzania following the dissolving of the East African Community. The trip ends in **Mokowe**, where one can catch a motor boat to the island of Lamu.

NORTH COAST
Accommodation

LUXURY: **Nyali Beach Hotel**, PO Box 90581, Tel: 471551. **Mombasa Beach Hotel**, PO Box 90414, Tel: 471861. **Severin Sea Lodge**, PO Box 82169, Tel: 485001. **Serena Beach Hotel**, PO Box 90352, Tel: 485721. **Intercontinental**, PO Box 83472, Tel: 485437. **Flamingo Beach Hotel** (ASC), PO Box 81443, Tel: 485777. **Al Wahat Beach Hotel**, PO Box 90224, Mombasa.
MODERATE: **Silver Star Beach Hotel** (ASC), PO Box 81443, Tel: 472542. **Reef Hotel**, PO Box 82234, Tel: 471771. **Whitesands Hotel**, PO Box 90173, Tel: 485926. **Travellers' Beach Hotel**, PO Box 87649, Tel: 485121. **Bamburi Beach Hotel**, PO Box 83966, Tel: 485611. **Kenya Beach Hotel**, PO Box 95748, Tel: 485821. **Neptune Beach Hotel**, PO Box 83125, Tel: 485701. **Dolphin Beach Hotel** (ASC), PO Box 81443, Tel: 485801. **Shanzu Beach Hotel** (ASC), PO Box 81443, Tel: 485604. **Palm Beach Hotel** (ASC), PO Box 81443, Tel: 485520/1.
BUDGET: **Silver Beach Hotel** (ASC), PO Box 81443, Tel: 471471. **Bahari Beach Hotel** (ASC), PO Box 8144, Tel: 471471. **Giriama Beach Hotel**, PO Box 86693, Mombasa, Tel: 485726. **Ocean View Beach Hotel**, PO Box 81127, Tel: 485601.

Restaurants

Claudio's Italian Restaurant, Mtwapa Creek, Tel: 485208. **Imani Dhow**, Severin Sea Lodge, Tel: 4850001-5. **Il Dueto**, Nyali Golf Club, Tel: 472136. **Maxim's**, Nyali, Tel: 471861. **Porini Village Restaurant**, PO Box 58, Kikambala, Tel: (0125) 32148. **Galana Steakhouse**, near the Severin Sea Lodge, Tel: 485572.

Nightclubs

Bues, Hotel Nyali Beach. **Bora Bora**, near the Ocean View Hotel. **Le Club**, Hotel Intercontinental Shanzu. **Twin Star**, Hotel Palm Beach. **Starion**, near the Silver Beach Hotel, with casino.

Excursions

Bamburi Nature Trail, Bamburi, Tel: 485501. **Kenya Marine Land**, Mtwapa Creek, Tel: 485923. Sea Aquarium and Snake Park, trips on dhows.
Mamba Village, Nyali, Tel: 472709. At Kenia's one and only crocodile farm you can study and admire these impressive little dinosaurs from close quarters. Restaurant and snack bar, discotheque in the evenings. Nearby is the **Kipepo Aquarium,** with exhibits of local marine life.
The Ruins of Gedi in the region of Malindi/Watamu are worth a visit. The town "died" in the 16th century and was taken over by the jungle for a while. The excavation area is open daily from 7 a.m.–6 p.m.

Sports Fishing

Mtwapa Creek, James Adcock, PO Box 95693, Mombasa, Tel: 472066. **Kilifi**, Mnarani Hotel, PO Box 81443, Mombasa, Tel: Kilifi 2318.
In **Watamu** and **Malindi** several agencies offer day trips on diesel-powered boats for those wishing to engage in a spot of deep-sea trollfishing. Your catch of the day may include shark, sailfish, tuna, marlin and bonito, to name only a few of the many species of fish populating the sea here.

WATAMU
Accommodation

MODERATE: **Turtle Bay Beach Hotel**, PO Box 457, Tel: Watamu (0122) 32622. **Hotel Hemingway**, PO Box 267, Watamu, Tel: 0122/32006. **Ocean Sports Hotel**, PO Box 100, Malindi, Tel: 0122/32008. **Watamu Blue Bay Hotel**, PO Box 163 Watamu, Tel: 0122/32095. **Watamu Beach Hotel** (ASC), Watamu, Tel: 0122/32010.

Excursions

The hotels Turtle Bay and Ocean Sports arrange excursions to the Malindi National Marine Reserve.

MALINDI
Accommodation

MODERATE: **Lawfords Hotel**, P O Box 20, Malindi, Tel: Malindi (0123) 20440. **Blue Marlin Hotel**, PO Box 20, Malindi, Tel: 0123/20440. **Eden Roc Hotel**, PO Box 350, Malindi, Tel: 0123/20480. **Coconut Village**, PO Box 868, Malindi, Tel: 0123/ 20928. **Vasco Da Gama Lodge**, PO Box 639, Tel: 0123/21027. **Stephanie's Sea Horse**, PO Box 583, Tel: 0123/20430. **African Dream Village**, PO Box 939, Tel: 0123/20442.
BUDGET: **Driftwood Club**, PO Box 63, Malindi, Tel: 0123/20155. **Ozi's Bed & Breakfast,** PO Box 60, Malindi.

Restaurants

A multitude of small restaurants tempt the visitor in Malindi, or you can relax in a genuine German beer garden.

Banks

Barclay's Bank, PO Box 100, Tel: 0123/20036. Additional banks on Government Road.

Rental Cars

Avis, Tel: 0123/20513. **Glory Car Hire**, Tel: 0123/20065.

Excursion

To the Malindi National Marine Reserve, Malindi-Watamu. Ticket Office behind Casuarina Point.

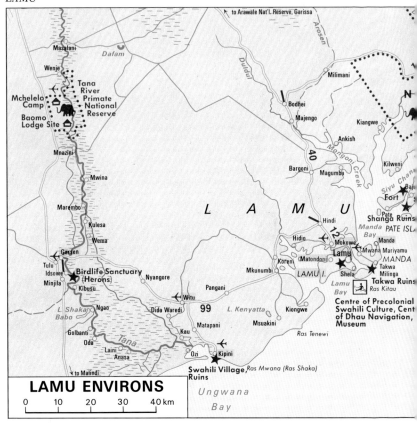

LAMU ENVIRONS

0   10   20   30   40 km

THE LAMU ARCHIPELAGO AND ITS VICINITY

The Lamu Archipelago is located on the northernmost reaches of the Kenyan coast. This group of islands, which consists of Lamu, Pate, Manda and several smaller islands owe their special character to their exposed location, which has kept the flood of tourists out of this corner of Kenya up to now.

The archipelago has been witness to a long and turbulent history of over a millenium, sometimes marked by armed confrontations, and at other times by long periods of cultural blossoming and flourishing trade. Arabs, Portuguese and Persians established themselves in the archipelago's bustling trading ports. Just as they did from the other port cities on the East African coast, heavily laden dhows sailed from here carrying ivory and slaves, setting a course toward Arabia, India and China, returning with the winds of the winter monsoons bringing spices, rugs and other precious oriental wares to Africa. Rivalries were the order of the day between the two aspiring coastal cities of Lamu and Pate, which repeatedly changed their fellow allies. However, it wasn't until the Oman Arabs had managed to extend their area of influence ever further that the hitherto independent city-states forfeited their autonomy. The unstoppable economic decline of the archipelago began with the

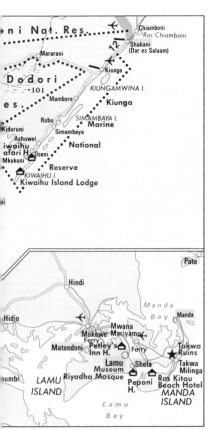

Lamu

To this day the island of Lamu is a living piece of old Arabia in the midst of Black Africa. Both the island and city by the same name are only accessible by sea, albeit, sailing time from **Manda Island** is limited to a few minutes. Visitors who arrive directly from Mombasa, Malindi and Nairobi touch down on the sand landing strip at the small airport on Manda. If coming via the land route, the drive ends in Mokowe, from where the trip continues by ferry as well.

The majority of visitors stay only for a day in Lamu and with these few hours can only get a vague idea of the full magic of the island. A walk through the city conveys the impression of living in another time – even another world. There are no automobiles clogging its maze of narrow streets and alleyways, since driving a car is forbidden on the island. The only institution excepted from this prohibition is the police prefecture itself. Who should be surprised, then, to learn that alongside the ten thousand human residents on Lamu, there live about 6500 donkeys, who solve every transportation problem. There is even a clinic for all these beasts where they are treated free-of-charge, of course.

The connections with the other islands are maintained with sailboats. From the picturesque harbor, from which the sailing ships struck out to sea to make their journeys to distant countries in earlier days, a few dhows still sail loaded up with wares. However, nowadays they only cover the jaunt to Malindi or Mombasa. Occasionally they take passengers along.

The section of the city of Lamu that faces the sea consists predominantly of stone buildings which were constructed in the 18th and 19th centuries. Their thick walls provide welcome protection against the heat, and the stone benches next to the entrances are the places where the neigh-

elimination of the slave trade by official prohibition in the 19th century. However, the islands didn't fall into the deep sleep (which has continued to the present) until Mombasa took over its preeminent function as the gateway to East Africa. This happened after the construction of the railroad and the digging of a new deep-bed harbor, which is also able to accomodate large ships.

The island's well established mercantile connections of the past had brought not only affluence and modernity, but also the teachings of the Koran. It is thought that the Archipelago is indeed the place of origin of the Arabic-Islamic hued Swahili culture, that spread all along the East African coast.

bors meet to chat in the evenings. The distinction of seeing these houses from the inside is won at the latest when you seek accomodations in one of the numerous guesthouses. The style and atmosphere are compensation enough for the simply furnished rooms. Picturesque interior courtyards overgrown by blooming bougainvilleas, old carved Lamu furniture and terraces with a grandiose view over the city are only a few of the pleasures they offer. The western section of the city, in which the poorer population lives, consists of simple mud huts with Makuti roofs and directly borders the fields which surround the city.

In order to come to grips with Lamu's labyrinthine streets, the best orientation points are **Harambee Avenue**, the main street that leads to the fort and the market place; and the street that runs along the harbor. The **Tourist Office** and the bank

Above: Islamic hue in Lamu's Old Town.
Right: The sun quickly dries the streets in Lamu after brief rain showers.

are located there, and the **Hotel Petley's Inn**, a Lamu institution steeped in. It is situated in a stylish 19th century manor and offers rooms which satisfy even the most demanding visitor. There is even a swimming pool at the guests' disposal. In the evenings the hotel's bar is usually crowded to bursting. Thirsty vacationers and some locals allow themselves the pleasure of one of the bar's more-or-less high-proof drinks. The reason is that the other restaurants do not sell any alcoholic beverages, in accordance with the decrees of Mohammed. However, they have other things to offer: Arabic-African delicacies such as spicy meatballs with aromatic herbs, or fried tigerfish in coconut sauce along with incomparable fruit juices of freshly-pressed lemon, mangos or tamarinds.

A few steps away from Petley's Inn the **Museum of Lamu** awaits its visitors. Household devices, furniture, jewelry and – the museum's big attraction – two gigantic *siwa*, long horns of ivory and copper, blown only on special occasions, give an impression of the craftsmanship of the Swahilis. A glimpse into the splendid marriage suite reveals the magnificent world of the One-Thousand-and-One Nights. For an adequate obulus the museum is prepared to present an informative slide-show covering the history and renovation of Lamu.

Little alleyways lead from the sea-side up to **Harambee Avenue** and further on through the city. Lots of shops in the whitewashed two-storied buildings conjure up the image of an oriental bazaar, and outside on the heavy wooden doors hang the multicolored *kangas*. In the street one comes upon men clothed in the floor-length white *kanzus* or the *kikois* (a type of wrap) and wearing the traditional *kofia* on their heads. The women are enveloped from head to foot in their black *buibuis;* only their expressive eyes can be seen under their protective veils.

The city is filled with brisk activity into the late hours of evening. And it is completely safe for tourists to mix in with the hustle and bustle as well. However, some consideration is expected by foreigners as far as clothing is concerned. You should conform at least somewhat to the Islamic conceptions.

In purely Islamic Lamu there are two dozen mosques which one may only enter with permission. Among the more interesting is the 16th century **Friday Mosque** in the north of the city. Lamu's most famous Islamic temple is the **Riyadha Mosque** located to the southwest of the market. It is where the *Maulidi-al-Nabi* festival takes place each year, at which the Moslems celebrate the birthday of the Prophet. As many as 10,000 pilgrims come from throughout East Africa, from the Comoro Islands, the Arabian peninsula and even from India come to the island on the occasion of the festival. During that week Lamu is overflowing with visitors; they are offered meals free of charge in a public kitchen behind the Riyadha Mosque. The high-point of the

week-long celebration is a *Ziyara*, a procession to the **grave of Habib Swaleh**, a holy man who gave the religious life of Moslems a new impetus after settling in Lamu some time after 1880.

Excursion to Shela and Matondoni

On the northeast end of the island of Lamu is the village of **Shela**, unmistakeable with its white minaret towering in the sky like a lighthouse. There are two possibilities for getting there: One can either take a boat or use the three kilometers for taking a walk on the beach.

Main attraction of the sleepy village, which was the stage for a bloody battle between the Pate and the Lamu at the beginning of the 19th century, is the small but exclusive **Hotel Peponi** and the dream-like beauty of its sandy beaches. Bordered by high dunes, the beaches extend 12 kilometers up to **Kipungani.**

Matodoni, where the dhow is still built using traditional means, is located on Lamu's west coast. If one sails to the vil-

lage it might well happen that the trip will take a lot longer than planned, since, if the wind doesn't cooperate, the seamen must tack for hours on end before they are able to lay in at Lamu again.

The Islands of Manda, Pate and Kiwayu

The most important connection to the outer world for the island of Manda is the little airport across from Lamu. Otherwise it is only possible to get there by boat. Nearby, in the little village of Manda, some scarcely excavated ruins provide a reminder of the oldest settlement on the East African coast, originating from around the ninth century. The ruins of **Takwa** are more interesting. They are hidden away in the mangrove swamps at the end of an inlet, and constitute the remains of a city from the 16th

Above: Walking the plank, as it were, on one of the numerous dhows that cruise along Lamu's coast.

or 17th century. The ruins themselves are comparable with Gedi in both structure and archeological significance.

The southern peninsula **Ras Kitau** has alluring, paradisiacal beaches. In the quiet grounds of the **Ras Kitau Beach Hotel** the vacationer can enjoy utter seclusion from the outside world.

Girded with dense mangrove forests, the island of **Pate** is located 32 km to the northeast of Lamu. Dangerous reefs and shoals make the approach by boat difficult, and the little airport has only irregular flights. Accordingly, the number of visitors is quite low, although Pate has a couple of nice things to offer: There are the **excavations** of **Nabhani** and **Shanga** and the fortress of the small oriental village of **Siyu**. The biggest town on the island is **Faza**, with 1500 inhabitants. The fishing village of **Kizingitini** is renowned for its gorgeous beaches and the shellfish caught there. It is possibble to explore the island either on foot or by donkey. The only overnight accomodations are rooms in private houses.

The situation is entirely different on the island of **Kiwayu** situated to the north. It, too, boasts splendid beaches and fascinating coral cliffs. This paradise for a vacation by the seaside, spent snorkeling or fishing on the high seas also offers the more affluent vacationers comfortable lodgings at the luxurious **Kiwayu Island Lodge**.

The Boni, Dodori, Tana River and Arawale Reserves

The hinterlands along Kenya's north coast have scarcely been developed, and besides are no longer safe with the civil war raging in Somalia. The **Boni** and **Dodori** wildlife reserves, located near the Somalian border, were not established until 1976. These are intended to offer protection in particular to the numerous elephant herds and the topi antelope. Observing the animals is made more difficult by the dense vegetation of the virgin forest and brush, and the few trails cut across the land are virtually impassable.

The two wildlife reserves to the west and east of the Tana River are somewhat more accessible. The **Tana River Primate National Reserve** lies on the west bank of the Tana river on the road from Garsen to Garissa (which is frequently difficult to drive during the rainy season). The wildlife protection area was primarily established for the rare colobus monkey and the mangabey, which are otherwise found only in the Western part of Africa. The **Boama Lodge** has the only comfortable sleeping accommodations in the whole reserve. It is possible to make canoe excursions from there to observe crocodiles and hippopotami.

The **Arawale National Reserve** is located on the direct (but poor) road from Mokowe to Garissa along the east bank of the Tana River. Unique to the Arawale Reserve is the Hunter's hartebeest although they are, unfortunately, almost never seen in this virgin landscape.

LAMU ARCHIPELAGO
Access
By air: A regular flight service connects Manda Island with Nairobi, Mombasa and Malindi. Daily air service between Kiwaiyu Island, Lamu and Nairobi. *By boat:* A post boat calls daily at Pate. From Manda airport, ferries run to Lamu after the arrival of a flight. A boat service connects Lamu and Shela several times daily; boats stop at the Ras Kitau Beach Hotel on request. *By car/bus:* Take the overland route to Mokowe for the ferry to Lamu. Travel agencies in Nairobi, Mombasa and Malindi organize day trips or excursions to Lamu.

LAMU
Accommodation
MODERATE: **Petley's Inn**, PO Box 4. **Yumbe House Lodge**, PO Box 81. **Lamu Palace**, PO Box 193, Tel: 0121-33272/33164. **Stone House**, PO Box 193, Tel: 0121-33149.
BUDGET: A local guide will take you to any of these budget hotels – all in the vicinity of the harbor: **Bahati Lodge, Rainbow Lodge, Castel Lodge, Jannet House**.
Restaurants
Yogurt Inn, inexpensive snack bar and café in town. **Bush Gardens**, fish eatery at the harbor. Many small restaurants in the streets of the old town with amazingly good food at reasonable prices. **Hapa-Hapa Restaurant**, Promenade. **Petley's Inn**, Promenade, close to Lamu Museum.
Camping
Camping is not allowed on Lamu.
Bank
Standard Bank, PO Box 100, Tel: 3265.
Museum
Lamu's museum at the dock features numerous exhibits of handicrafts of wood and silver. Models of boats are also displayed. Open from 8 a.m.–6 p.m.
Hospital
The new, large hospital is situated at the fringe of town, in the direction of Shela.

SHELA
Accommodation
Hotel Peponi, PO Box 24, Tel: 0123-3029.

MANDA ISLAND
Accomodation
Ras Kitau Beach Hotel, PO Box 99. **Blue Safari Camp**, PO Box 3250.

KIWAYU ISLAND
Accomodation
Kiwayu Island Lodge; Reservations: PO Box 48287, Nairobi, Tel: 331231.

GREEN CITY IN
THE SUN

NAIROBI

NGONG HILLS

GIKOMBA

NAIROBI NATIONAL PARK

NAIROBI

It hasn't even taken a single century for **Nairobi** to evolve from a solitary railroad support station in the East African wilderness, into a modern city numbering over two million inhabitants. The name Nairobi, by the way, was derived from the Masai words *enkare nyarobe*, or "sweet water".

Since its founding, Nairobi, situated at a considerable altitude of 1645 meters, has developed at a fantastic speed. From a small pioneer town, it has grown into a metropolis that can scarcely be distinguished from the big cities of Europe or America, with all of the advantages and disadvantages that accompany them. Modern hotels and corporate skyscrapers put their unmistakable stamp on the cityscape, just as much as the elegant upper-class suburbs or the slums on the city's outskirts. Of course, there's one special feature that makes Nairobi incomparable: Just a couple of kilometers past the city limits herds of giraffes rove across the steppes, lions wait in ambush for their prey, and zebras graze in the pristine wilderness.

Preceding pages: Nairobi, a city that grew from a shack to a metropolis in less than a century. Left: In the lanes of Nairobi.

Nairobi, the largest city in East Africa, is not only Kenya's leading industrial and trade center, it also has great significance on an international level as both a convention city and the seat of various bureaus of the United Nations.

The demographic development of Nairobi is keeping up with the urban housing growth rate: Today the population count exceeds the two-million mark and for the year 2000 the city is expected to have between up to three and four million inhabitants.

100 Years of History

Kenya's development into a nation was hastened dramatically by the construction of the Kenya-Uganda Railway. The line which was to connect Mombasa on the Indian Ocean with Lake Victoria and Uganda reached the spot where Nairobi stands today in 1896. Despite the surrounding swamp this place was chosen as a permanent camp due to the fact that the difficult task of laying tracks in the steep discontinuity of the Rift Valley was just a little up the way. In only a few years, the up-and-coming little city of Nairobi developed from what started as a couple of wooden shacks.

During this period, white settlers, real estate speculators and adventurers came

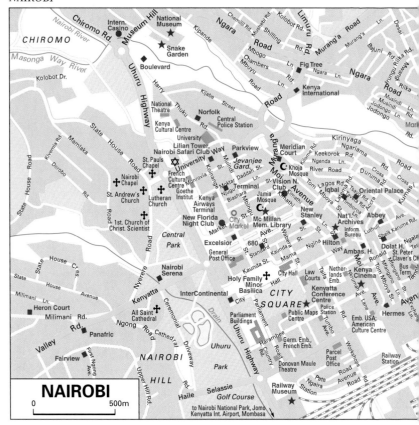

streaming into the country and established themselves in Nairobi, while a number of big-game hunters made the city a base for their safaris. A lively social life rapidly developed, offering a wide variety of entertainment to the farmers and hunters who often lived in isolation for months at a time. In 1907, only a few years after its founding, Nairobi became the seat of the British administration for East Africa and consequently the capital of Kenya. The population had already grown to 12,000 by the year 1910.

The breathtaking speed of the city's development has persisted to this day. Greater numbers of surrounding towns were incorporated and villagers from the whole country flocked to the city in the hopes of better wages and a higher living standard. These hopes, though, soon proved to be false for the majority, since there was neither housing nor employment to be had. As a result, huge slums formed on the city's outskirts that has in the meantime become a nightmare for the city's politicians and planners.

A Look Around the City

The best way to establish one's bearings in Nairobi's inner city are by locating the skyscraper of the **Kenyatta International Conference Center** and the conspicuous cylindrical tower of the **Hilton Hotel**. Close to these, the **Tourist In-**

ganizers keep offices and/or representatives in the particularly larger hotels and shopping centers. One should, however, beware of the tricksters who lure the unsuspecting visitor with seemingly inexpensive tour offers and, along the way, attempt to pursue out their illegal currency and drug operations.

As soon as you know your way around the city just a bit, you will be able to discover a lot more by going on foot. The majority of interesting sights can be comfortably reached this way, and following a simple itinerary in the Nairobi grid is child's play. During the day, Nairobi is as safe as any other large city, although valuable items, be it a gold wristwatch or even an attaché case with important papers shouldn't be brought along on a stroll through the city. Furthermore, leave nothing in an unattended automobile, nor in its locked trunk!

As a rule, the four-hour-long tour of the city starts off at the **Kenyatta International Conference Center** in the heart of the city. The building complex was constructed in 1972. Rising up alongside it is one of the oldest governmental buildings in the city, the Neo-Classical **Courthouse** with its austere façade above the entrance supported by a colonnade.

Next stop is the **Parliament Building**, whose certainly most exciting feature is the twelve-story pillar of its **clock tower**. A collection of 49 linen and wool carpets, sewn and stitched by the East African Women's League, hangs in the Long Gallery of the Parliament. They tell the story of Kenya's colonial past. At the intersection of **Parliament Road** and **City Hall Way** stands the Catholic **Holy Family Minor Basilica**. A variety of Protestant churches are located on the other side of **Uhuru Highway** near the Central and Uhuru Park. On the south side of the latter, the Neo-Gothic structure of the **All Saints' Cathedral** stands out as a prominent feature in the modern urban landscape.

formation Center is located on **Moi Avenue** on the same level as the Hilton Hotel. The **railroad station**, Nairobi's most important transportation node, is located at the southern end of Moi Avenue. All the cross-country trains arrive here from Mombasa, Kisumu and Malaba at the Ugandan border. The majority of foreign visitors, however, arrive at the **Jomo Kenyatta International Airport**, which is located about 14 kilometers outside of town.

One of the ideal opportunities for the newcomer to Nairobi to get an initial first overview and to review what might be worth a visit later on, are the very informative organized city tours. A number of reliable travel agencies and tour or-

The Cathedral and the churches are not the only religious sights in Nairobi: Numerous mosques, and temples of the Hindu and Sikh religions, in the metropolitan area still testify to the city's cultural diversity. By far the most beautiful place of worship, however, is the city's huge Friday Mosque, the **Jaima Mosque** designed in Indian style in 1925. With its two minarets and gleaming silvery dom, it looks like the perfect backdrop for a fairy tale out of *The 1001 Nights*. Right around **Banda Street**, where the mosque is located, one comes upon the picturesque **City Market**, an agglomeration of stands offering colorful fruit and flowers for sale.

Another of Nairobis more popular markets, which is also visited in the various tours of the city, is located in the district of **Kariokor**. There you can

Above: The colorful and bustling market in Nairobi. Right: The great bull elephant Ahmed in effigio in the National Museum in Nairobi.

sample a lot of charcoal-broiled specialties – indeed delicacies – of beef, goatmeat or even tripe.

An extensive walking tour of the city usually calls for some form of relaxation. Here Nairobi has to offer a number of pleasant parks or lawn-covered spaces. Even though they may not be quite as well groomed in the past few years as they used to be – due to the drastic and uncontrolled increase in population – the nickname for Nairobi, "Green City in the Sun", is nonetheless still quite applicable.

Right in the city center one can relax or row about on artificial ponds in the **Central and Uhuru Park** on Uhuru Highway. Those who are in the mood for some genuine peace and quiet, however, must undertake a somewhat longer journey and drive to the **City Park** on **Limuru Road**. It is located a ways outside of the center near **Parklands**. The city Park graduates almost seamlessly to an old forest with jacaranda and other indigenous tree species, and is currently attracting an increasing number of monkeys, who are quite happy to put on a bit of a show in return for some peanuts or crackers. Also of interest is a visit to the **Boscawen Memorial Collection** of rare plants, situated in the area of the Limuru Road park entrance; another amusing activity might be a walk through the **labyrinth** at the opposite end of the park.

Interesting Museums

Kenya's more recent history is amply displayed in the **Railway Museum** next to the train station. It features historical photographs, elegant parlor cars and old locomotives from the pioneer days of the Kenyan railroad that are sure to quicken the heart of any devoted railroad fan. In addition, the most widely told cock-and-bull story from the days of the railroad's construction is vividly documented in the museum: the man-eater tale of Tsavo. It concerns a pride of lions that consider-

ably delayed the construction of the *Lunatic Express*, in that it ate up the track layers. The construction supervision engaged a courageous hunter, who, however, fell victim to the lions himself. The railroad compartment from which the luckless huntsman was pulled by one of the predators also stands in the museum for all to examine.

The **National Archive** shelters a collection of documents from Kenya's history as well as a significant exhibition of Africana. Joseph Murumbi himself, the country's former vice president, was the one to compile the latter. The museum building with an arcade is located on Moi Avenue across the street from the Hilton Hotel.

One further outstanding collection is housed in the Neo-Classical building of the **McMillan Memorial Library** next door to the Jamia Mosque. In addition to exhaustive newspaper and parliamentary archives, it also has an extraordinary collection of books which is located on the upper floor.

Without a doubt, however, the best overview of the country's history, culture and natural science is conveyed by the **Kenya National Museum** on **Museum Hill**. The collection of articles of prehistoric, ethnological and natural history interest enjoys worldwide renown as the most extensive documentation of East Africa. The department of prehistory and early human history is particularly noteworthy for its collection of important archeological finds made, above all in Kenya, by the archeologist Leakey family. Dr. Richard Leakey is the current director of the museum. A jewel in the natural history department is the extensive collection of African bird and butterfly species. Museum visitors with an interest in ethnology should certainly not pass up the beautiful collection of tribal portraits of the writer and wildlife conservationist Joy Adamson. Kenya's more recent past is impressively documented with photographs and manuscripts as well as numerous other exhibits. A service of the Kenya Museum Society offers highly informative guided tours through individual exhibits (Monday through Friday).

In the museum's open-air courtyard an immense elephant (or rather, to be more precise, a replica of the mastodon) stands as a memorial to the famous bull Ahmed who lived in the Marsabit Animal Reserve. His right tusk was no less than three meters long!

Next to the National Museum is the Snake Park, where animals from all over Kenya have been gathered. A sign warns those with evil intentions in the following, blunt fashion: "Beware, intruders will be eaten!"

From Museum Hill and the Snake Park it's merely a few steps to another of Nairobi's history-drenched places: The legendary Norfolk Hotel on Kipande Road.

The Norfolk – Relic of the Past

The old, traditional **Norfolk Hotel** was ready for guests on Christmas, 1904, and is just as much a part of Nairobi's history as the railroad. After its destruction in a bombing in December, 1980, it was restored at great cost, but true to the original design, which was in the style of an English manor. In 1904 as well as today, the hotel is considered among the best in the country. In earlier days the Norfolk accomodated such celebrities as Ernest Hemingway and Winston Churchill, who probably sipped their drinks at the **Lord Delamere Bar** like everyone else. This famous bar, which is still a popular meeting-place today, was named after the notorious Lord Delamere. The spokesman for the white settlers arriving in droves from Europe was in the habit of parking his stiff upper lip, and going on benders with his "Kenya Cowboys". Now and then he would invade the Norfolk and shoot it up with his pistols.

Right: One of the best places to go snake-watching is in the Snake Park in Nairobi.

Another place with tradition is the **Thorn Tree Café** in the old New Stanley Hotel at the intersection of Kenyatta Avenue and Kimathi Street. People who patronize the place generally enjoy a bustling crowd and jolly fellowship. Its centerpiece is a genuine thorn tree on which visitors to Nairobi can leave messages for friends and other travellers.

Souvenirs, Souvenirs

The remarkable **African Heritage Gallery** on Kenyatta Avenue across the street from Hotel 680 is a good address for people shopping for souvenirs. The best of African craftsmanship and African works of art have been assembled here from every corner of the continent. There are extraordinary woodcarvings, masks, textiles, baskets and jewelry. A restaurant has also been opened in the gallery, offering specialties from around the continent as well.

Naturally enough, Nairobi has a great number of curio and antique dealers, although the prices are in many cases well above the threshold of tolerance. Occasionally one finds beautiful pieces from the estate of a colonial lord, though it is an open secret in the business, that the majority of dealers acquire their wares mainly in Europe.

Caution is urged in the purchase of woodcarvings! Many of the galleries have beautiful pieces, but frequently cracks in the wood ruin the pleasure of ownership after a relatively short time. The reason for this problem is that the woodcarvers work mostly with uncured materials, in other words, with wet wood. Since the pieces often lay unprotected under the equatorial sun while they are being worked on, the wood dries out far too quickly, and this is what causes these cracks. On the other hand, it is also possible that the objects don't take so well to life in centrally heated European rooms. This is usually due to the fact that

the pieces, particularly the larger works, arrive to Europe with a relatively high moisture content and dry out within a rather brief period in heated rooms. This also results in cracks and fissures in the material. Therefore, as a matter of course, those wishing to acquire woodcarvings should limit their purchases to smaller and/or unfinished pieces. The colorings and waxes applied by the artists, combined with the finishing polish, prematurely seals the wood, causing the aforementioned phenomenon.

The **Watatu Gallery**, which is located on Standard Street, regularly organizes exhibitions with the works of indigenous artists, whose creations can also be admired in the rooms of the **Alliance Française** (Kenyatta Avenue) or the **Goethe Institute** (in the Mandaleo House on Monrovia Street).

Aficionados of private galleries should keep a watchful eye out for the paintings of Joseph Katembo. The concise abstract pliancy of his brushstroke is unmistakable. This renowned painter from Zaire, who has already been living in Nairobi for many years, has a particular liking for market scenes and depictions of Africa's animal kingdom as motifs for his oil paintings.

Cuisine for Every Palate

It's pretty tough to decide where one should go for lunch or an evening meal in Nairobi. There are countless choices for every taste and financial condition.

The **Tate Room** on the first floor of the New Stanley Hotel is still the most exclusive restaurant in all of Nairobi. Admittedly, the interior – pink silk fabrics and bleached oak – is rather reminiscent of a 19th-century brothel, however, the food is simply outstanding.

For a long time there was a civilized contest between the Tate Room and the Ibis Grill, flagship of the Norfolk Hotel: Who offered the better, more sumptuous and abundant Sunday brunch? The New Stanley finally wound up the victor with a four-hour brunch, including cham-

pagne, and the byword "Eat as much as you want!"

On Friday evenings the Café Maghreb, situated by the swimming pool of the Serena Hotel, puts on a large buffet at which Nairobi's social elite gathers. The Hilton Hotel features several good restaurants; the Intercontinental can boast of its first-rate rooftop restaurant **Le Chateau**. However, many guests even of these exclusive hotels prefer the countless larger and smaller specialty restaurants spread throughout the city.

The restaurants of Rolf Schmidt are highly recommended. Both of them, **The Horseman,** in the Karen district, and **Le Chevalier,** in Muthaiga, are located a ways from the city center. The Horseman is reminiscent of an English hunting lodge, while the cuisine of Le Chevalier maintains a French tradition.

Nairobi's best fish restaurant, however, is the **Tamarind** in the building of

Above: The Carnivore's slabs and hunks of meat are a gastronomic experience.

the National Bank on Harambee Avenue. Their private trout farm has helped give them a major quality advantage over the competition.

The managers of the Tamarind also supervise the **Carnivore**, a restaurant past the airport on Langata Road. As might be expected from the name, it specializes in meat dishes, be it entire animals or cuts of beef, pork, lamb, mutton, or chicken. Such exotic beasts as zebra, antelope, giraffe and ostrich are roasted on large skewers and served to the customers is such large amounts that they never leave the place hungry. Over time the Carnivore has become so popular that some tour organizers have made it part of their itineraries.

The hotels Norfolk, Fairview and Ambassadeur regularly offer an "African buffet", although insider information has it that the best buffet of this sort is considered that of the Utalii Hotel on Thika Road, about five kilometers out of town. By the way, the Utalii Hotel is a part of the national hotel technical school that supplies all of Kenya with qualified personnel. On Sundays the hotel puts on an immense buffet in European style, which is set up either in the air-conditioned dining room or by the swimming pool. Nairobis's cosmopolitan demographic configuration is reflected in its selection of restaurants: There are Italian, Chinese, Japanese, Mexican, Korean, French, German, Indian, Ethiopian and, of course, Kenyan restaurants.

The smallest restaurant in town must certainly be Alan Bobbe's **Bistro** on Koinange Street. It has marvellous food and a very pleasant atmosphere. It's harder to say which restaurant most truly deserves the title "genuine Italian": the **Trattoria** on Kaunda Street, **Marino's** on the Aga Khan Walk next to the American Embassy, or **La Foresta Magnetica** with piano bar, on Mama Ngina Street.

There is a large number of Chinese restaurants, each of which has its own loyal circle of Chinese and Kenyan clientele. One can eat plentifully at the **Rickshaw** in the Fehda Towers on Standard Street and in the **China Plate** on taveta Road; very authentically at the **Mandarin** on Tom Mboya Street, but the majority of visitors patronizes the outstandingly managed **Dragon Pearl** in the Bruce House on Kenyatta Avenue. The service is very friendly in the **Panda** in the Imenti House on Tom Mboya Street.

Local connoisseurs of Indian cuisine tend to prefer the non-vegetarian *Mughlai* dishes. The best Indian restaurants are probably the **Minar** on Banda Street or the restaurant going by the same name in the Sarit Center near the Westlands as well as the **Safeer** in the Ambassadeur Hotel. On the other hand, pure vegetarian dishes are fairly frequent in the **Mayur** (corner of Keekorok Road and Tom Mboya Streeet), and at the **Satkar** on Moi Avenue, which specializes in South Indian cuisine.

Since there is practically no theater life to speak of in Nairobi the restaurants also close relatively early for a large city. This means that optimally one should have placed the final orders by 10 P.M. The exceptions are in the larger hotels, the Trattoria and the Foresta Magnetica.

Visitors to Nairobi who don't quite feel like throwing in the towel at that early have a choice between three casinos and various nightclubs. This brings to mind a curious Kenyan institution that should be mentioned, which exists in all of the larger cities: the day and night club. They generally consist of a bar that stays open 'round the clock, although most of them are dives the tourist would be better off steering clear of. Of course, there exist in Nairobi two or three such clubs that are definitely worth a visit because of their pleasant, friendly atmosphere and African clientele. One of these is located in the **Kenya International Hotel** at the beginning of Murang'a Road. African dishes are also served here in the middle of the night.

The **JKA Resort Club**, on Mombasa Road past the turn-off to the airport, offers its customers a dance floor and a house band. The **Hillock Inn** is indeed a bit difficult to find, located in the industrial zone on Enterprise Road. Everywhere in this neighborhood one comes across Nairobi's African middle class, that offers visitors a warm welcome. **Buffalo Bill's Bar** in the Heron Court Hotel on Milimani Road is a western-style nightclub, which has a reputation for attracting numerous generously endowed ladies without escorts. This sort of nocturnal butterfly stays here till around 11 and then migrates to the **New Florida**, **Visions**, **Hollywood**, **Florida 2000** or **Annabel's**, in other words the clubs in the city center, or to **Bubbles** at the International Casino.

One can dine in all of the nightclubs, dance until dawn, or simply have a drink at the bar. The musical spectrum moves back and forth between rock, jazz, heavy metal, African top-tens and romantic

tunes. Each club has its own particular crowd of regulars. **Visions** is especially popular.

The Hotel Intercontinental on Uhuru Highway and the Safari Park Hotel on Thika Road both house gambling casinos and thus pose some competition to the older **International Casino** on Museum Hill. The government supervises the activities of the casinos. They close at 3 A.M. on weekdays and a half-hour later on weekends. It is expected of visitors from Europe and America that they place their bets in hard currencies. Whatever the winnings, they are paid out in the same.

Accomodations for Every Pocketbook

The price for a room in one of Nairobi's international hotels is only insignificantly less than for comparable accomodations in a European metropolis.

Above: Busses are a popular mode of transportation. Right: Genuine city life beyond the air-conditioned hotels.

There are, however, hotels with bath and comfortable furnishings for only a fraction of the cost of a five-star hotel. Nairobi hosts quite a number of international conferences, therefore advance reservations are recommended. Among the luxury hotels, the **Nairobi Serena** on Central Park is not only the best in the city: It is also considered one of the world's finest hotels. Those who particularly enjoy the nostalgia of a historical ambience should in any case take lodgings in the **Norfolk Hotel**. In addition, there are hotels belonging to the international **Hilton** and **Intercontinental** chains, and the state-run **Panafric**, the centrally-located **Hotel 680**, the **New Stanley Hotel** and, finally, the palatial **Nairobi Safari Club** and the **Windsor Golf Hotel**.

Travellers with tighter budgets are best off choosing one of the less expensive hotels, such as the **Hotel Boulevard**, which has its own swimming pool; the **Fairview**, which also has a reputation for good food or perhaps even one of the dozens of establishments like the **Hotel Africana**, where a double room with shower (including breakfast) starts for around twelve US dollars. Many backpack tourists are satisfied with a place to sleep in dormitory-style rooms, for example at the **Iqbal Hotel**, where a bed only costs two dollars a night.

Although one can naturally book full board at any of the larger hotels, and frequently have a choice between several restaurants in the process, experienced visitors usually take only a room with breakfast. As a rule the hotels are located within a really convenient distance from Nairobi's city center, where there are more than 60 first-class restaurants at one's disposal.

NGONG HILLS

Travellers to Kenya familiar with the books of Karen Blixen (who also published using Tania as her Christian name), are fre-

quently interested in visiting her house and the grave of her lover, Dennis Finch-Hatton. Her former residence now belongs to the grounds of the *Karen Cooperative College*, which also extends over a section of the former coffee farm. Tour organizers offer trips to the **Blixen Museum**, although the majority of participants are truly disappointed, since the house is not very impressive. Less than ten years ago it exhibited virtually nothing with any direct connection to Blixen. Only the props which have been assembled here for the popular film *Out of Africa* convey to the visitor a (halfway authentic) portrait of the Danish authoress. Incidentally, Karen, a suburb of Nairobi, was also named after her.

Those wishing to pay a visit to the Blixen house can well combine this with an excursion to the Ngong Hills and/or to the **Bomas of Kenya** in the suburb of Langata. Every afternoon and evening, traditional African dance performances are held in the Bomas. In addition, one has the chance to study the various ways

of life of individual tribes in the local open-air museum.

For a trip to the **Ngong Hills** one should plan on taking about one-half day. They can already be seen in the distance when you leave Nairobi's city-center on the Langata Road. The drive continues through the suburbs of Langata and Karen, passing by the **Ngong Forest**. Beyond the town of **Ngong** you turn right to the Panorama Route, which is indicated with signs. At the very top the visitor is confronted with two completely antithetical kinds of scenery. The view back toward Nairobi includes the skyscrapers in the downtown as the backdrop to the small farmer settlements of the Kikuyu, then the green suburbs of Langata and Karen – a pretty, though almost prosaic sight. However, the view in the other direction, toward the Great Rift Valley offers an overwhelming panorama extending nearly 100 kilometers over an isolated piece of wild Africa with all of its primeval power only spotted now and then with isolated patches of haze.

GIKOMBA

A few kilometers out of town, just to the east of Nairobi lies the village of **Gikomba**, where the woodcarvers of the Wakamba tribe ply their trade. Most visitors will have already come here as part of a sightseeing tour of the city. Otherwise it's really recommended to hire a taxi for this little excursion. The price for the ride shouldn't exceed 80 shillings, sightseeing time included. Of course, it's also possible to reach Gikomba with public transportation, however, there are unusually many pickpockets working the busses on this route!

The number of woodcarvers in Gikomba fluctuates, although there are usually not less than 500 of them working here, crowded together in little workshops. Many of them come from the small town of **Wamunyu** in the district of Machakos. The training of the wood-

Above: Wakambas are famous for their woodcarving skills.

carvers takes place as they work, without theoretical instruction. The apprentices begin their period of schooling by polishing the figures with sandpaper, and then, step by step, learn how to handle the tools of the **Wakamba** carvers. While they work, often singing, the craftsmen sit in special chairs and use their knees or feet as a vice. The majority of the woodcarvers are members of a cooperative, which both purchases the raw materials wholesale and takes over the marketing of the finished pieces. Located not far from Gikomba on Landhies Road is the **Workshop for Applied Arts**. It is under the direction of the *Undugu Society*, which works on behalf of street children in the poverty-stricken quarters. A second workshop of this sort is managed by the *National Christian Council* in **Pumwani**. It produces toys and leather goods as well as textiles. Of course it isn't necessary to make the entire journey to Pumwani to have a chance to admire their work, since the organization also has a show-room in Standard Street in Nairobi's Center.

NAIROBI
Accommodation

LUXURY: **Norfolk Hotel**, PO Box 40075, Nairobi, Tel: 335422. **Nairobi Safari Club**, PO Box 43564, Nairobi, Tel: 330621. **Serena Hotel**, PO Box 46302, Nairobi, Tel: 725111. **Nairobi Hilton**, PO Box 30624, Nairobi, Tel: 334000. **Hotel Intercontinental**, PO Box 30667, Nairobi, Tel: 335550. **Panafric Hotel**, PO Box 30486, Nairobi, Tel: 720822. **New Stanley Hotel**, PO Box 30680, Nairobi, Tel: 333233. **Safari Park Hotel**, PO Box 45038, Tel: 802493. **Windsor Golf and Country Club**, PO Box 74957, Tel: 219784/217497/ 217499.

MODERATE: **Jacaranda Hotel**, PO Box 14287, Nairobi, Tel: 448713. **Six Eighty Hotel**, PO Box 43436, Nairobi, Tel: 332680. **Boulevard Hotel**, PO Box 42831, Nairobi, Tel: 27567.

BUDGET: **Fairview Hotel**, PO Box 40842, Nairobi, Tel: 711321.

Restaurants

The Tamarind, Tel: 338959, 220473. **Alan Bobbe's Bistro**, Tel: 336952. **Ibis Grill**, Norfolk Hotel, Tel: 335422. **The Horseman**, Karen, Tel: 882033. **The Carnivore**, Langata Road, Tel: 501779.

INDIAN: **Minar**, city center, Tel: 29999. **Minar**, Westlands, Tel: 748340. **New Three Bells**, Tel: 20628. **Dhaba**, Tel: 334862. **Nawab Tandoori**, Tel: 740209. **Supreme**, Tel: 25241.

ITALIAN: **Marinos**, Tel: 557404. **Arturos**, Tel: 26940. **The Galleria** (in the international The Toona Tree), **Casino**, Tel:742600.

CHINESE: **Hong Kong**, Tel: 28612. **Rickshaw**, Tel: 333229. **China Plate**, Tel: 20900. **Mandarin**, Tel: 20600. **Panda**, Tel: 331189.

JAPANESE: **Shogun**, Tel: 720563. **Akaska**, Tel: 220299.

Additional Restaurants

African Heritage Café, Tel: 222010. **Jardin de Paris**, Tel: 336435. **Foresta**, Tel: 223662. **Bangkok**, Tel: 751311. **Hard Rock Café**, Barclays Plaza, Loita St., Tel: 220802.

Excursions from Nairobi

The most interesting excursions from Nairobi take you to the Nairobi National Park, the Ngong Hills, the Wakamba woodcarvers in Gikomba, the Karen-Blixen-Museum, the Snake Farm or **Giraffe Farm** (Gogo Falls Lane, 1 km from the main entrance of the Nairobi National Park). The Giraffe Farm is open to the public Mon–Fri 4–5.30 p.m., weekends from 10 a.m.–5.30 p.m.

Animal lovers will delight in the **Animal Orphanage** run by the David Sheldrick Wildlife Trust, where orphaned elephant or zebra babies are nursed with love and care. These cuddly

animal babies can be visited on their afternoon walk, daily 4–6 p.m. The Orphanage is situated on the left hand side of the road, past the main entrance of the Nairobi National Park.

Banks

Official banking hours are from 9 a.m.–2 p.m.; however, some banks offer foreign exchange services all day and, additionally, on the second and/or last Saturday of the month. The banks in the Jomo Kenyatta International Airport are open 24 hours a day.

Post / Telecommunication

Post offices in the center and in most suburban shopping centers open Mon–Fri 8 a.m.–7 p.m., with a lunch break from 12.30–2 p.m.

Hospitals

The most important hospital is the **Nairobi Hospital,** Arwings-Kodhek Rd., Tel: 722160. As many private doctors have their surgeries within the hospital complex, fast expert help can be provided in most cases of emergency or illness. The hospital has a 24-hour emergency ward, a well-equipped, modern intensive care unit and a laboratory (open daily).

The **Aga Khan Hospital** has excellent equipment and facilities too, and a well-trained staff offers expert care. The hospital is on Limuru Road, opposite the City Park, Tel. 740015.

Police

The **Central Police Station** is situated on University Way and can be reached by foot from the Norfolk Hotel and the Nairobi Safari Club, Tel: 22222. In case of theft, inform the police immediately. Although the formalities at the police station can be a frustrating, nerve-racking experience, you'll just have to bear them with the patience of Job – you'll need the documents for your insurance claim.

Galleries and Souvenirs

Browse through the small art galleries for good quality art objects at reasonable prices. **African Heritage** on Kenyatta Avenue offers the largest selection of African crafts; **Gallery Watatu** on Standard Street shows exhibitions of well-known local artists.

African spears, shields, masks and jewellery can be purchased in the market and at various stores, i.e. **Hut Ltd**, **Cottage Crafts** and **Dewansons**. Before investing your money in souvenirs don't forget to look around and compare, as quality and prices can vary enormously.

Festivals and Special Events

The famous **Safari Rallye** (start and finish in Nairobi) begins a week before Easter. End of September: **Nairobi International Show** in the Jamhuri Park. October 20: **Kenyatta Day.** December 12: **Independence Day**.

NAIROBI NATIONAL PARK

The solely 120 square kilometer Nairobi National Park is located only a stone's throw away from the gates of the city and can easily be reached by automobile within 15 minutes. Alongside a great diversity of other wildlife the park serves as shelter to four representatives of the so-called "Big Five", namely lions, rhinoceroses, buffaloes, elephants and leopards. Only the elephant is missing, since such a small park could only handle their somewhat destructive way of life with the greatest of difficulty.

The north, east and west sides of the park are enclosed with a 36 kilometer-long fence; the open south side leads directly into the **Kitengela Conservation Area**, through which roam large herds of zebras, whitebeard gnus and antelopes on their annual herd migrations.

The small park, which opened in 1946 against considerable local opposition, is supposed to be – in the words of the first park administrator – a legacy for the world of the future, a place where people can communicate with nature and find peace of mind.

Before the state declared the region a national park, it served as a military camp for the army and as pastureland for Somali herdsmen. After the Somalis were resettled, the present day infrastructure was gradually built up, including roads, dammed lakes, buildings and fence enclosures. Any motor vehicles with a plain two-wheel drive can make it nearly year-round on the roughly 150 kilometer-long road network of the park.

Two large entrances lead into the park. In order to reach them, you have to drive from either Nairobi's final traffic circle at the Nyayo National Stadium about three kilometers straight ahead to the **Mombasa Road Gate** (to the right of the main

Left: The ostrich, a bird at home in almost every national park.

road across from the Firestone tire factory); or take a right onto Langata Road, which leads to the **main entrance** of the park. Besides these there are three more entrances: The **Langata Gate** and the **Banda Gate** are located on the park's west side several kilometers beyond the main entrance. To the **Cheetah Gate** you must drive 15 kilometers down Mombasa Road until the junction towards Namanga and Amboseli.

Many interesting paths criss-cross the park in all directions, so that visitors can put together an individual route according to their own tastes entirely. Those coming in with their own vehicle should by all means purchase a map of the park, stay strictly on the marked trails, and carefully observe the speed limits.

An astonishing number of animal species have settled in the park, which also provides them with a great variety of landscapes. For example, a forested plateau with splendid Kenyan highland tree species, including the croton and the Cape chestnut, extends along the western edge of the park in the neighborhood of the main entrance.

Somewhat further to the east beyond the forested area, there is a terrific view stretching over the savannah, with a vegetation consisting partly of acacias and date palms. Narrow rivers periodically flow through this valley. The umbrella acacia sometimes grows along their banks – a typical river tree –, known to earlier visitors to Kenya as the "fever tree". The reason was that this tree grows in wetland regions and is a favorite breeding ground for the malaria-carrying mosquito.

The **Mbagathi Athi River**, which has a continuous flow of water the whole year, cuts across the entire southern edge of the park, at some places plummeting through deep rocky gorges with steep rock walls. Later it turns into an easygoing river that meanders lazily through flatlands with swamp vegetation.

The animal habitats have been enlarged considerably not least by the many dams of varying size in the park's interior. The lake formed in the area of the main entrance by the **Narogomon Dam**, for example, extends over a length in excess of a kilometer, while other bodies of water are no wider than ponds, though they nonetheless attract hordes of aquatic birds and wild animals who either drink from or wallow in their braken waters.

Nairobi's Peaceful Oasis

Nairobi's skyline, with its high-rises, the castle-like Kenyatta Hospital, the screens of the drive-in cinemas and the industrial complexes, is etched against the park's northern horizon. To the east, beyond the Jomo Kenyatta International Airport, one can make out the **Mua Hills** off in the distance and to the west the

Above: A cheetah at rest – for once – in the Nairobi National Park. Right: The rhinoceros, a member of the Big Five.

Ngong Hills. The Nairobi National Park not only provides the layman with an outstanding introduction into Kenya's animal kingdom. Experienced animal researchers also come back to the little piece of wild Africa ever and again.

The black rhinoceros is one of the very special features among the members of the big five that live here. These rare beasts, whom one hardly never spots in other Kenyan national parks, were captured roaming free in the wilderness and resettled here, where they can live in peace and multiply under the supervision of wildlife conservationists, protected from poachers, their most dangerous enemies. Visitors have a fairly good chance of discovering one of the more than 40 black rhinos, which, of course usually avoid humans by making lengthy deviations over the shortgrass savannah.

The Kaffir buffalo prefer to live in the western forest district. A section of the East African Trench runs through this area, and the parklands descend precipitously to the lower-lying plain.

Unlike, the leopard, which also inhabits the forest, can be seen now and then in the trees and cliffs of the river gorges.

As it used to be, the open savannah is still the hunting grounds of the lion, for whom the herds of animals grazing there mean a good catch. When the weather is hot, the lions, whose sand-colored coats virtually melt into the surroundings, like to rest under isolated trees or on the rocks of dried-out riverbeds.

Also, the savannah is the preferred terrain of another predatory feline, namely the cheetah, which, with its phenomenal sprinting speed, can even outrun the swift Thomson gazelle. With a little bit of patience the safari participant may also catch a glimpse of the shy serval cat, the desert lynx, or the African wildcat.

With a passionate, ravenous hunger, the conspicuous Maasai giraffe munches on the leaves of bushes and trees. The peculiarly shaped leaves of many date-palms can be traced to the diligent "styling" of the giraffes' hard-working chomping apparatus.

During the year's dry seasons, in January, February and March, and in the months of August and September, huge herds of savannah dwellers, closely encircled by hungry predators looking for a catch, cross over the river and migrate across the **Kitengela Plains** in order to mingle with the cattle of the Maasai. To the disappointed park visitors it seems as though at these times even the very last animals had disappeared into thin air, especially since the long grasses successfully conceal almost every animal which is more than a few meters from the road. An attentive observer can, however, still discover many interesting animals during the wildlife migration seasons. For example, the graceful impala, a species of antelope with lyre-shaped horns, is among the animals that isn't given to wandering. They like to while away the hours in areas with a scattered growth of trees, while the bushbuck, with its beautifully colored markings, only leaves its home in the dense forests in the early mornings or late evenings.

Besides the waterbuck, which has a preference for long swamp grasses, with a bit of luck and persistence, one can also catch a glimpse of the dikdik, the reed buck, capricorn and other smaller species of antelope.

Contrary to all expectations, the small stock of hippopotamui only rarely spends any time at the dammed lakes, preferring the soutern edge of the park instead. After passing the second third of the **Athi River** one arrives at the **Hippo Pool**, where hippopotamui, crocodiles and aquatic turtles coexist in simply beautiful harmony.

The five-kilometers-long path running all the way around the pool, provides some welcome relief from the noise and dust produced by the automobiles. It also gives information on the park's nature. Finally, the passionate ornithologists among us can also observe, at their

Above: A macabre, but nonetheless fascinating scene in the Nairobi Park – vultures with their prey.

leisure, the almost 500 species of birds, that's more than have been counted in, for example, all of Germany; and even if one only has a flighting interest in our feathered friends, they still merit at least a brief look. Some of the birds, which have settled in the Nairobi National Park, are not very large, but with that, breathtakingly beautiful. The largest bird in the park, the ostrich, crosses one's path on almost every visit. Also, the slender gray secretary bird with its long dark feathers on the back of its head, which sometimes stick out, frequently struts over the savannah and keeps watch after a snack of snakes, grasshoppers and other large insects.

The reservoirs are a popular abode for aquatic birds including various subspecies of the stork and heron, and sometimes one might even get to see a royal crane, the heraldic animal of Uganda.

Perhaps the most impressive type of bird, however, are the birds of prey. For many visitors they represent the quintessential element in the classic African picture: The view over the wide, flat steppes with vultures circling in the sky high overhead.

All six of the vulture species living in Kenya are represented in the park. Since their visual faculty is vastly superior to that of humans, they are able to spy out an animal cadaver from an altitude of thousands of meters. A group of circling vultures is usually an indication that somewhere below, on the expanse of the savannah, a large predatory animal has caught and killed its prey. When the lion or cheetah has eaten its fill, the vultures descend and meticulously clean the bones of the remaining scraps of flesh. These proceedings, which frequently appear both macabre and simultanously fascinating to the foreign visitor play a significant role in balancing the savannah's ecosystem.

From a distance, when the vulture is in flight, with its characteristic bald head, it bears a strong resemblance to various species of eagle and to the somewhat smaller buzzard when they, too, circle in the sky above. The most commonly seen are the brown martial eagle and the mostly black and white fish eagle, whose cry rings in one's ears long after the bird has vanished. The East African cliff buzzard with its red tail feathers is commonly seen in the entire park, and from October through April great flocks of augur buzzards, the pigmy falcon and other predatory birds head off for southern Africa, where there is an ampler supply of food and where also the climate is warmer. There are many different weaver-bird species living along the riverbanks or in the luxuriant vegetation near the reservoirs; among the most conspicuous of these is the honey-eater or sunbird, which seems magically drawn to every blooming plant. It's difficult, however, for the layman to discriminate between the little brown larks, the myriad passerines, the bee-eaters and others who populate the savannah.

NAIROBI NATIONAL PARK

Access

Drive on Uhuru Highway until – passed the Animal Orphanage – you come to the main gate of the park. The drive takes no more than 20 minutes.

Accommodation

Masai Lodge, PO Box 81443, Nairobi.

Excursions
Bomas of Kenya

An open-air museum with dance performances and souvenir sales. Forest Edge Road, 2 kilometer from the main park entrance. Opening times Mon–Fri 9 a.m.–5 p.m.; Sat and Sun 1–6 p.m.

David Sheldrick Wildlife Fund

The **Animal Orphanage** (Magadi Road, just past the main entrance at the southwestern corner of the park) was called into life by the late gamekeeper of the Tsavo National Park David Sheldrick with the purpose of raising and nursing orphaned animal babies, mainly elephants and zebras. Open daily from 4–6 p.m.

The park's numerous snake species are only too glad to avoid the probing eye of the visitors. On the other hand, there is a vast number of lizard species that can be observed on hot, sun-drenched days taking a sun-bath on the cliffs.

The slower one drives through the park, the greater the chance is to discover something exciting or unusual. If driving in your own car, plan on taking at least several hours. You may want to mark a route out on the map that will lead you through the most varied landscapes. The chances of encountering a correspondingly varied fauna will be all the greater.

A crowd of vehicles at any particular spot is a sure sign that there is something to see, but there is a special charm to discovering the animals for oneself, and observing them quietly in their natural surroundings.

To the right of the parking area by the main entrance stands the eminently visitable **Animal Orphanage**. Baby animals that have lost their parents and sick animals are raised here and cared for.

111

A PARADISE AT KILIMANJARO'S FOOT

AMBOSELI NATIONAL PARK
LAKE MAGADI
TSAVO NATIONAL PARK
TAITA HILLS
LAKE JIPE / LAKE CHALA

Two of Kenya's most famous and interesting wildlife conservation areas are located in the southeast section of the country: The **Amboseli National Park** and the **Tsavo National Park**. Towering up between them is Mount Kilimanjaro, which, of course, stands across the border in Tanzania, but which nevertheless provides the Kenyan landscape with a majestic alpine backdrop. The parks are easily accessible from both Nairobi and the port city of Mombasa, and record increasing numbers of visitors every year. As a result, on the one hand, the financial means required for the maintenance of the wildlife conservation area are secured, of course. On the other hand, however, by its very nature the heavy tourism also takes its toll on the plant and animal life of the parks.

In addition to the large national parks, the region along the Tanzanian border has a few other special attractions to show for itself: the bird paradises on **Lake Magadi** and **Lake Jipe**, for example, and the Hilton chain's private **Taita Hills Game Sanctuary**, which is embedded in a broad glade of the Tsavo Park.

Preceding pages: Giraffes reaching for the sky with the massive hulk of Mount Kilimanjaro as a backdrop. Left: A thorny delicacy for the gerenuk, an inhabitant of the bush.

AMBOSELI NATIONAL PARK

Perhaps the greatest attraction of a visit to the Amboseli Park is the breathtaking view of the eternal snows capping the summit of Mount Kilimanjaro. Many have already succumbed to this mountain's powers of attraction, among them Queen Victoria, who made a gift of it to her nephew, Germany's Kaiser Wilhelm II, or Ernest Hemingway, whose travels to the mountain inspired his tale *The Snows of Kilimanjaro*.

On top of that, the Amboseli has such an overwhelming abundance of bird and animal species that one feels transported to a veritable Garden of Eden. When the numerous animals spend their days at the three swamps during the dry seasons, it's possible to catch a glimpse of every member of the so-called "Big Five" in the course of a single hour's drive through the park.

From Nairobi, the roughly 240 kilometers to Amboseli lead over **Athi River** and the good road in the direction of **Namanga** on the Tanzanian border. A somewhat lengthier approach leads from Nairobi onto the Nairobi-Mombasa National Highway until **Sultan Hamud** or **Emali**, at which point you turn off onto the road to **Loitokitok**. The suggested route from Mombasa would be either the

115

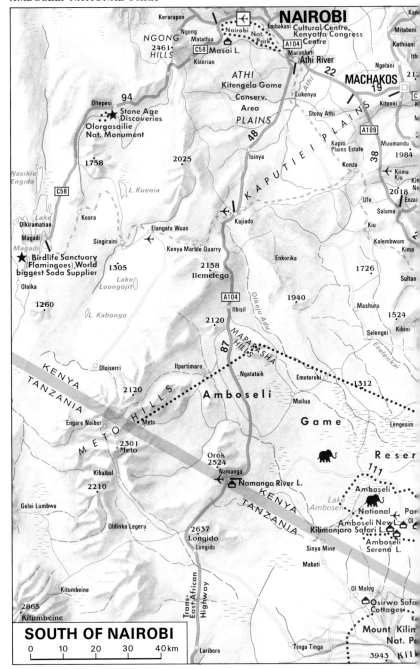

SOUTH OF NAIROBI

0   10   20   30   40km

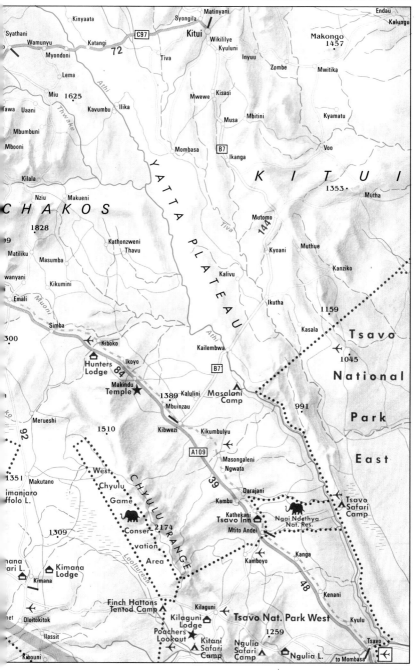

drive to Emali, or else taking the direct way through Tsavo West from the village of **Tsavo**. There are also flights from both Mombasa and Nairobi to the Amboseli Park.

In its present form the national park is all that remains of the Southern Game Reserve, which was established in 1906 in an area of 27,700 square kilometers. In 1948, the conservation area was reduced to only 3200 square kilometers, and re-named the Amboseli Game Reserve. In the Masai language, *amboseli* means "salty soil". Cut in size yet again in 1973, the present-day Amboseli National Park now extends over an area of only 392 square kilometers.

The southeastern tip of the park almost touches the foot of Mount Kilimanjaro, whose snow-capped cone watches over the landscape from an altitude of 5894 meters. It should be mentioned though, that it takes a bit of luck to catch this postcard motif in its full beauty, since mists and vapors often veil this highest of Africa's mountains. In the early mornings one has the best chance to get a clear view of both of Kilimanjaro's peaks, **Kibo** and **Mawensi**.

The vegetation of the park varies drastically depending on the availability of water and the salt content of the soils. A spare growth of reed grasses is found in the vicinity of **Lake Amboseli**, which is dried out most of the time. Further to the east, the vegetation has a greater abundance of species: A belt of acacia trees extends over the alkaline soils of the shortgrass lands, while the open savannah – the heart of the park – has only scattered bushes and shrubs besides the sparse acacia forest.

In the south and east, extensive stands of papyrus reeds are found near watering holes and in the reservation's swamplands. The melt water of Kilimanjaro

Right: Baboons are cute and playful creatures, but sometimes get annoyed and bite.

flow in countless subterranean channels down to the papyrus-reed and cypress grass swamps **Enkong Narok**, **Oltukali** and **Longinye**. They are of extraordinary importance to the ecological balance of the park, since, during the dry periods, 95% of the reservation's wildlife lives here, leaving the reservation only during the rainy season and wandering to the neighboring ranches. The swamps are the ideal location to spot great numbers of gnus, Grant's and Thomson's gazelles, elephants, rhinos, lions, cheetahs, baboons, buffaloes, impalas, and more.

An indeed very special sort of experience awaits the visitor at the viewpoint of **Observation Hill**: When Lake Amboseli is dried out, the glow of the midday sun causes bizarre silvery forms to grow out of the parched lake-bed, the savannah starts to shimmer in the blazing heat, and the Fata Morgana tricks the eye into seeing a stretch of water.

Amboseli's first lodge, **Ol Tukai**, was built in the middle of the park to house the film team that made *Snows of Kilimanjaro* in 1948. In 1992 the complex was entirely renovated. Those with no great demands for comfort can rent one of the simple and inexpensive bungalows in **Ol Tukali Bandas**. Also in the neighborhood, **Kilimanjaro Safari Lodge** was built with a view of the mountain; further north is the **New Amboseli Lodge**.

In earlier times the Masai pastured their herds of livestock in this area. Today they are forbidden by law to come into the national park with their animals. This measure seems rather incomprehensible to the Masai, and they don't always observe it. During the dry season the swamps are the only sources of water, and if wild animals are allowed to drink it, why not domestic animals, they argue.

The **Amboseli Serena Lodge**, further to the south, is situated on the **Enkongo Narok** – the Black River – a popular wildlife passageway. Ernest Hemingway is said to have set up camp at the **Kili-**

manjaro **Serena Lodge**. Outside the park in the direction of the Tsavo National Park is the comfortable **Kilimanjaro Buffalo Lodge** as well as several well developed **campgrounds**.

Besides its abundant stock of wildlife and the charms of its landscape, the proximity of the reserve to the capital city of Nairobi has lead to the fact that it attracts many, perhaps too many visitors. The unauthorized departure from the prescribed trails – whether in private vehicles or because the drivers of tourist busses are pressured into it – has in many places caused serious damage to the already meager sod. The consequence of this is, that the stock of animals, for which these pasturelands are the primary source of food, have started to decrease in recent years. It's unclear what the future of the Amboseli Park will look like if its vegetation continues to be destroyed in this manner. It can only be hoped that this renowned conservation area will again become what it once was: a paradise for man and animal alike.

OLORGESAILIE AND LAKE MAGADI

The bird sanctuary on **Lake Magadi** comfortably fits into a day-trip from Nairobi, whereby those with an interest in archeology may wish to drop in on the prehistoric excavation site of **Olorgesaile**. For lodgings, there are some simple huts at Olorgesailie, but the guests must bring their own food and water.

Starting out from Nairobi, the tour leads first of all down Magadi Road, through the Ngong Hills, and into the Rift Valley. The junction to Olorgesailie is another 66 kilometers along the road. According to geological and archeological research, in the Paleolithic age a large lake extended here. Nomads and hunters set up their camps along its shores. In the 1940s, the Leakeys, the world-renowned Kenyan archeologist couple, discovered – in the four-square-kilometer excavation area – hundreds of stone tools with ages ranging from one-half to one million years. They also discovered animal

bones, some belonging to already extinct species. Olorgesailie turned out to be one of the most fertile sites for archeological finds from the Paleolithic period. Even the layout of camp sites of the period could be reconstructed with the aid of modern archeological methods. Some examples of the finds are on exhibit in the little **Olorgesailie Museum**.

Having returned to the main road, it's about another 30 kilometers to Lake Magadi, which can usually be smelled before you can see it. From a distance its alkaline waters shimmer in hues ranging from rose to white, though when examined close up it turns out to be merely a wide expanse of salt-saturated water. The great economic significance of soda, which is among Kenya's most important export goods, laid the foundations for the town of **Magadi**: This settlement, constructed for the roughly 500 employees of

the **Magadi Soda Company** amidst the hot, sterile wasteland doesn't have any particular appeal for tourists.

A toll bar marks the limits of the premises belonging to the soda company. After registering one can enter and drive along the embankment to the south side of the lake, where hot springs bubble up with waters up to 40 °C. These are supposed to work wonders for rheumatism and articulatory complaints.

Be this as it may, most visitors come here because of the birds: Marabous, pelicans, plovers, geese and ducks romp about in the water, and the beautiful rose-red flamingos also glide to the shore in great flocks when they can no longer find sufficient food at Lake Nakuru.

ACROSS THE TSAVO PARK
– From Nairobi to Mombasa –

Above: This road makes a bee-line toward Taita Hills. Right: Field glasses are often the only way to get close to the animals.

The main highway from Nairobi to Mombasa is one of Kenya's most important traffic arteries. It cuts across the **Tsavo Park**, Kenya's largest wildlife reserve, between **Mtito Andei** and the **Manyani Gate** southeast of the city of Tsavo. Thus, people who prefer to take the land route instead of flying into the national park will – no matter where they start out – still cover a part of their route on the 490 kilometer long highway. Although this stretch is well maintained, serious accidents take place time and again due to the high concentration of traffic and the break neck driving style typical in this country. People doing the driving themselves should keep a sharp eye out for animals crossing the road and for people driving without lights. Exceeding the speed limits is punished with unpleasantly high fines!

From the highlands around Nairobi the road passes through a plain and after that into the industrial town of **Athi River** (on the waterway of the same name), and then further on to **Sultan Hamud** and **Kiboko**, an attractive oasis with a small lake. From there excursions are available from **Hunter's Lodge** to the (volcanic) caves in the **Chyulu Hills**. This mountain chain, which reaches an altitude of 2170 meters at its highest point, is one of the youngest volcanic ranges in the world, and is peppered with numerous caves, some of them rather grand.

Not much further on the traveller arrives in **Makindu**, 160 kilometers from Nairobi. The city's prime landmark is the **Sikh Temple**. Its golden cupola in the midst of the African savannah looks very peculiar indeed. But the temple is an important monument in Kenya's history – or more precisely in the history of the great railroad construction at the end of the 19th century. At that time thousands of Indian laborers came to the country, among them a large number of Sikhs. They built their temple next to one of the railroad's firewood depots. After construction on the railroad was completed the temple served as a hospice for travellers irrespective of their race or religion. It has been expanded several times over

the decades, and now includes a dining room and sleeping rooms to accomodate the visitors. Those who accept this hospitality only have to pay what they can afford.

One reaches **Mtito Andei** by way of **Kibwezi**. Even though the name has the rather unsettling meaning "Forest of the Vultures", Mtito Andei is nonetheless a popular resting spot at the halfway mark between Nairobi and Mombasa.

From Mtito Andei one can also get to the romantic **Tsavo Safari Camp** in Tsavo East. However, visitors wishing to spare themselves the fatiguing drive on the secondary roads can also travel to the camp with small charter aircraft flying directly from Nairobi and Mombasa. The jolting road to the camp ends for the time being at the **Athi River**, which has to be crossed on a rubber raft. Usually, the arrival of a vehicle is noticed so quickly on the opposite side that the waiting time for the ferry seldom exceeds a half-hour. The former means of crossing the river was a kind of cableway that hardly inspired any

confidence. A man allegedly fell victim to crocodiles when the cable broke.

Visitors to the camp stay in comfortable tents, enjoying the evening hours by campfire. At most, the quiet of night is broken by the croaking of the frogs.

You shouldn't pass up your chance to take the camp's jeep excursion up to the **Yatta Plateau** at sunset. The absolute solitude and the expansive view across the undisturbed landscape, with the evening sun sinking behind the hills makes this little trip into an unforgettable experience. It is also compensation for the fact that because of the dense vegetation usually only few animals can be seen in the camp's vicinity.

Back again to the Nairobi-Mombasa highway: The next stop is the little town of **Tsavo**, which achieved a certain fame during the construction of the railroad.

Above: Elephants always have the right-of-way in and out of the national parks. Right: Among the finest places to stay in Kenya, the Salt Lick Lodge.

All one finds here nowadays is a train station, a petrol station and a bridge. The latter had to be built over the **Tsavo River**, a job that was impeded for a couple of months by man-eating lions. The bridge spans the Tsavo at its confluence with the Athi River, which then becomes the Galana and flows east for some distance before emptying into the **Sabaki River**. The latter then pursues its journey to the Indian Ocean. Located outside of the Tsavo Park, surrounded by sisal plantations, is the town of **Voi,** the railroad junction of the Mombasa-Nairobi and the Taveta-Tanzania lines. Its market is a good place to buy fruit as provision. The next train station is the town of **Mackinnon Road**, named after the Scotsman Sir William Mackinnon who had this section of the railroad line built at his own cost. An unusual sight and important destination for pilgrims is the **Holy Man's Grave**, built in the fifties in Persian-Indian style; it belongs to the **Pir Padree Mosque**.

From here, the trip continues to **Mariakani**, which is known primarily for

being on the Safari Rally itinerary. The closer one comes to the coast the more fertile and heavily settled the land becomes. Banana trees and coconut palms hem the edges of the road as little suburbs announce the proximity of Mombasa.

TSAVO NATIONAL PARK

Tsavo was opened in 1948 as the first of Kenya's wildlife reserves. With an area of 21,283 square kilometers, it still is Kenya's largest national park until today, accessible by way of a road network some 2000 kilometers long. It owes its international popularity not least to the many films about elephants that have been shot here. At one time the largest elephant herds in Africa lived in this region; unfortunately, however, periods of drought and poachers have decimated their numbers. Only since the appointment of Dr. Richard Leakey as director of the Kenya Wildlife Service in 1989, has it been possible to contain the poachers and begin rebuilding the pachyderm

population again. The famous "red" elephants, whose color is due to the park's laterite dust, have certainly caused heavy damage to the spare vegetation. This has resulted in the former forestlands of the national park becoming largely savannah overgrown with brush today.

The Tsavo National Park is especially popular among those enjoying a sea-side vacation. A brief safari gives a first impression of the animal kingdom and of Kenya's landscape as well. The approximately two-hour drive from Mombasa makes even one-day excursions possible. Since the Nairobi-Mombasa highway runs right through the park, the conveniently-located Tsavo attracts visitors by the hundreds of thousands each year. It's hardly surprising, therefore, that on the heavily-travelled main routes of the wildlife sanctuary, there is no longer much to be noticed in the way of wilderness, and that the popular **Kilanguni Lodge** resembles an amusement park around lunchtime. However, those who head off onto the side trails or perhaps a little

deeper into the Tsavo East will sometimes come upon nary a soul for the whole day. Caution is therefore urged concerning flat tires, which are no rarity on the dirt roads. You should always have damaged tires repaired as quickly as possible, so as not to be dependent on the help of others in the case of another flat.

There are over 50 different species of mammals and almost 400 bird species living in a surprising diversity of vegetation, despite the considerable damage it has suffered. In contrast to other regions, the Tsavo has up to now always somehow been able to regenerate after periods of drought, floods and the destruction by elephant herds.

If you are doing your own driving, make sure you have an accurate map. They can be purchased in Mombasa, Nairobi, or at petrol stations with a shop, but not generally at the entrances of the park. All routes and intersections are indicated on

Above: To each his own, leopards like to hang around in trees.

the maps. Always keep in mind during a drive through the park that it is only permitted to get out of your vehicle at specially identified places. This prohibition exists not only for the protection of the animals, but for your own safety as well!

Tsavo West

The western section of the Tsavo Park extends from the Nairobi-Mombasa highway out to the Tanzanian border. Travelling along a well-developed road network one passes through hilly savannahs and acacia forests, through fascinating volcanic mountains whose lava flows aren't even 200 years old yet. There are several possiblities for the trip into the western park, depending on the starting point: Either turn off from the highway into the park at Mtito Andei or Tsavo, or drive from Voi through the Taita Hills Reserve to the **Maktau Gate**. Coming from the Amboseli Park take the route via **Kimana**.

Sometimes it happens that tourists already make their first acquaintance with

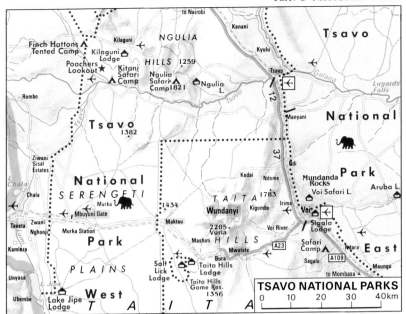

a wild animal at a park entrance. Curious baboons are only too glad to romp on or around automobiles, or attempt to commit petty larceny on the packed lunches they so very often contain. Never forget that the bite of a baboon can be very dangerous.

The **Kilanguni Lodge**, located in the middle of the park, is the starting point for the majority of reconnaissance trips. It was opened in 1962 as the first lodging for tourists in the Tsavo Park. With its splendid outlook over the Chyulu Hills located nearby, the lodge is still just as popular today as it ever was. The nearby watering holes are visited with pleasure by elephants, zebras and buffaloes and other wildlife. Sitting on the terrace to sip a cup of coffee or tea, one can relax and watch the animals passing by as if looking at a film. Many lizards, mungos, rhinoceros birds and glossy starlings feel just as much at home on the grounds of the lodge as the tourists.

To the south of Kilanguni are the **Mzima Springs**, situated in the middle of a picturesque, small oasis with palm trees and acacias. The crystalline fresh-water springs idyllically lined with stands of papyrus reed, are a true paradise here in the arid Tsavo Plain. More than 240 million liters of water per day bubble forth from the springs, supplying the city of Mombasa with drinking water through a 150-kilometer-long pipeline. Visitors may leave their vehicles at the parking area and cover the little stretch to the springs on foot. There is a remarkable underwater observatory in the small lake from which one can watch hippopotamui and crocodiles as well as tropical fish from close up.

Hippopotami spend the greater part of their days under water. They can remain under the surface for up to five minutes before coming back up, snorting upon arrival, to get some air. In the evenings and nights they leave the water to graze on the shores. Even though hippos are generally considered to be rather peaceful beasts, it is not advised to stand in the way of these massive heavyweights in

125

case one of them should stray onto land during the day. Also, one might meet up with a crocodile on the shore – in other words, be careful!

Some other worthwhile spots to visit in the park are the **Poachers' Lookout** with a splendid view over the bushland of **Ol Turesh** in the neighborhood of the **Kitani Lodge**, or a drive through the craggy **Rhino Valley** over the untrodden and rather impassable stretch from Kilanguni to the **Ngulia Safari Camp**. There is no guarantee, however, that you will catch a fleeting glimpse of the rare rhinoceroses, even in the hermetically fenced-in **Rhino Sanctuary**. Of course, the rangers at the entrance are always pleased and at the ready to go off on a rhino search with the park visitors, but this is absolutely no guarantee of success.

Beyond Rhino Valley the road winds steeply uphill to the **Ngulia Safari Lodge**.

Above: Quite literally tons of Hippopotami wallow together. Right: Voi Lodge provides a good lookout for wildlife watching.

This romantically situated lodge is enthroned above a precipice in the **Ngulia Mountains**. A heavily used wildlife trail runs through here, and in the night a floodlit watering hole below the lodge attracts many animals. An attempt to lure leopards is made every evening by depositing a piece of meat in a tree – usually a successful undertaking. The entire proceedings can be watched at leisure from the lodge's dining room. A journal is kept in the lodge with information as to where and when which animals were most recently sighted.

Both the Kilaguni and Ngulia Safari Lodges are fully equipped with all the creature comforts. These come at a price, naturally. The bandas (simple bungalows) in the Ngulia Safari Camp and Kitani Safari Camp are ideal for travellers with a tighter budget, although everyone is requested to bring along his own food and drink. In general, advance reservations are recommended.

A little-travelled route with beautiful landscapes leads from the Kilanguni

Lodge toward the north to the **Chyulu Hills**, and past the lava fields of the only recently extinguished **Shetani Volcano**.

Tsavo East

The substantially larger Tsavo East Park, which extends off to the northeast from the Mombasa-Nairobi highway, is only partially accessible to visitors. The arid region north of the Galana River is connected along its northern reaches to the adjacent **South Kitui National Reserve**, a plant and animal conservation area. Only limited excursions can be made into the protected zones from the Tsavo Safari Camp, in the area of **Mtito Andei** (see page 124). The parklands to the south of the river are open for visitors: endlessly broad, arid region, the very (quint)essence of untamed Africa.

Standing only a few kilometers away from the park entrance at Voi is the **Voi Safari Lodge**, on a hill high above the plain from which one can survey three watering holes. A subterranean passage begins at the lodge, and ends at an observation stand only a few meters from one of the watering holes. It supplies a very close-up view of the animals. With a bit of luck, from the lodge you may also be able to observe the huge buffalo and/or elephant herds on their migrations.

Stretching off to the north of the Safari Lodge are the low **Mundana Rocks.** This geological formation is one-and-one-half kilometers long. Through centuries water has gathered beneath this precipitous rock ledge, creating an outstanding place to observe wildlife.

An especially beautiful stretch leads along the **Galana River**, Kenya's second-largest waterway. The banks of the river are fringed with papyrus and palms, and only a few safari busses disturb the region's seclusion.

Named after their discoverer, Captain Frederick Lugard, the **Lugard Falls** are worth a visit – not for their height, but because of their idyllic location. A bit further on at **Crocodile Point,** one can watch crocodiles dosing in the sun in

127

relative safety. As long as you don't leave the observation platform, you will be keeping the respectful distance necessary for personal safety.

Remaining on the road along the river, which is named the **Sabaki** on its course out to the ocean, one arrives to the **Sala Gate**. From there it's still another 115 kilometers to the coastal city of Malindi. The majority of visitors take the more popular route by way of the **Aruba Lodge**, located on an artificial lake, which draws a great deal of wildlife, then leaving the park through the **Buchuma Gate** and returning to the Nairobi-Mombasa highway.

TAITA HILLS

The most common access route to the **Taita Hills Game Sanctuary**, the private wildlife park owned by the Hilton

Above: Bateleur eagles can be spotted in the savannah, often ogling a prey from a great height.

Hotel chain, begins in Voi, and follows the road to Taveta on the Tanzanian border. After passing through the little towns of **Mwatate** and **Bura** – known for a battle in the First World War in which the German General Lettow-Vorbeck was fighting with British troops – you arrive at the intersection leading to the reserve. Living in the hilly forest region making up the Taita Hills are gnus, elephants, buffaloes and zebras as well as predatory beasts such as lions and cheetahs.

Lodgings can be had in one of the two Hilton lodges opened in 1973, which offer every conceivable comfort to their guests. The luxurious lodge **Taita Hills Hilton** is located at the entrance of the park, surrounded by an ocean of flowers and equipped with a swimming pool, a putting green and its own landing strip for light aircraft. A billboard in the lodge informs the guests comprehensively as to when and where which kind of animal was last spotted. Day-guests are also welcome to a highly recommendable lunch in the lodge.

The **Salt Lick Lodge** was constructed atop pilings in the midst of this wildlife park, which has an area of 113 square kilometers. Its recreational activities cover a manifold spectrum, ranging from watching wildlife from subterranean observation posts to dinner by candlelight. Many interesting animal species come to the lodges's watering hole.

LAKE JIPE AND LAKE CHALA

If you stay on the main road between Voi and Taveta, a few kilometers before the border you arrive at the junction to **Lake Jipe**, coming soon afterwards upon the road to Lake Chala. It's well worth leaving the usual route for once to pay a visit to this, as yet relatively unknown part of Kenya, since not only do both of these enchanting papyrus-fringed lakes have particularly alluring landscape, but Lake Jipe also offers passionate bird lovers an extensive field of observation. The border with Tanzania runs right through the lake.

The wild, romantic **Lake Chala** is a 100-meter-deep crater lake, which surely would be a hot item among scuba divers for its underwater caves – but only if they could momentarily suppress the thought of the crocodiles that populate it.

Situated in the midst of primeval wilderness, Lake Jipe is a unique paradise for birds. It has an area of roughly 40 square kilometers and is fed by the **Lumi River**, which has its source on the Kilimanjaro. There are countless aquatic birds living on its shore among the reeds and rushes, papyrus stands and waterlilies. The birds can be best observed on a boat tour.

Whereas the shore on the Kenyan side is flat and accessible, the **Pare Mountains** tower into the heavens at altitudes of up to 2100 meters along the Tanzanian shoreline. Accordingly, the panorama is most breathtaking from the **Lake Jipe Safari Lodge**.

One can also pitch a tent along Lake Jipe's shore – as long as one isn't bothered by the smacking noises emanating from the grazing hippopotami at night. From their point of view, these pachyderms don't have an especially high opinion of unwelcome disturbances either. In other words, be careful!

Bird species come in virtually innumerable quantities, but larger mammals are precious few. The animals here are considerably shyer than in the more heavily frequented tourist areas. Nonetheless, this untouched nature conveys a fairly good sense of what true wilderness really means.

Those not wishing to drive back on the same route can, with the aid of a precise map, take one of the smaller trails through the Taita Hills back onto the main road between Nairobi and Mombasa, and – with a bit of luck – wind up coming out at Mackinnon Road.

AMBOSELI NATIONAL PARK
Accommodation

LUXURY: **Amboseli Serena**, PO Box 48690, Nairobi. **Kilimanjaro Buffalo Lodge**, PO Box 72630, Nairobi.
MODERATE: **New Amboseli Lodge**, PO Box 30139, Nairobi. **Kilimanjaro Safari Lodge**, PO Box 30193, Nairobi.
BUDGET: **Ol Tukai Lodge**, simple self-catering bandas with grocery store. **Camping facilities** at the New Amboseli and the Amboseli Serena Lodge. Two additional camping sites outside the park near Kimann Lodge.

Checkpoint Namanga – Tanzania

At the small border town of Namanga most people cross over to Tanzania by foot. Good transportation on both sides of the border.
Reasonably priced accommodation at the **Namanga River Hotel** or **Five Star Hotel** instead of the expensive lodges in the Amboseli.

TSAVO NATIONAL PARK WEST
Accommodation

LUXURY: **Kilaguni Lodge**, PO Box 30471, Nairobi. **Ngulia Safari Lodge**, PO Box 340471, Nairobi.
BUDGET: **Ngulia Safari Camp** PO Box 30471, Nairobi. **Kitani Safari Camp**, PO Box 1498, Nairobi.

Checkpoint Taveta – Tanzania

Buses from Mombasa and Nairobi run to the Tanzanian town **Moshi** near the Kilimanjaro. Simple accommodation at the **Taveta Hotel**.

TSAVO NATIONAL PARK EAST
Accommodation

MODERATE: **Voi Safari Lodge**, PO Box 30471, Nairobi. **Aruba Lodge**, PO Box 14982, Nairobi. **Galana Game Ranch**, PO Box 20139, Nairobi, north of the Salana River at the eastern fringe of the Tsavo East Park. **Tsavo Safari Camp**, PO Box 30471, Nairobi.

TAITA HILLS
Accommodation

LUXURY: **Taita Hills Hilton**, PO Box 30624, Nairobi. **Salt Lick Lodge**, PO Box 30624, Nairobi.

LAKE JIPE
Accommodation

Lake Jipe Safari Lodge, PO Box 31097, Nairobi.
Tip: Reservations for all listed lodges and camps can be made through your tour operator or travel agencies in larger towns.

THE GREATEST
ANIMAL SHOW
ON EARTH

MASAI MARA

The **Masai Mara Game Reserve**, a natural continuation of the Serengeti National Park in Tanzania, extends over an enchanting, undulating grassland with gently rolling hills and beautiful acacia forests, through which the **Mara** and **Talek Rivers** wind their way. For many travellers to Kenya, a visit to the Masai Mara is the crowning touch of an East African safari. And when the enormous herds migrate over the broad area of this wildlife paradise it puts each and every visitor in a state of awe and reverence. While the Masai are permitted to pasture their animals in the outer parts of the Masai Mara, the reserve's heart, however, is reserved for wildlife and safari visitors alone.

How to Get There

Airplanes, flying in from Nairobi or Mombasa, have a choice of several landing strips in the Masai Mara. For travellers with a sense of adventure who aren't scared off by the rather poor road conditions, the overland drive starting out from Nairobi is an attractive alternative.

Preceding pages: The gnu migration across the Masai Mara is one of the great experiences of Kenyan wildlife. Left: Peaceful coexistence in the savannah.

The route follows along the road to **Limuru** until the old **Kijabe Road**. There is a truly stupendous vantage point over the Rift Valley and **Mount Longonot** before the road – which at this point is hacked into a precipice – starts slithering down into the valley in breakneck style. On the way down towards the valley, the road passes by the chapel **St. Mary of the Angels**, and a few kilometers further the road to **Narok** forks off to the left. The asphalt road, which runs almost straight-as-an-arrow through the bottom of the valley brings one past **Mount Longonot** and a satellite station.

On the 82-kilometer drive from Kijabe to Narok stands the **Mount Suswa**, a beautiful, extinct volcano. In this desolate, inhospitable region, travellers encounter the Maasai for the first time, and on both sides of the road they can already catch sight of the first herds of gazelles, giraffes and zebras.

In Narok the road continues up to a T-junction: The right turn leads through **Mau Narok**, **Elmenteita** and **Njoro** to Nakuru; the left turn crosses the **Ewaso Nyiro River**, passing by Narok's landing strip and continuing on to the Masai Mara. Just past the landing strip there is a checkpoint of the Game Department, after which the road makes a lefthand turn into the Mara region. A junction to

133

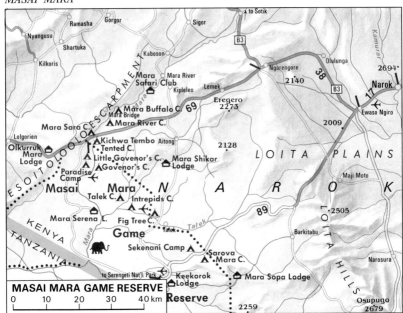

MASAI MARA GAME RESERVE

0 10 20 30 40 km

the left heads off to **Cottar's Camp**, and continues on to the **Sarova Mara Camp** and to **Keekorok**. The first road, though, leads a little further to an unforgettable landscape impression as compensation for the dust and poor road condition: Immeasurable wheat fields suddenly stretch out before the weary eyes of the unsuspecting traveller.

The wheatfields come to an end in **Ngorengore**, and even though the park entrance is still miles ways, one already comes across many wild animals. In particular lions seem to feel quite at home here, and if you should have a flat tire at night on this road, you must by all means stay in the vehicle until daybreak before attempting to replace it, or setting out to seek assistance.

After Ngorengore the road leaves **Mount Eregero** to the left and runs through the sleepy little trading settlement of **Lemek** to a fork a couple of ki-

lometers up the way. The left-hand road leads one through another little trading post, **Altong,** up to the beginning of the actual park. The right-hand road proceeds through the country of Senior Chief Lerionka Ole Ntutu, crosses the Mara River, and finally arrives in **Sotik**.

Masai Mara Game Reserve

As a result of the fortunate circumstance that the great plains of East Africa were Masai country, here – more than in the rest of Kenya – it was possible for an extraordinary abundance of flora and fauna to be preserved. Lions, leopards and cheetahs slink through the underbrush, while gazelles, zebras, antelopes and gnus graze contentedly on the savannah. Extended families of hippopotamui wallow about in the shallow waters of the Mara River, crocodiles lounge about basking in the sun on the sandy riverbanks, and catfish or other fish species skitter around unmolested in the bodies of waters in the Masai Mara.

Right: The river crossings by herds during the migrations is a dramatic sight.

According to a 1995 census 1.5 million whitebeard gnus, a half-million gazelles, 200,000 zebras and 70,000 impalas were recorded in the Masai Mara Reserve. Since the elephants have become very irritable due to human encroachments on the habitats, the greatest of caution is always a necessity when coming anywhere near their herds.

In July, when the dry season hits the Serengeti, the animals migrate to the grasslands of the Mara for three or four months. They cross the Mara River in the direction of the Masai Mara in stamping, snorting multitudes. Predatory animals, hungry for prey, including the slender Masai lion, tirelessly run circles around the forward crashing beast throngs. The grasslands and the gently rolling hills of the Mara practically disappear beneath the herds.

Hard on each others hooves, the beasts stream to new foraging lands in masses that frequently reach out to the horizon. Up to a million gnus and several hundred thousand zebras and buffaloes, accompanied by antelopes and gazelles populate the Masai Mara at this time. As the rainy season begins at the beginning of November, and the Serengeti becomes green again, the animals move back south.

The dramatic river crossings of the herd are an overwhelming experience. After a lengthy search the leaders decide on a spot along the river that seems suitable to the entire herd. They then plunge over sheer slopes into the river after the leaders. Many of the weaker animals aren't strong enough for the powerful currents and soon are pulled helplessly downstream. Others are unable to find a foothold on the opposite embankment and are pushed aside by stronger members of the herd. Frequently access to the rescueing shore is so narrow that a part of the herd fails to find it and desperately attempts to reach the other side by ways of an inaccessible spot, usually to no avail. In this manner, river crossing by a herd can last several hours.

During the migrations one often sees antelopes nonchalantly grazing only meters from a pride of well-sated lions. They are fully aware that they have nothing to fear from the king of beasts as long as they are occupied with digesting their regal dinners and can scarcely get up off the ground with their swollen bellies.

The film **Out of Africa** was shot against the tremendous natural backdrop of the Masai Mara.

On a Game Drive

The most advantageous times to take a "game drive" are in the early hours of the morning and in the late afternoon. What's more, watching the sunrise in the midst of the wilderness is an experience that is most certainly worth setting one's alarm clock for.

Predatory felines, for example, are known to take their siestas during the midday hours. They are at their most active – and one is thus most likely to catch sight on them – in the mornings and evenings. The cooler hours of the day are used by the animals for grazing, hunting for prey and visiting the watering holes for a drink or a swim.

Nowhere else in Kenya are there as many lions per acre as in the Masai Mara. Frequently, the visitor comes across entire families, whose playful cubs seem perfectly oblivious of all the spectators. With a bit of luck you might also get to see some cheetahs or leopards. By and large, the local drivers of the lodges and camps know exactly where to find these shy animals. They know their habits and also get information from other drivers. Unfortunately, due to the throngs of visitors to the park, it can also happen that the drive ultimately turns into a regular car chase, since each driver strives to snare the best spot for taking photographs for his passengers. You should never incite the driver to pull up just a little bit

Right: One way to see the Masai Mara is by hovering over it in a hot-air balloon.

closer to the animals. Mother cheetahs sometimes feel so distressed that they indeed leave their young in the lurch, and cheetah cubs are a very popular delicacy among baboons.

Countless hippopotami live on the Marek and Talek Rivers. In the early mornings they loll around dosing in the sun on the sandy riverbanks. Later on in the day, they can only be detected when they come back up to the surface giving off loud snorts in the process. The population of rhinoceroses, however, has been almost eradicated in the reserve. There are only a few specimens still living here under the protection of the gamekeepers.

When visiting the Masai Mara, one should always bring along a warm sweater or jacket. In the highland plain, which reaches altitudes of 1700 meters in places, it can get rather cold in the mornings and evenings. In addition, visitors are usually driven around in open all-terrain vehicles.

Luxury and Adventure

An overnight stay in one of the camps or lodges is, of course, a part of any safari in the Masai Mara. The selection of accomodations ranges from do-it-yourself camps to the ultimate in luxury lodges. "Game drives" through the reserve are available at all lodges and camps. Wake-up time for an early morning game drive is before the crack of dawn, but with a cup of tea or coffee. The second game drive usually takes place toward noon, the third in the late afternoon. The day's wealth of experiences can be topped off with a romantic evening by a campfire.

It's virtually impossible to find lodging in the Masai Mara without advance reservation. Despite the numerous lodges and camps, the demand far exceeds supply, and for the time being the government has stopped the construction of further tourist complexes for the protection of the wildlife.

The lodges and tent-camps of the Masai Mara place not only their own vehicles at visitors' disposal for the game drives; several even offer rides in hot-air balloons, in which one can float silently over the savannah and gaze in wonder at the grandiose spectacle of the herds migrating. Depending on the time of year, several camps organize raft safaris on the shallow, most of the time lazily winding Mara River, which finally oozes off into the **Mararua Swamps** and, as it were, disappears into nothing. The Mara River is fed by several tributaries with their sources in the Mau Escarpment, transforming it into a wild, ravaging torrent during the rainy seasons. Within only a few hours the water level can leap five or more meters, and the subsequent inundation sweeps tree and beast into a seething maelstrom of brown mud.

The **Mara Buffalo Camp**, one of the oldest in the Masai Mara, provides a relaxing atmosphere and the best in Swiss cuisine as well as a most splendid vantage point over the river below. The watering hole near the camp is illuminated at night so that visitors are able, from the bungalow verandas, to observe the beasts of the savannah at close range as they quench their thirst.

At this point, the Mara River flows relatively swiftly. If you should feel the need to go fishing for a couple of tranquil hours, the camp management will be pleased to provide the necessary equipment, and later on the cooks will prepare your catch most appetizingly. At some places on the river the catch can weigh as much as seven kilograms; here, however, you have to be satisfied with fish weighing around one-half kilo.

Just as in every camp, there is also a game scout here, whose task is to keep a lookout for dangerous animals for the sake of the guests' safety. Nonetheless, caution should be exercised when walking around the camp at night (even if only from tent to tent), and always bring along (and use) a flashlight. Hippopotami and buffalo, with which run-ins can have deadly consequences, frequently visit the

camps at night, sometimes not leaving again until the break of day.

In comparison to the modest, relatively inexpensive Mara Buffalo Camp, the **Governor's Camp**, opened in 1972, appears the very summit of comfort with its 36 luxury tents. The high standard of the service and the excellent cuisine would have been inconceivable in the bygone days of the big safaris. In the last few years the style of the Governor's Camp has been yet further refined, and the enthusiastic regulars return here over and over again. In addition, in 1976, the management opened the **Little Governor's Camp** on a small lake which is sought out by great multitudes of birds and wild beasts. A boat transports visitors to one of the 17 tents of the romantically situated camp with its bewitching atmosphere.

Like an oasis, the **Keekorok Lodge** is located amidst the migrating herds of the

Above: A bloody scene, but only man kills for the sake of killing or for profit.

savannah, and its guests can select between single, double or triple occupancy rooms or luxury tents. The cool stone entrance path leads past the reception and onto a veranda with a view on a broad meadow and a watering hole which lures hordes of wildlife during the day.

Since the Keekorok Lodge is a member of the Block Hotels chain, its cuisine can be measured against the finest hotels in all of Kenya. Its guests can unwind in (or by) its beautiful swimming pool, and a hiking path takes the guest's breath away with its wildlife and splendid panoramic views. In the evenings, Masai from the surrounding regions perform traditional dances or tell of their traditions and legends.

The **Mara Serena Lodge** is located in the northwestern section of the wildlife preserve. It's an imaginative reproduction of two *manyattas*, the traditional villages of the Masai. This lodge, built high up on a rocky ridge, has a splendid view over the savannah. There are 78 rooms and a landing strip. Visitors with their own vehicles can easily reach the lodge from Narok by way of a good road. The terrace above the swimming pool is a marvelous platform from which to survey the herd migrations and the Mara River.

The **Masai Mara Sopa Lodge** on the slopes of the Oloolaimutia Valley (60 double rooms and 12 suites) has an equally overwhelming panorama over the valley and the wildlife reserve.

The **Sarova Mara Camp** (double tents) extends over a natural height between two rivers, and its watering hole (also natural) attracts plenty of wildlife.

Located deep in the bush, the outstanding **Kichwa Tembo Camp** offers its guests not only luxurious comfort, but also the excitement of a "real safari" and the fascination of camping in the wilderness. The wilderness hiking tours, lead by experts, provide a unique opportunity to experience (and photograph) primeval nature at very close range.

The pleasant **Fig Tree Camp** in the neighborhood of the **Talek River** is operated by the owners of the Nairobi Oakwood Hotel, while the near luxury camp **Mara Intrepids** was founded by the Kashoggi family. This camp is situated directly on the Talek River, which literally teems with crocodiles and hippopotami. Each group of tents has its own bar-tent with refrigerator and attendants. The swimming pool gives much-needed refreshment from the tribulations of the journey. In the evenings people meet at the **Champagne Terrace**, a roughly ten-meter-high observation platform, to see what the local wildlife is up to. A spotlight is shone far out into the plain, making the eyes of the passing gnu herds look like the lights of a big city.

The newly opened **Olkurruk Mara Lodge** is located on a hill amid bewitching landscape, providing a view of great beauty over the Masai Mara. This stylish lodge was on one of the shooting locations for the film *Out of Africa*.

MASAI MARA GAME RESERVE
Accommodation

LUXURY: **Keekorok Lodge**, PO Box 47557, Nairobi. **Mara Intrepids Club**, PO Box 74888, Nairobi. **Governor's Camp**, PO Box 48217, Nairobi. **Sekenani Camp**, PO Box 61542, Nairobi, Tel: 333233. **Mara Serena Lodge**, PO Box 48690, Nairobi. **Olkurruk Lodge**, PO Box 30471, Nairobi. **Mpata Safari Club**, PO Box 45895, Nairobi, Tel: 337200. **Mara Shikar Lodge**, PO Box 10773, Nairobi, Tel: 336551/336833.

MODERATE: **Kichwa Tembo Camp,** PO Box 58581, Nairobi. **Masai Mara Lodge**, PO Box 72630, Nairobi. **Sarova Mara**, PO Box 30680, Nairobi. **Mara Sopa**, PO Box 72630, Nairobi. **Mara Fig Tree Camp**, PO Box 40683, Nairobi. **Masai Mara River Camp**, PO Box 48019, Nairobi. **Mara Buffalo Camp**, African Safari Camp, PO Box 81443, Nairobi.

Camping facilities at the Keekorok Lodge and outside the Game Reserve. Lodgings at camping places must be booked in advance at the **National Park Headquarters**, PO Box 4021, Nairobi, Tel: 501081.

Balloon Safaris

You can book balloon safaris in the luxury lodges Keekorok Lodge, Mara Serena Lodge, Mara Fig Tree Camp and Governor's Camp, or through Balloon Safaris, PO Box 47557, Nairobi.

Entrance Fees

The parking fee varies according to the duration of your stay: per day per person 50 Ksh, per vehicle 50 Ksh.

Climate

As the Masai Mara Game Reserve is situated at a height of approximately 2000 m above sea level, nights tend to get a bit chilly. You will need a jumper, cardigan, or a light anorak, especially on early morning game viewing tours.

Petrol Stations

Most of the lodges have their own petrol pump which can also be used by non-residents. However, it's cheaper to fill up your tank in Narok, outside the Game Reserve.

NAROK
Accommodation
Valley View, on the main road.
Banks
Barclays Bank, on the main road.
Buses
Daily buses to Nairobi and Nakuru. Two or three times a week there is a service to Western Kenya (Sotik and Kisii) and to Seronera in Tanzania.

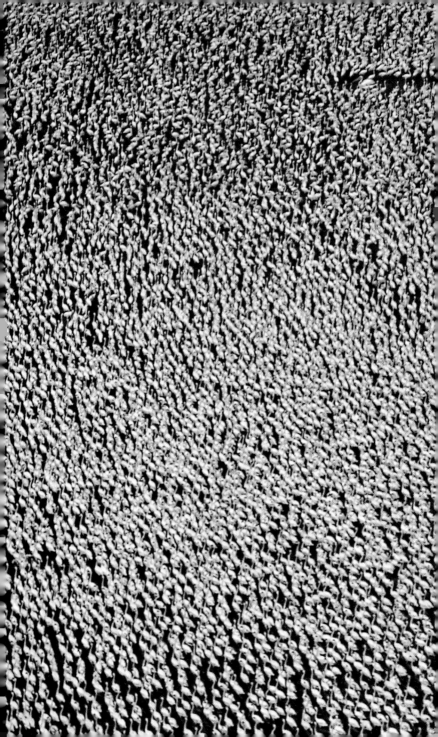

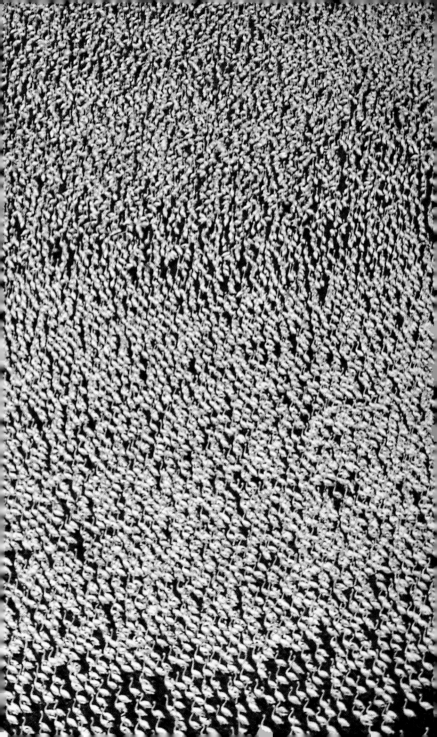

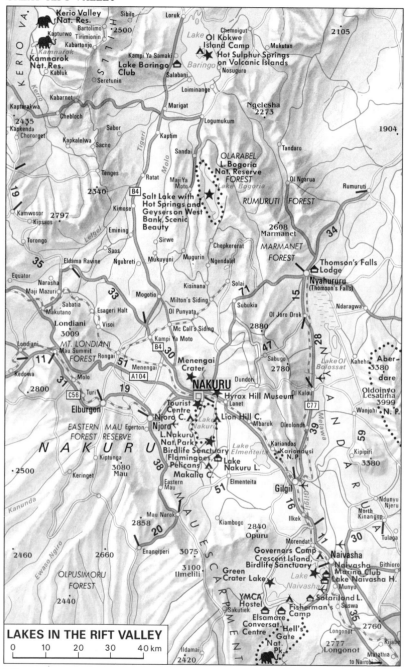

LAKES IN THE RIFT VALLEY

0   10   20   30   40 km

LAKES IN THE GREAT RIFT VALLEY

LAKE NAIVASHA
LAKE NAKURU
LAKE BOGORIA
LAKE BARINGO

The massive Rift Valley is a fault running on a north-south axis created millions of years ago when Earth's crust collapsed after being pushed up by volcanic activity. The depression begins in the Jordan Valley and crosses the Red Sea, Ethiopia, Kenya and Tanzania, before ending at the Zambezi Delta in Mozambique. As a result of two parallel plates crashing up against each other, the softer rock sank and formed the trench bottom with a chain of salty lakes, while the harder rocks were forced upward, where they remained standing as part of a steep trough. Even today, the countless volcanic cones of the Rift Valley region are a reminder of this agitated past.

The extinct **Suswa** and **Longonot** volcanoes stand south of **Lake Naivasha**, and the lake's shore itself is studded with volcanic rocks. One can find glittering shards of jet-black obsidian, which was crafted into axheads and knives by our ancestors. The valley bottom around **Lake Elmeteita**, further to the north, is dotted with numerous small volcanoes; and volcanic rubble extends between **Nakuru**, **Borgoria** and **Baringo**.

When looking down from the lofty heights of the Rift's escarpment over the

Preceding pages: More than enough pink flamingos to go around at Lake Nakuru.

valley plain, one begins to grasp what immense perturbations and shifting of the Earth once took place here. Springs and small rivers feed the chain of lakes which extends the entire distance from Lake Naivasha to **Lake Baringo**. Each one of these lakes possesses not only a unique chemical composition; they also have a charm of their very own. The vicinity surrounding them is no less interesting. The lakes are easily reached from Nairobi and attract both Kenyans and foreigners in search of relaxation. They are also popular stop-offs for people on safaris to Lake Turkana.

LAKE NAIVASHA

The entire route from Nairobi to Lake Naivasha, located in Kenya's northern reaches, is also the main transportation artery to western Kenya and to Uganda. The first turn-off is the old road to **Naivasha**, which is used today primarily as a detour for trucks.

It is in extremely poor condition, although the drive through the idyllic landscape is certainly worthwhile for anyone with some extra time, and interested in a "shake-up tour". On the way is the **Chapel of St. Mary of the Angels**, which was built by Italian prisoners-of-war – a good spot to take a breather.

143

If the itinerary of your excursion includes climbing **Mount Longonot**, south of Naivasha, then the old road is the right route to follow. The relatively easy ascent of this old volcano rewards the visitor with an impressive panorama of the surrounding countryside. When the weather is clear, the view reaches out to the Aberdares mountain range and into the Masai steppes. The well-worn path around the edge of the crater, which leads over Longonot's highest point (2776 meters), is rather strenuous. For those few, who still haven't had enough, however, there's the steep descent to the base of the crater. Ascending Longonot takes from one to two hours; the path around the crater approximately three hours.

To reach Naivasha in the shortest time, one must pass up the picturesque detour on the old road and continue driving straight ahead on the new expressway, which also has observation spots. This route to Naivasha basically consists of one single large ascent to the highest point on the road and a shorter and even steeper downhill drive to the lake. A left turn (well indicated) points the way from the bottom of the valley to the town of Naivasha.

Lake Naivasha is a popular destination for people in Nairobi wanting to make day-trips or a weekend vacation for fishing, boating and relaxation. It is also conveniently located as a rest-stop along the way for people trekking to **Lake Nakuru** or even further into the northern reaches of Kenya.

Lake Naivasha, at 1890 meters above sea-level, is the highest lake of the Kenyan Rift Valley. People were already living here in prehistoric times. Their over 4000-year-old artifacts are still being discovered in the vicinity.

When, in 1883, the German natural scientist G.A. Fischer arrived as the first European in Naivasha, the region around the lake was still inhabited by the Masai.

Above: When the food supply dwindles, the flamingos seek their fortune elsewhere. Pelicans over Lake Naivasha.

Naivasha is a transmogrification of the Masai word *en-aiposha*, which means flowing or else fluid. The Europeans were mostly unable to pronounce this word correctly.

In other respects, however, the new arrivals were more skilled, since after the resettlement of the Masai who were living around the lake, they forcibly occupied the entire lakeshore area during the colonial period. Still in private hands today, the land surrounding the lake is heavily irrigated, used for the cultivation of vegetables and flowers which are destined primarily for export. Also, Kenya's only commercially produced wine is made from grapes cultivated on the lake's southern shore since 1980.

Depending on the amount of rainfall, the water-level of the lake – and thus the shoreline – is in constant motion. The lake, which has an average depth of about eight meters, even washed over Naivasha's railroad tracks in 1917 and, in contrast, once dried up almost completely during the fifties.

The deepest point of Naivasha is the small crater lake in the southeast, which has a depth of about 20 meters. The edge of the crater emerging from the lake is attached to the mainland by a rock ridge. Depending on the water level, **Crater Island** – as it is called – is either a peninsula or a "real" island.

The lake is fed by two rivers: The **Melawa**, which has its source in the eastern **Nyandarua Mountains**, and the **Gilgil**, which winds through the Rift Valley from the north. Since the lake has no visible outlet at all, the freshness of its water can probably be ascribed to the presence of subterranean drainage channels. The water levels of most of the remaining lakes in the Rift Valley are reduced exclusively through evaporation. This fact explains the very high alkalinity of their waters.

It takes strong nerves to handle driving the exceedingly rugged trail around the lake, and what is more, by and large it runs so far from the lakeshore that one can only catch an occasional glimpse of the water. The only public access to the lake is on the premises of hotels and campgrounds along the southern shore.

The **Moi South Lake Road** branches off from the old Naivasha road three kilometers from the town of Naivasha. This trail, which is merely fatiguing at the beginning, turns into a driver's nightmare after a few kilometers.

All the hotels stand on the right at this point. First off is the **Lake Naivasha Hotel**, situated in the middle of a beautiful garden. It satisfies the most demanding customers. The Lake Naivasha Hotel as well as the **Safariland Lodge** (five kilometers further) both offer boat tours on the lake and ornithological safaris. The Safariland Lodge certainly doesn't achieve the level of service of the Lake Naivasha Hotel by a long shot, but it is nonetheless a comfortable base for exploring the surrounding region.

The YMCA hostel, shortly before the turn-off to the **Hell's Gate National Park,** offers outstanding lodging to the self-reliant traveller; located just a little further down the lakeshore is the **Fisherman's Camp,** which includes campgrounds, boat rental and bungalows for do-it-yourselfers.

The **Elsamere Conservation Center** (the last tourist establishment) is located beyond the campgrounds. It provides lodging and full board for a clientele consisting primarily of professional biologists. This was originally the site of Joy Adamson's home, the writer artist and animal researcher, who enchanted countless readers with her books about the tame lioness Elsa. Advance reservations are an unconditional must.

No matter where you "pitch a tent" for the night, be it in a comfortable hotel or on the campgrounds, prophylactic measures against mosquitos – which also like the lake environs very much indeed –

Right: Termites, the busy little builders of limited empires.

are an absolute necessity. Especially at dawn and dusk they come humming to their victims with bloodthirsty glee.

A large number of hippopotamusses have chosen to make the lake their home; on the other hand, crocodiles are scarce. Sport anglers will experience some great moments here fishing for black perch (introduced from North America) or the delectable tilapia.

The lake's edge is surrounded with a thicket of delicate and feathery and papyrus reeds, which were already used by the ancient Egyptians as paper. The objects, which appear from a distance to be small islands moving over the water in the wind, are in reality clumps of papyrus plants that have grown together in rafts. Bird-watching travellers will discover, much to their frustration, that it's virtually impossible to observe the activities of their feathered friends on the lake when the water level is extremely low. The view is cut off in particular by the papyrus thickets and these wandering clusters of reeds. A boat tour is imperative for those not willing to limit themselves to watching the birds in the trees and surrounding wetlands. In this manner, it is also possible to get to the bird sanctuary located in the middle of Lake Naivasha, admiring, along the way, the water lilies and the hippopotami that surface to greet the passers-by with their loud snorts.

During the months of winter in Europe the local flocks of birds are increased by the "newcomers" from more northerly realms. It can happen that a few of the duck and stilt-legged species will appear oddly familiar. On the other hand, the sight of pelicans fishing next to each other like soldiers, is sure to be a completely new experience.

Hell's Gate National Park

One of the significant sights near the southern shore of Lake Naivasha are the

spectacular cliffs, gorges and wildlife of the **Hell's Gate National Park.** It has been possible, with the help of a United Nations research program and the support of the World Bank, to channel the hot springs of the "Gates of Hell" for the production of electricity; today the geothermal generating plant covers a noteworthy portion of Kenya's electricity demand. The drillings went down to depths of as much as 1700 meters. The highest temperature measured there is 304° Celcius.

Past the YMCA hostel, a route branching off from the opposite side of the road leads to the main entrance of the Hell's Gate Park and, shortly beyond it, a volcanic rock, the **Fischer's Tower** (named after the aforementioned German explorer) juts up into the heights. Its jagged cliffs are home to the yellow-spotted dassie and many unusual species of birds. With a bit of luck you might even spot the increasingly rare lammergeier, which builds its nests in the cliffs, as well as herds of zebras, antelopes and Grant's gazelles as they run across the flat, broad plain in the valley far below.

The occasion finally arises again to go for walks on some beautiful paths. However, one should without question, observe the marked paths and stay on them, so as not to get lost. Dyed-in-the-wool automobile freaks can make a trip through the park from the main gate and depart again through the second entrance at the geothermal power station. Its appearance is a veritable jolt into the present: The network of piping and plumes of snow-white steam it emits before the wild African scenery could almost be out of some science fiction film. A good asphalt road leads from the plant back to the southern lake road.

For those whose thirst for adventure has not yet been quenched, an excursion to the **Mau Escarpment** on the west side of Lake Naivasha, and on to **Sakutiek** can still be recommended. The Mau Escarpment, which reaches altitudes up to 3100 meters, forms the imposing, precipitous slopes of the Rift Valley at this

point. The trip on rutted paths up to the high plateau is for all-terrain vehicles only. Soon, the landscape turns into a cool, green mountain idyll. If you don't feel like taking the same road back, Saku-tiek can also be departed toward the north, via **Njoro**, through beautiful and richly variegated farmland to Nakuru. The road between Nairobi and Narok lies to the south.

LAKE ELMENTEITA AND LAKE NAKURU

A good road starting from the town of Naivasha runs around the western edge of Gilgil, site of a large military base, and after travelling 30 kilometers further you might get a first glimpse of Lake Elmen-teita. At this point the road begins to de-scend easily into the valley, and the dusty trail, branching off on the left-hand side

Above: Its not refuse, not plancton, but a pink ribbon of flamingos. Right: A mosquito net serves as camouflage as well.

(suitable for vehicles with two-wheel drive), leads to the entrance of the Lake Nakuru National Park.

After turning off to the right at the in-tersection to the village of **Elmenteita**, the next junction on the road (nine ki-lometers further on the left-hand side, clearly signed) leads directly to the **Ndarit Gate** and into the park itself. In rainy weather, it might be a better idea to refrain from taking the picturesque dirt trail and continue instead on the main road.

After a while, Lake Elmenteita comes into view on the left-hand side. Just as is true of Lake Naivasha, **Lake Elmenteita** is surrounded by private land for the most part. It originally belonged to the vast es-tate of the infamous Lord Delamere. The shore of the lake, which occasionally dries out, is hemmed by a narrow band of pink flamingos, giving the visitor a little foretaste of the natural theater awaiting him or her at Lake Nakuru. The lake is so alkaline that not very much other life has been able to develop in it.

Kariandusi and Hyrax Hill

Those for whom the beauty of nature alone doesn't quite fill the bill, should pay a visit to the **Kariandusi** prehistoric excavation site, located on the other side of the main road to the east of Lake Elmenteita. A lot of stone tools and fossils, several hundred-thousand years in age, which were discovered here, can be viewed in a small museum. The shore of a huge lake that extended far into the Rift Valley roughly ten thousand years ago, is supposed to have been here.

Another excavation site is located two kilometers to the southeast of Nakuru. The museum of **Hyrax Hill**, a 50-meter lava crest excavated by Mary Leakey in the 1930s, has interesting finds of earlier periods of settlement on exhibit, including tools and earthenware. The ground-plan of the settlement as well as tombs from the Neolithic Period and the Ice Age have been preserved. This place was probably settled by the Kalenjin, semi-nomadic herdsmen from the Nile Valley, who have since moved further into the country's western reaches. The Neolithic tombs are of particular archeological significance. Solely the burial places of the women contain gifts, from which it might be inferred that womens' social position was higher than mens'. The view out over Lake Nakuru is also quite splendid. Both of these excavation sites are among the most significant in the country.

Lake Nakuru National Park

Lake Nakuru National Park is one of the most beautiful bird "paradises" in the world. Millions of dwarf flamingos hem the edge of the lake like a pink ribbon. In 1961, the lake was proclaimed a national park and bird sanctuary, the first of its kind in East Africa. However, the incomparable pleasure of viewing the flamingos is becoming increasingly rare. This is explained in part by the fact that the

flamingos don't breed on Lake Nakuru, but migrate instead to build their nests, sometimes all the way to Natron Lake on the border between Kenya and Tanzania. It also appears that the birds side-step Lake Nakuru when its water level is too low, since this causes an increase in the alkalinity with the result that the flamingos' preferred foods – larvae, aquatic insects and algaes – are not present in sufficient quantities. At these times, the birds head for **Lake Bogoria** to the north or to the more southerly and somewhat cooler Lake Naivasha. According to season, visitors to Lake Nakuru may only get to see a few birds and may, naturally, be accordingly disappointed.

Alongside the flocks of dwarf flamingos one can also admire the rare great pink flamingo and another 450 species of birds. Fishing pelicans plunge their beaks in the water with the hope of catching a couple of the delicious tilapias that were introduced here some time ago in order to eradicate – as far as possible – the larvae of encroaching swarms of mosquitos.

One pelican can consume up to one kilogram of fish per day, and if you consider that on this lake some 5000 pelicans manage to feed themselves easily, it's not hard to imagine how quickly the introduced tilapias became accustomed to their new home.

Extending along the southwestern edge of the lake is an acacia forest along with the various arboreal birds indigenous to it. On the other hand, completely different species of birds inhabit the rocky hills on the eastern shore, which is totally overgrown with candelabra euphorbia.

The chances of seeing a leopard in Nakuru are good, especially on the southeastern edge of the park between the two lodges. The Rothschild giraffe, which has become rare in Kenya's hunting grounds, has been resettled in the park, as has the black rhinoceros.

This animal, which is among the oldest species on earth, is the second-largest land mammal. These colossi have existed in Africa for 60 million years. Whether they are roaming about in the thickets, running over the plains, or quietly taking a drink at a watering hole, their massive bodies are imposing, and their two horns demand respect, plainly and simply. These voluminous beasts win the affection of the majority of tourists, in spite of their absentmindedness, unsociable character, short-sightedness and "pachydermousness". Their poor visual faculty is a probable explanation for their high degree of irritability and constant readiness to attack. Much has been written and philosophized about the fact that a rhinoceros might simply forget a tourist whom he was charging, and suddenly pause to graze. Nonetheless, this isn't very reassuring when two armoured tons are racing toward you at 50 kilometers per hour.

Right: Water is a most precious commodity and often has to be carried great distances.

The black rhinoceros was decimated so extensively that the animals which have survived in Kenya would supposedly not even be enough to supply North Yemen with horn for a year. On the other hand, the so-called white rhinoceros, which was saved just before it became extinct, isn't white at all. Its name is traced back to the Afrikaans word for wide, a good description of its nostrils, which are rather like a horse's. Likewise, the material referred to as horn isn't horn at all, rather densly compressed hair.

The current population of both species amounts to some 4000 specimens. In 1970, there were still about 65,000 black rhinos alone. When undisturbed they move ponderously around their accustomed territory and live according to a simple pattern of behavior: relaxing, wallowing, drinking and eating. The food of the black rhino consists of bushes and grasses, which it tears off with its sharp movable grasping lip, paying no attention to the thorns and spines that the plants have developed to protect themselves.

The acacia forests around Lake Nakuru are also home to the colobus ape; bohor marsh-goats graze on the steppe to the south of the lake, while herds of Defassa waterbucks roam around its northern edge. In the north too, where the lake is deepest, small groups of hippopotami loiter about. On the other hand, impalas appear throughout the lake area.

A good road runs all the way around Lake Nakuru. Various turn-offs lead to the observation points along its shore, which make a close-up look at the various aquatic birds possible.

To be sure, caution is advised on the western shores when the water level is low. At these times the birds are very far away and you might be tempted to drive closer to the water over the flat alkali plains. If you don't want to spend the rest of the day shovelling the vehicle out of the mud it's best to drop this idea as quickly as possible.

There are two lodges in the park: **Lake Nakuru Lodge** and **Lion Hill Camp**. The lodge is located on a hill on the southeastern shore, right alongside an old farmhouse; the standards and comfort of the Lion Hill Camp (tents) in the eastern hills beside the lake are just as impressive as the picturesque views.

Two camping grounds are located in the midst of beautiful acacia forests: The first is in the neighborhood of the main entrance, the second somewhat further to the south. In the town of Nakuru, however, one can select among a variety of reasonably priced accomodations. The **Midland Hotel** can be highly recommended among these.

Nakuru, capital of the Rift Valley Province, is located only a few kilometers away from the park. This attractive town is an important nodal-point for trade, and the center of the agricultural hinterlands. Not only is Nakuru the fourth-largest city in Kenya, it is also the oldest in the interior. The first settlers came here as early as 1903.

In addition to Lake Nakuru and Hyrax Hill, there is one more interesting sight in the neighborhood of the city. The volcanic cone of the **Menengai Crater**, at an altitude of 2278 meters, towers over the whole surrounding region. The tremendous crater has a diameter of some twelve kilometers and is up to 300 meters deep. Only well practiced rock climbers should brave the steep descent into it. The crater was given its rather repulsive name Menengai, which means "Place of Corpses", late in the last century by Masai warriors as they threw members of another Masai tribe over the cliffs down into the abyss.

Thomson's Falls

The extreme contrasts in Kenya's geological strata have created many waterfalls. **Thomson's Falls** in Nyahururu thunder downward in a single powerful cascade from a height of 72 meters. On the route from Nairobi to Maralai an asphalt road leads over Gilgil to Nyahu-

ruru; from western Kenya a *murram* (undulating washboard track) leads from Nakuru to the falls. The town of Nyahururu, which was also named Thomson's Falls until 1973, is the center of an agricultural region in the Aberdares. It has a market, a sawmill and is also the terminal station of the railroad. The beautiful old **Thomson's Falls Lodge**, which is constructed out of local timbers, is located at the falls and offers comfortable lodging in addition to good quality board. With the exception of the falls there's really nothing to be seen in the city. The brisk stream of visitors who come to see the waterfall is due primarily to its convenient location.

The way to Thomson's Falls, which is situated merely about 500 meters from the center of the town, is well indicated with signs on the right-hand side. The only secured observation platform is located on the premises of the lodge (access to outside visitors), which provides both

tourists and the ubiquitous souvenir sellers a spectacular view of the falls. An unsecured path leads (at your own risk) to the basin under the falls. This most powerful of Kenya's waterfalls turns into a meager trickle during the dry season.

There are several climbing paths, certainly not secured, leading to the top of the falls. Caution is advised on these since the rocks might be slippery. You must return on the same path as the cliffs are too eroded to offer a safe hold. A visit to Thomson's Falls can be combined with a drive through the **Aberdare National Park** and a relaxing drink or snack at the lodge there. It can be cool here during the day, so don't forget a sweater or a jacket.

LAKE BOGORIA

Lakes Bogoria and **Baringo**, located to the north of Nakuru, are reached via the D 365, which branches off from the main road in the town of Nakuru. The direction signs show the way to the **Lake Baringo**

Above: The ubiquitous souvenir stands in Kenya, here near Thomson's Falls.

Club and the **Baringo Island Camp**. Until it reaches Baringo, the road, which is very good, runs through a landscape that clearly shows the devastating consequences of overgrazing. Whenever you're nearing larger herds of goats and sheep you should, in your own interest, drive slowly and carefully.

In **Mogotio**, a bumpy trail branches off the main road to the **Lake Bogoria National Park**. A high-riding vehicle with two-wheel drive can most certainly manage this stretch.

From a topographical viewpoint, Lake Bogoria is quite distinct from the more southerly lakes, since it is deeper and located at the bottom of a valley with spectacular precipices descending 600 meters. Its high alkalinity content is due to the fact that it has no drainage, rather only a trickle of an inflow in the south, and only during the rainy season does it receive its minimal amount of fresh water. Since there are no fish in this lake, the pelicans pay it only brief visits at best. On the other hand, the pretty flamingos are exceptionally at ease here, and travellers who haven't had their fill yet in Nakuru have one more opportunity to take their pleasure in full measure at Lake Bogoria.

On the western shore of the lake hot springs pop up out of the ground in the form of little geysers and propagate peculiar, rather putrescent odors. One should walk over the crust of earth here rather carefully, since it is thin – and the water beneath is boiling hot! At a little distance from the springs the water is a bit cooler, in fact an ideal temperature for a warm bath.

Drivers with four-wheel-drive vehicles shouldn't pass up their chance to take the bumpy trail along the eastern shore, since each evening the greater kudus, a species of antelope, scramble down the precipices to drink at the watering holes. If you're travelling with camping equipment you can spend the night in the park

without hesitation. There's scarcely a better place in all of Kenya to observe the majestic great kudu with their spiral-shaped horns.

In local legends, Lake Bogoria is still spoken of as the place of the lost tribe: "In this region there were two tribes, the Sokomos and the Kamales, which lived here many centuries ago, long before there was a lake here.

The hospitable Sokomos were always ready to welcome travellers passing by and offer them food and drink. The miserly Kamales, on the other hand, complained of the "demands" of the travellers and served them sour milk, rotten meat and moldy vegetables. This angered the god Chebet, who let heavy rainfalls beat down upon them. Under the weight of the deluge, which lasted for days, the land broke asunder. The water, in contrast, continued to rise incessantly, forming a lake which flooded the villages. The Sokomos were able to reach safety on the heights, whereas the village of the idle Kamales perished under the floodwaters. Even today you can still hear the wails of the Kamales."

The legend is being spun yet further today as well. One safari entrepreneur – who has seen just about everything – set up camp here not long ago. At midnight, he was suddenly awakened by the clanging of pots and the bewildered cries of women and children. He assumed that his licentious employees were having a roaring party, so he got out of bed to remind them of the rest all the safari participants had earned so well. His astonishment was great when he found both his employees and his guests in a deep sleep: He had heard, without the shadow of a doubt, the lost tribe of the Kamales.

You can easily set out on a day-trip to Lake Bogoria from Nakuru or Baringo; one alternative might be an excursion to the lake on the Nakuru-Baringo route, which passes along the western shore of Lake Bogoria.

153

LAKE BARINGO

Lake Baringo is located 40 kilometers to the north of Bogoria and 110 kilometers away from Nakuru. A well-marked right turn leads from the main road to the **Lake Baringo Club** (western lakeshore) and the Island Camp. On the pier, located two kilometers past the club entrance, there is a boat waiting, even late in the evening, in order to transport travellers to the island of **Ol Kokwe** with its enchanting **Island Camp**. The trip takes about 20 minutes.

The water of this lake, which has no visible drainage at all, like that of Lake Naivasha, is comparatively fresh, leading to the conclusion that it also has subterranean drainage channels. The small herds of hippopotami and crocodiles, which are indigenous here, are apparently satisfied with the selection of food at the lake. They are only a relatively

Above: It takes a great degree of skill to paddle and fish from this precarious vessel.

slight danger to the local tribes of the Pokot, Njemps and Tugen. Swimmers, windsurfers and waterskiers need not suffer from too many anxiety attacks over them either.

Romping about in the waters of the lake are barbels, catfish and tilapias, and one can rest assured that these tasty fish are being served up prepared all sorts of ways in the Lake Baringo Club or the Island Camp.

Baringo isn't exactly famous for its wild animals, although, as a consolation prize, you'll be able to get a good look at the hippopotamui who come to fertilize the grasses of the club; and relaxation is certainly no problem in the midst of this mighty natural scenery. Passionate ornithologists, on the other hand, will feel transported to paradise here. In the Baringo region more than 460 species of birds have been recorded.

In the periods with plentiful rain one should by no means miss the opportunity to take a boating tour on the **Molo River**, especially since you can get a close-up look at sun-bathing crocodiles and observe quite a lot of beautiful birds, including flocks of ducks, herons, stilt-legged birds, lapwings and kingfishers. They don't seem to be much bothered by the boat, not even when it passes fairly close to them. Also, the birds in the Club's garden and at the Island Camp are used to a lot of visitors, with or without field glasses.

Short strolls outside of the Island Camp can be rather frustrating occasions, in that environmental protection doesn't seem to exist yet, and garbage (through which goats rummage with apparent glee) is dumped everywhere. You have to walk a bit further on to leave "civilization" behind, although the difficult hike to the highest point on the island will reward your efforts with a splendid panoramic view over the lake, and perhaps you'll even find the rose-colored, stone "desert rose".

In the mornings and evenings, guided tours are offered to bird lovers by the club's ornithologist. The morning tours stray about three kilometers from the club to the foot of a sheer cliff where one can observe the broad variety of bird species living in these arid regions, while the evening tour provides a closer look at the birds on the lake's southern shore.

The Island Camp organizes boat tours and can also provide visitors with water skiing and wind surfing gear. Of course, during the day there's rarely enough wind to fill the sails, but in the evening there is often a stiff breeze to make up for it.

The camp also offers tours to a Njemps village, where amateur – and professional – photographers have an opportunity to fire away to their hearts' desire without feeling that they're disturbing anyone. Another tour brings visitors to the ruins of a fortress built around the turn of the century on the east shore of the lake. It was abandoned shortly after its completion, since the mosquitos there gave the residents a good taste of living hell.

LAKES IN THE RIFT VALLEY

NAIVASHA
Accommodation
La Belle Inn, PO Box 532. **Hotel North Kinangop**, Moi Avenue. **Governor's Camp**, PO Box 48217, Nairobi, Tel: 331871.
Camping at Burch's, PO Box 40.

LAKE NAIVASHA
Accommodation
Lake Naivasha Hotel, PO Box 15, Nairobi. **Safariland Lodge**, PO Box 72. The International Youth Hostel Association's **Youth Hostel** (with camping and bandas) is at the south shore of the lake. **Fisherman's Camp** at the south shore of the lake offers **camping facilities** and rental bandas. Information: PO Box 14982, Nairobi.
Transportation
Bus service Nairobi – Nakuru. Train station with connections to Nairobi and Nakuru.
Excursions
Crescent Island (rental boats at Lake Naivasha Hotel, Safariland Lodge and Fisherman's Camp). Hell's Gate. Fischer's Tower. Mount Longonot. Mau Escarpment. Elsamere Conservation Centre, Museum and Research Station.

LAKE NAKURU
Accommodation
Lion Hill Camp, PO Box 30680, Nairobi, Tel: 333248-51. **Lake Nakuru Lodge**, PO Box 70559, Nairobi, Tel: 220225/226778.

NAKURU
Accommodation
Mau View Lodge, PO Box 1413, Nakuru. **Midland Hotel**, PO Box 908, Nakuru. **Mukoh Hotel**, PO Box 238, Nakuru.
Transportation
Train station with connections to Nairobi, Eldoret and Kisumu. Bus service to Nairobi, Eldoret, Nyahururu, Narok and minibuses to Lake Baringo.
Excursions
Prehistoric sites Kariandusi and Hyrax Hill (with museum). Menengai Crater.

NYAHURURU
Accommodation
Thomson's Falls Lodge, PO Box 38.

LAKE BARINGO
Accommodation
Island Camp PO Box 42475, Nairobi.
Lake Baringo Club, Tel: 2259, radio-telephone call Nairobi.

SUDAN ETHIOPIA
Lake Turkana
SOMALIA
Marsabit Nat'l. Park
UGANDA
Maralal Nat'l. Sanctuary
Samburu Nat'l. Park
Kampala
KENYA
Meru Nat'l. Park
Jamame
Kisumu Nakuru
Aberdares Nat'l. Park
Mt. Kenya Nat'l. Park
Lake Victoria
Nairobi
Arusha
Malindi
INDIAN
TANZANIA
Mombasa
OCEAN

CENTRAL KENYA

THIKA AND VICINITY

AROUND MOUNT KENYA

ABERDARES

MOUNT KENYA

MERU NATIONAL PARK

SAMBURU / MARALAL

MARSABIT

The central highlands of Kenya extend from north of Nairobi out to the **Laikipia** and **Embu Plains**. Both the twin peaks of Mount Kenya, and the Aberdares mountain range are located in the heart of the country. By the beginning of this century European immigrants had already settled the fertile highlands and driven out the native Kikuyu. The moniker for this region, "White Highlands", was also coined during this period. Nowadays the area is once again populated predominantly by people of African heritage who live here as farmers and herdsmen.

In the mountainous regions, two national parks help protect the abundance of flora and fauna: the **Aberdares National Park** and the **Mount Kenya National Park**. At the edge of the highlands the renowned **Meru National Park** and the smaller **Oldoinyo Sabuk National Park** also merit a visit. The most important transportation routes leading from Nairobi to the highlands in the north are, on the one hand, the stretch via **Thika** and **Nyeri** to **Nanyuki**; and on the other via Thika to **Embu** and further to **Meru**. Both of them have been properly de-

Preceding pages: The patchwork quilt of villages and fields over the undulating landscape around Nyeri. Left: Mount Kenya with its shawl of mist.

veloped and passable in all seasons. The most important artery for traffic heading west out of Nairobi goes through Thika to **Garissa**.

THIKA AND VICINITY

The small town of Thika, which isn't very far from Nairobi, derives its significance primarily from the fact that it is an important nodal point for transportation bound not only to the north but also to the western reaches of Kenya. It has also won some renown from the book *The Flame Trees of Thika*, which tells of the first European settlers. In addition, it is known for its numerous pineapple plantations, the fruit of which is marketed worldwide primarily by the US corporation Del Monte.

Otherwise, the town doesn't have a whole lot to offer – with the exception, perhaps, of a pleasant stop-over in the **Blue Posts Hotel**. The establishment is also called "the Hotel between the Waterfalls", since on its premises two impressive waterfalls thunder down into the depths: The **Chania Falls** to the right of the hotel's entrance, and the **Thika Falls** to the left. The Blue Posts, one of the oldest hotels in Kenia, has a well-tended park with ancient trees. Winston Churchill stayed here in 1907. The Chania

159

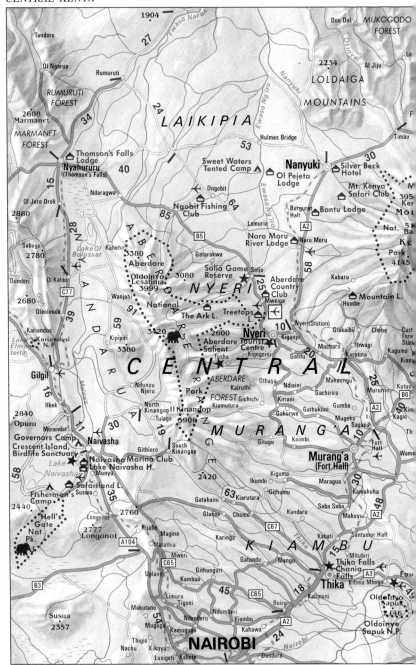

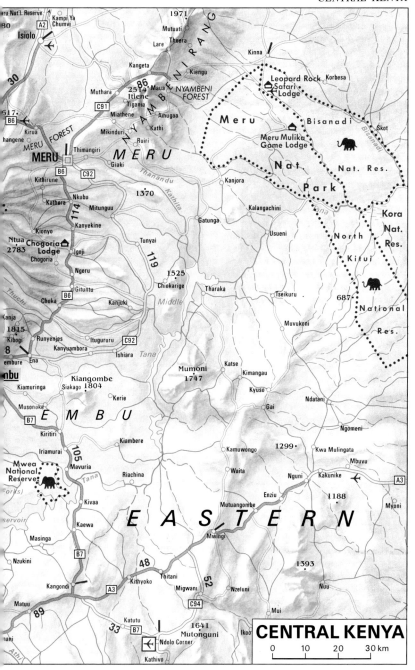

CENTRAL KENYA

0   10   20   30 km

Falls, fed by the Thika River, tumble from a height of 25 meters. They are fringed with magnificent specimens of indigenous tree species. A path leads from the hotel to the Thika Falls 200 m away. Its's surprising how drastically this waterfall contrasts with the nearby Chania Falls. The Thika Falls are almost completely screened off from the hotel by dense growth of tall trees; it has a wilder and more somber appearance than the Chania Falls, even though both are of roughly the same proportions.

Sapuk National Park

From Thika it is possible to drive to the Oldoinyo Sapuk National Park or to take an excursion to the **Fourteen Falls**.

Mount Kilimambogo is visible to the right off the road to Garissa; winding around its base is the **Athi River**. After about 15 km a right-hand turn (behind the post office) is indicated with a sign pointing to **Kangundo**. The junction for continuing to the waterfalls is marked. This trail, covered with a layer of red dust most of the time, is drivable in all kinds of weather, although low-riding vehicles have to be driven slowly and carefully (big chunks of rock!). The large parking area to the side of the falls is guarded by armed policemen. Ten years ago a group of tourists making a picnic here were held up and robbed by a gang equipped with bows and arrows. Fortunately nobody was injured, but ever since the police post stationed in the nearby settlement of Oldoinyo Sapuk has sent a team to guard the area around the waterfalls and to the national park up in the higher elevation. Since the beginning of the patrols there have been no more similar incidents.

Nobody quite knows for certain how the Fourteen Falls received their name.

Right: This coffee plantation looks like a peculiar, vegetal army in the Kenyan highlands.

One supposition is that the falls descend over fourteen thresholds where the water is dammed up, but when one has begun to count it quickly becomes apparent that there must be far more. Nevertheless, nobody has managed to determine the exact number. From the edge of the falls there is a breathtaking view of the tremendous masses of water crashing down 27 meters. Continuing on the little-travelled road in an easterly direction one passes through thinly-settled regions before reaching Garissa.

Situated only 80 km to the northeast of Nairobi, not far off the road between Thika and Garissa is the small (scarcely 18 sq km) **Oldoinyo Sabuk National Park**. The road to the park runs along the fascinating Fourteen Falls and then ascends almost to the summit of **Mount Kilimambogo** (2148 m). From the mountain there is a splendid view clear out to the snow-capped summits of Mount Kenya and Kilamanjaro. The park is home to large herds of buffaloes, bushbucks or guibs, and the koba or waterbuck as well as countless birds.

AROUND MOUNT KENYA

The road from Thika to Nanyuki leads along the valley between Mount Kenya and the Aberdares Mountain Range. The first larger town on the way is **Muranga**, formerly Fort Hall. Hanging there in the St. James Church you can find the impressive works of the Tanzanian painter Elimo Njau; they convey an impression of contemporary East African art. Several roads lead from Muranga to **Nyeri**, located to the northwest. The road going through Sagana winds through fertile green fields and finally ends in the busy little city of **Karatina**. The *matatu* and bus station is the central point of the market bustle in the town center.

Continuing further north on the road one is soon faced with a choice between the direct route to **Nanyuki** and the

somewhat longer one which passes through Nyeri, the main town of the whole Kikuyu region.

Lord Baden-Powell, the world-famous founder of the Boy-Scout "movement", lived here for a couple of years from 1938 until his death in 1941. His grave is located in the city center. The **Outspan Hotel** was built around his old house.

The Outspan is exceptionally popular because of its beautiful gardens, sports facilities and extensive, manifold selection of tours and excursions. It offers, for example, hikes along the banks of the Chania River, which originates in the Aberdares. Furthermore, the Outspan offers excursions to the Aberdares, a number of traditional dance performances, several golf courses and the opportunity to do some fishing.

Returning to the main road from the little town amidst the verdant hills, you can take in the impressive view of Mount Kenya's volcanic massif, provided that it is showing its usually cloud-shrouded summit.

Nearby the next village, **Naro Maro**, is the Naro Moru River Lodge, which is the main point of departure for climbing expeditions to Mount Kenya. Some kilometers further on, a large yellow sign and several souvenir shops bring to the attention of passing travelers that the equator is supposedly located here. In truth, it is located a bit further on at the southern entrance to Nanyuki, the center and shopping crossroads for the surrounding farmlands.

Still further on along the road around Mount Kenya, one of the most important connecting routes to the rugged northern reaches of the country branches off to the left towards Isiolo.

From this point it is still about 30 km to **Meru**, a city of about 75,000 inhabitants which is also the trading and business center of the area. The primary crops cultivated in the surrounding lands are tea, coffee, corn (or maize) and tobacco. From the entrance of the town it's still a good 80 km to the Meru National Park. If you continue on the road around Mount

Kenya, the only larger town before you get back to Thika and Nairobi is **Embu**, a small city named after the Embu tribe which lives in this area. To the south of Embu, the Tana River has been dammed up into several gigantic lakes, which also ensure the generation of a large part of the country's electricity requirements. The **Mwea National Reserve**, located on the edge of the water reservoir, is not accessible to tourists.

ABERDARES

Wild, romantic mountain landscapes, sheer cliffs and green valleys await the visitor to Aberdares National Park. The mountain range, almost 70 kilometers long, extends along the East African Trench and has peaks reaching altitudes as high as 4000 meters. During the rainy season, the roads through the park are barely passable.

Above: The elephant, extinct in parts of Africa, comes in herds in the Aberdares.

In the north, the Aberdares reach heights of 4000 meters at the upland moors of **Oldoinyo Lasatima**. 40 miles to the south of them the summit of **Kinangop** towers 3906 meters. In between is the upper moorland plateau, a region overgrown with tufted hair-grass and heather. Off toward the east is a fantastic view of distant Mount Kenya, and to the west one can, with ease, discern the broad Great Rift Valley and further off into the distance Lake Naivasha and the Mau Escarpment rising behind it.

One particularly wonderful natural phenomenon in the Aberdares are the waterfalls. **Gura Falls**, Kenya's highest, plunge down 300 meters into the Gura River. Almost opposite, the **Karura Falls** travel down a 275-meter precipice to end in the **Chania River**.

Visitors to the Aberdares have a good chance to see elephants, buffaloes, water-, bush-, and reed-bucks, the cape elk (also called eland antelope), bongos, duikerbok antelopes, sunis, river and wart hogs, lions, baboons and hyenas.

The roads which criss-cross the park were constructed for the most part by British troops during the War of Independence in the fifties. The most important of all these is a partially asphalted route which ascends to an altitude of 3170 meters, and leads all the way from Nyeri to Naivasha.

Travel via Nyeri to the Aberdares is facilitated by numerous hotels, which were originally constructed as observation posts and viewpoints.

The Outspan Hotel in Nyeri is a starting point for expeditions to the **Treetops Lodge**, located near a watering hole in a forested region of the Aberdares. The Treetops is the most famous lodge of its sort in the world. Only by way of ladders does one reach the lodge in the gigantic trees. A commemorative plaque reminds us of the stay of Princess Elizabeth and the Duke of Edinburgh in this hotel. During the night they once spent here, the high-born guest received some rather significant news: King George VI had passed away, and the Princess had suddenly become Queen Elizabeth II of England.

The elegant arboreal lodge The Ark has far more luxury to offer to its guests than even the Treetops. The hotel is reached by way of the **Aberdares Country Club**. This "tree-hotel" can accomodate up to 79 guests in single and double rooms. In addition to the birds, at nightfall bush-bucks, elephants and buffaloes show up at the watering hole near the Ark. Each of its levels has an observation platform with a comfortable glassed-in lounge where one can spend the entire night watching the animals.

The **Aberdares Country Club** has outstanding grounds for trout angling on the section of the river located along its premises. But it also provides for a broad variety of recreational activities including hiking, riding, bird-watching and playing tennis. There is also a swimming pool. The guests of the Ark and the Aber-

dares Country Club can come in from Nairobi by automobile or be picked up after their arrival by aircraft at the nearby **Mweiga** airstrip.

Solio Game Reserve

Any account treating the smaller parks of Kenya would be incomplete without mentioning a remarkable place, easily reached from the Aberdares Country Club: the **Solio Game Reserve**.

The renowned Parfet family lives here on a 25,600 hectare parcel of land situated between Mount Kenya and the foothills of the Aberdares. These remarkable nature conservationists have had extraordinary success in rhinoceros breeding. In a period during which the rhino was being rapidly exterminated by hunters throughout Asia and Africa, Count Parfet and his wife Claude managed to breed both black and white rhinos on their 5600-hectare private animal reserve. Success has been achieved in the preservation and breeding of more rhinos per square kilometer in this area than in any other place in the world.

Solio shares its wealth with the state-controlled animal reserves whose rhino populations have been heavily decimated or completely exterminated, as well as animal reserves in private hands, where rhinos for breeding and the propagation of the species are urgently needed. With a stock of over 100 animals, they have been able to provide several specimens to other parks, including Lake Nakuru, in addition to other animal reserves in private hands. As part of this effort 15 rhinos were resettled from Solio into the Nakuru Rhino Sanctuary. There had been merely one lonely rhino living there. Three others were taken to Lewa Downs, four to Ol Pejeta and three to Ol Jogi, north of Nanyuki.

Organized groups of tourists coming in from the Aberdares Country Club are allowed access to the area, which is pro-

tected by an electric fence and is closely guarded.

The Solio Wildlife Conservation Area offers one of the last remaining possibilities to observe the animal life of the high plains in secure and natural surroundings. Among its residents are lions and leopards as well as cheetahs, gazelles and zebras. Besides the ostrich there are many other species of birds, some examples being the osprey or fish-hawk, the crested guinea-hen and the brown parrot. On the plain and on the edges of the swamp in the center of the Solio Reserve there are, among others, bush bucks and ibexes, duikerboks, oryxes, eland antelopes and the great wild boar.

Almost every nook and cranny of the wildlife reserve can be reached by way of its approximately 300 kilometers of well maintained roads. The carefully preserved

Above: Mount Kenya reaches even higher than the clouds most of the time. Right: The exclusive Mount Kenya Safari Club, founded by actor William Holden.

habitats in the Solio have brought about an increase in several species, including the buffalo and the zebra, which graze quite peacefully alongside the rhinoceroses.

MOUNT KENYA NATIONAL PARK

The first European who laid eyes on Mount Kenya was the German missionary-explorer Dr. Johann Ludwig Krapf. No one at the time (1849) believed that there could be a snow-capped mountain at the equator. Not until 34 years later was his discovery confirmed, by Joseph Thomson, a Scotsman.

On clear days you can enjoy a wonderful view of the mountain's three peaks, **Batian**, **Nelion** and **Lenana**. They have been described as the most perfect "design" for an equatorial mountain in the world. Mount Kenya is also the only place anywhere around the equator which has continuous snow-cover.

The sweeping mountain is surrounded by farmland and savannah. From dense

rain forests, bamboo jungles and highland moors, the landscape changes to heaths with huge lobelias and cruciferous plants in the higher elevations, finally culminating in a zone of naked rocks and mere snow. The feathered world of this mountain is exceptionally diverse and ranges from huge eagles to the brilliantly colored sun-bird.

In the forested regions below the moors there are also large numbers of animals roaming free in the wilds. One unusual aspect of this area is that the lions share the moorlands with the zebras that come up from the lower-lying plains. There are also numerous species of reptiles here including the mountain viper, which is found exclusively in the regions of Mount Kenya and in the Aberdares.

Hiking and mountain-climbing tours on the snow-covered peaks start out, for the most part, at the **Naro Moru River Lodge**, where it is also possible to rent mountain climbing equipment.

The **Mountain Lodge** is located in the midst of a dense rain forest in the south-western foothills of Mount Kenya, which are also a part of the National Park.

One more crowning jewel of this area is the luxurious **Mount Kenya Safari Club**, located in a garden of some forty hectares before the majestic background created by the fog-shrouded mountain massif. This exclusive club was founded in 1958 by Hollywood star William Holden. Celebrities from all over the world appear on its membership list, although non-members are also welcome to spend some time in this paradise. The remarkable selection of recreational options at the club include a number of bird observation towers, several swimming pools, restaurants, bowling lanes, putting greens, a nine-hole golf course, a pavilion and several tennis courts.

MERU NATIONAL PARK

The **Meru National Park** is located to the north-east of Mount Kenya. Up until just a few years ago it was still a public hunting grounds.

The park, located in Kenya's southeastern reaches, covers an area of 870 square kilometers, and is interspersed with swampy areas, volcanic rock and pasture lands. It is a typical African bush landscape, serving as home for a great number of freely ranging wild animals.

Elsa, the famous lioness raised by zoologist and author Joy Adamson, was born in the Meru National Park. The book *Born Free* is a memorial to her; it also provided the material for the film as well as a popular song by the same name. 30 years have already gone by since the lioness Elsa was released back to the wilds to roam free again. For many years, Joy and her husband George Adamson were in the habit of taking lions from captivity and returning them to freedom.

A few kilometers downriver on the Tana the Meru National Park connects with the **Kora National Reserve** where

Above: The Grevy zebra can be spotted most often in the Meru and Samburu National Parks in the northern part of Kenya.

George Adamson spent the last years of his life. He was killed in a shootout with bandits in 1989; his wife had already been murdered in 1980. The Elsa Wildlife Trust plans to construct a museum which is to be dedicated to the Adamsons and their beloved lions.

The **Kora National Reserve** has not been developed for tourism, as is also true of the **Bisanadi**, **Rahole** and **North Kitui Reserves**. They are only accessible with four-wheel drive vehicles.

The southern border of the Meru Park, which is located at the equator, is formed by Kenya's largest waterway, the **Tana River**. Fifteen more rivers, all of which have their sources on Mount Kenya, snake through the remote wilderness of the Meru. The result: an immense diversity of vegetation and landscape for such a small area. The broad African savannah, dense closed-canopy alpine forests and swampy regions lay the groundwork for an incomparable wealth of mammals, reptiles and birds. Even though the biggest attraction of the Meru is the outstanding opportunity for observing lions and cheetahs, this national park had also been known for its small herd of white rhinoceroses. However, despite their having been guarded around the clock by armed gamekeepers, in a single day all five animals in the herd were slaughtered.

Among the fauna of the Meru is a large stock of Grevy zebras, which live primarily in Kenya's northern regions, the gentle reticulated giraffe, and a great number of Somalian blue-necked ostriches. In addition to the numerous mammals in the Meru National Park you can also observe about one-third of the altogether 1068 species of birds which have been recorded in Kenya.

The Tana River is populated by crocodile colonies and hippopotamui. The various tributary streams cutting across the park and ultimately emptying into the Tana River have dense forests of tamarind and fig trees growing along their banks. These serve as home to various species parrots and apes. The Tana suddenly becomes narrower when it reaches the picturesque **Adamson Falls**, and the overhanging poplar trees there provide much-coveted shade for what thereby becomes an ideal picnic spot.

The **Meru Mulika Lodge** is named after the nearby Mulika Swamp. From the balconies of the rooms one has a view of green marshlands with acacia trees, the feeding grounds of the koba or waterbuck, and herds of elephants, which are occasionally escorted by a horde of bellowing baboons.

Accomodations are also available in the Meru's **Leopard Rock Safari Lodge** or at one of the eight camping grounds at the traveller's disposal in the park.

Along the route to the Meru National Park there are well laid out tea and coffee plantations as well as flourishing agricultural enterprises of the central and eastern provinces of Kenya, and one could almost start to believe that there is one big Garden of Eden north of Nairobi.

CENTRAL KENYA

THIKA
Accommodation
New Blue Posts Hotel, PO Box 42.
Sightseeing / Excursions
Chania and Thika Falls. **Excursions**: Fourteen Falls (with accommodation **Fourteen Falls Hotel**). Oldoinyo Sabuk National Park (camp site).

NYERI
Accommodation
Outspan Hotel, PO Box 24 (point of departure for Treetops Lodge). White Rhino Hotel, at the outskirts of Nyeri.

ABERDARES NATIONAL PARK
Accommodation
The Aberdares Country Club, PO Box 59749, Nairobi. The Ark, PO Box 58581, Nairobi. Treetops, PO Box 23, Nyeri. Ol Pejeta Lodge, PO Box 58581, Nairobi.
Excursion
To the Solio Game Range.

MOUNT KENYA NATIONAL PARK
Accommodation
Mountain Lodge, PO Box 123, Kiganjo. Mount Kenya Safari Club, PO Box 35, Nanyuki. Naro Moru River Lodge (cheaper bandas and camping available on demand), PO Box 18, Naro Moru.
Excursion
To the Mount Kenya Game Ranch with Animal Orphanage, PO Box 288, Nanyuki.

NANYUKI
Accommodation
Sportman's Arms, PO Box 3. Nanyuki Sweet Water's Tented Camp, PO Box 58581, Nairobi, Tel: 216940.

MERU
Accommodation
Meru Country Hotel, PO Box 1386.
Sightseeing
Ethnological Museum.

MERU NATIONAL PARK
Accommodation
Meru Mulika Lodge, PO Box 42013, Nairobi. Leopard Rock Safari Lodge, PO Box 45456, Nairobi.

EMBU
Accommodation
Izaac Walton Inn, PO Box 1.

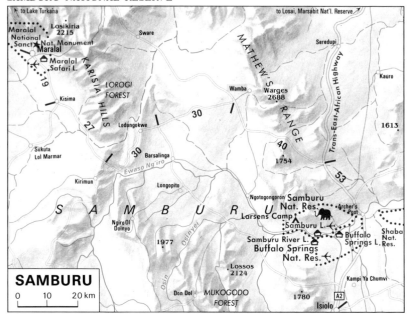

SAMBURU

0   10   20 km

SAMBURU, MARALAL AND MARSABIT

The traditional domain of the Samburu is the wild landscape to the north of Mount Kenya, in which the **Samburu, Shaba** and **Buffalo Springs Reserves** and the **Maralal National Sanctuary** are located. There are two additional conservation areas for animals and plants further to the north, the **Losai** and **Marsabit Reserves**. When taking a tour which includes these areas you will become familiar with Kenya's completely differing zones of vegetation, ranging from the green forests of the highlands to the semi-desert landscapes around Samburu with its volcanic hills and rivers.

When leaving the area around Mount Kenya in the direction of Isiolo one soon notices a considerable temperature increase and the first indications of the aridity of Kenya's northern desert, even

Right: The road to Maralal in the north is long and bumpy.

though here, in the transition zone on its border, there are still broad areas covered with grass and rounded hills do give the countryside a certain mellowness.

The paved road ends in **Isiolo**. The stretch to Marsabit has to be covered on a dusty, difficult dirt road. Then, in the neighborhood of **Archer's Post**, it gets even hotter. This is Samburu country.

The proud, tall Samburus with their reddish-yellow hair and their multicolored, toga-like *shukas* draped casually over their shoulders stand in the sun holding long-bladed spears, and guarding their large herds at pasture in order to defend against livestock thieves.

Samburu National Reserve

The trees extend like broad green ribbons along the river beds that meander through the Samburu National Reserve, an area 165 square kilometers in size with a wealth of contrasts. It is located to the west of Archer's Post, 315 kilometers from Nairobi. The Samburu National

Reserve is relatively small; its primary attraction lies in the density of its tremendous stock of wildlife. The animals living here move back and forth between this reserve and the 131 square-kilometer **Buffalo Springs National Reserve** on the other shore of the river.

At this place the immense fascination of Africa becomes clear: Here, the savannah with stunted thorn bushes, countless termite mounds and flattended rocky hills; there, the luxuriant centuries-old forest on the banks of the **Ewaso Ng'iro**. This river, which always has a flow of water, has been the life-giving – and preserving – artery of this region since the beginning of human history.

The balanced ecosystem of the savannah has created a habitat for many animal species, with which the Samburu have learned to co-exist. The Grevy zebra, which is exceptionally rare in other parts of Africa, is rather common here.

There are also the "Big Five" in Samburu: Elephants, rhinoceroses and buffaloes are not too numerous here, but the large stock of antelope has attracted many lions and leopards.

The **Ewaso Ng'iro River** is broad and peaceful here. It winds through the savannah and provides a habitat for fear-inspiring crocodile colonies (the beasts can be over six meters long) as well as the hippopotamui, who either lay around half-covered in the water or come up onto the muddy riverbanks to sunbathe.

There are accomodations for tourists in the **Samburu Lodge**, the **Samburu Serena Lodge** and the **Buffalo Springs Lodge** or at one of the many camping grounds which have been established along the riverbanks.

The third animal sanctuary, located as though on the third point of a triangle on the other side of the main road, is the **Shaba National Reserve**. It is the largest (239 square kilometers) of these three wildlife conservation areas. The primary reason it is less well-known than the others is that the roadways are for the most part in worse condition than in Samburu, so it's easy to get stuck when it

171

rains. The forest-covered hills and numerous springs are home to elephants, buffaloes, lions and zebras.

The famed animal researcher Joy Adamson raised cheetahs at the Shaba Reserve and successfully released them to the wilds again. She wrote a three-volume book about it. In 1980, Joy Adamson was murdered in the park leaving this major opus unfinished.

To the north of Isiolo a road leads to the Ethiopian border. Only a few kilometers away from Archer's Post is the little trading center of **Laisamis**, before the road descends into the dusty, godforsaken isolation of **Keisut** and the **Chalbi Desert**. The monotony of this black lava wasteland is interrupted only by bizarre, wildly cleft rock formations sprouting up like mushrooms on the desert floor.

Mountain lovers in this area might want to make an excursion to the ridges

Above: Crocodile sunning his – or her – tonsils in Samburu Park. Right: Surveying the landscape on the way to Lake Turkana.

of **Matthew's Range**. Among the Samburus, it is known as *Ol Doinyo Lengeyo*, which means "Mountain of the Child". In order to get to it, take the road leading from Archer's Post to **Maralal** and, after covering about half of the stretch, turn to the right into the little village of **Wamba**. The closest peak is the 2688-meter-high **Warges**, which can also be ascended fairly easily by people with no mountainclimbing experience. You should, however, take along one of the indigenous guides. If you continue to drive on over the trackless wastes further into the Matthew's Range region you come upon a lovely mountain landscape with green pastures and crystal-clear streams and ponds. The track is only passable with four-wheel drive vehicles. At its end one can start out on the rewarding ascent of the 2375 meter-high Matthew's Peak.

Maralal

A rocky road leads from Samburu National Reserve to the **Maralal Game**

Sanctuary, one of the world's smallest animal reserves. This conservation area is located inside the city limits of Maralal, the administrative seat of the district. One site interesting enough for a visit, is the inconspicuous bungalow in which the British held former Kenyan president Jomo Kenyatta prisoner in 1961. This rather inconspicuous abode has been declared a national monument.

The **Maralal Safari Lodge** is located a short distance from the town. It features cosy wooden cottages for its guests. In fact, it may well remind you more of the Swiss Alps than Africa. The fireplaces in the cottages will certainly be appreciated in the cool hours of the evening and night. It can start to feel pretty chilly on the plateau, which lays at an altitude of 1900 meters. The lodge was constructed a few meters from the parks constantly filled watering-holes, which means that its veranda offers an outstanding chance to observe the migrations of the thirsty beasts as they come to drink their fill.

In the Maralal National Sanctuary there are gangs of impalas, eland antelopes (Cape elk), buffaloes and zebras, packs of wart hogs and troops of baboons. There are also organized excursions which start out from the lodge to a place where meat is hung out for the leopards in order to attract the beasts – a successful effort, for the most part.

Drivers on their way north to Lake Turkana or east to Marsabit have their last opportunity to change money and tank up in Maralal.

Marsabit National Reserve

When driving from Archer's Post further to the north one cuts across the **Losai National Reserve** before coming to the village of Laisamis. It was opened in 1976, but it remains, as ever, scantily developed.

Further to the north, as one approaches the **Logo Logo** trading post in the early evening, the sun sometimes looks like a gigantic over-ripe orange gliding out of an invisible hand and sinking into a moon-like landscape on the horizon. This is the final stretch before Marsabit. A nocturnal drive in the moonshine is an unforgettable experience which really oughtn't be missed on a visit to Kenya.

The **Marsabit National Reserve** is 280 kilometers from Isiolo and 580 kilometers from Nairobi, although it appears to be on some other planet. The Marsabit National Park covers an area of 592 square kilometers within the 2088 square kilometer Marsabit Wildlife Reserve. One is richly rewarded for the fatiguing overland journey upon arrival in Marsabit. In the midst of the lava desert and somewhat flattened hills, the green **Mount Marsabit** towers up with its 1702 meters like an oasis.

The very nearly closed-canopy, secretive-looking green forest landscape of the mountain stands in stark contrast to the congealed igneous rocks of its surroundings. When driving in through the cool

173

air of night, about four kilometers out of town lights the Marsabit Lodge suddenly becomes visible on the mountain.

The moon, amidst countless constellations of glittering stars in the clear equatorial skies, shows the way through the whispering forest to a lodge in a very romantic location. It first appears as a silhouette on the horizon and is then reflected in the water on the southeastern shore of a small lake, the **Sokorte Diko,** as it is called in the Boran language. It was decided to build the lodge here in 1974, since the Sokorte Diko had always been a watering hole for free-ranging wild animals. In addition, there are three campgrounds, one of which is located on **Lake Paradise**. The other lake in Marsabit is the **Sokorte Guda**.

There are many interesting volcanic craters in the Marsabit, one of these is in fact the water-filled Sokorte Diko. On late afternoons, elephant and buffalo

Above: The famous giant elephants in the Marsabit National Reserve.

herds come to the lake. After they have quenched their thirsts, they come to graze on the lawn adjacent to the veranda of the dining room. Guests of the lodge can enjoy a close, prandial encounter with Kenia's wildlife, which here includes some of the largest elephants still extant on our planet.

Marsabit is indeed renowned as the home of gigantic bull-elephants with enormous tusks. When the region was proclaimed the Marsabit National Reserve in 1962, it was the protected (by presidential decree) turf of Ahmed, the patriarch of the pachyderms, who finally died in 1974 from old age. A plastic replica of Ahmed's body is on display in the National Museum in Nairobi. One of his tusks weighed 64 kilograms. After his death another huge elephant, Abdul (supposedly Ahmeds's brother) was named King of Marsabit.

The fascination of this remote, uncounterfeited outpost is strengthened even further by the presence of numerous other wild animals, including Grevy zebras, lions and leopards. The reticulated giraffe, which is seen on the slopes either individually or in groups is of particular interest.

Normally, giraffes prefer to live in broad, flat countryside. However, there are trees on the mountains, the only ones far and wide in this desert area, which have provoked the giraffes of Marsabit to give up their natural habits and adjust to their environment.

The inhospitable lava desert to the north has an irresistable power of attraction all its own. The route there leads through a sandy swatch of landscape with stunted acacia trees.

The Somalian ostrich is among the ornithological rarities of the **Dida Galgalla Desert**. It also is home to the majestic black-faced bustard and the graceful swallowtail falcon. The masked lark, which is considered exceptionally rare, is relatively common in this sea of lava.

When making a stay in Marsabit it is also quite worthwhile to direct your attention to the beauties of the long-extinct volcano craters, for example the **Gof Choba** and **Gof Bongole**.

In the Marsabit one also comes across the nomadic Boran, Rendille and Gabra tribes, who, just as they always have, drive their livestock to drink at the so-called "Singing Wells" of the once-powerful Laga Sagante River.

The name of the wells is based on the peculiar perception which you can experience for yourself on the edges of this huge rocky valley by listening to the hot, melodious winds of the desert. The sounds of the wind blend together in unique harmony with the rhythms of the shepherd's songs as they haul their water up from the depths.

The **Sibiloi** is Kenya's most remote national park, 320 km from Marsabit and 960 km distance from Nairobi. In between, the roadless **Chalbi Desert** extends on out to the northeastern shore of **Lake Turkana.**

ISIOLO
Accommodation
Bomen Hotel, PO Box 67, Isiolo.
Excursions
Camel rides in the surrounding countryside.
Transportation
Buses to Marsabit, Moyale, Meru and Nairobi.

SAMBURU / SHABA
BUFFALO SPRINGS
Accommodation
Larsens Camp, PO Box 31097, Nairobi, Tel: 335807. **Buffalo Springs Lodge**, PO Box 71, Isiolo. **Samburu Serena Lodge**, PO Box 48690, Nairobi. **Samburu Lodge**, PO Box 31097, Nairobi. **Sarova Hotel**, PO Box 30680, Nairobi. Several self-catering **camping sites**.
Excursions
Mountain-hiking tours to Matthew's Range, Matthews Peak or in the Warges.

MARALAL
Accommodation
Maralal Safari Lodge, PO Box 42475, Nairobi. **Buffalo House**, PO Box 28. Public camping site.
Transportation
Buses to Nyahururu, irregular service to the North. **Petrol**: Should you plan to venture into Northern Kenia, fill up your tank here – and don't count on petrol stations on the way.

MARSABIT
Accommodation
Marsabit Hotel, PO Box 110.
Transportation
Buses run several times a week to Isiolo, Moyale and the Ethiopian border (ca. 250 km).

MARSABIT
NATIONAL RESERVE
Accommodation
Marsabit Lodge, PO Box 42013, Nairobi. Several **camping sites** in exceptionally charming surroundings at Lake Paradise.

MOYALE
Accommodation
Simple accommodation only at the **Barissah Hotel** or **Bismillahi Hotel**.
Transportation
Buses to Marsabit, Isiolo and Wajir.
Crossing the Border into Ethiopia
Permission for entering Ethiopia is subject to the current political situation. Before planning a trip to Ethiopia it is advisable to check with the Ethiopian Embassy in Nairobi.

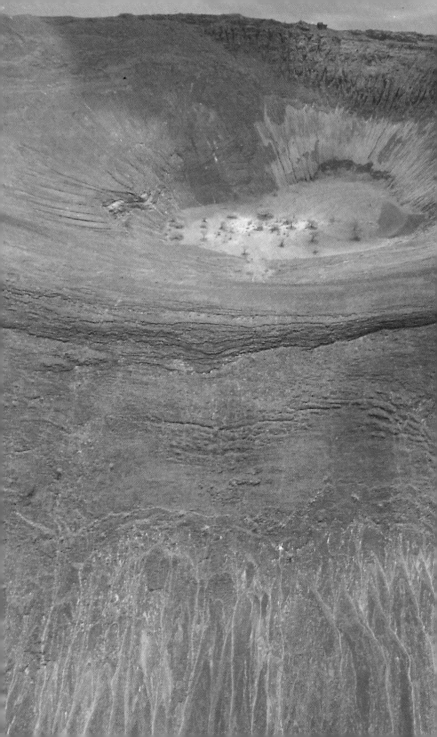

THE JADE LAKE

LAKE TURKANA
SIBILOI NATIONAL PARK

When the Hungarian explorer Count Teleki and Second Lieutenant Ludwig von Höhnel of the Imperial Austrian army crossed through Kenya in 1888, on March 6th, after an arduous voyage, they came upon a gigantic lake with water the color of jade. They named it Lake Rudolf in honor of their patron, Archduke Rudolf of Austria. They didn't forget Archduchess Stephanie either: Lake Stephanie, situated not far away to the northeast, was named after her. As part of "Africanization" efforts Lake Rudolf was changed to Lake Turkana in 1975.

One writer described this lake very fittingly: "An inland lake of incomparable beauty, surrounded by lava rocks and chains of violet-hued hills, covered with gleaming sunlight and overarched by star-spangled nights.

The plentiful algae in the lake transform the water into a colorful kaleidoscope ranging from slate grey to diamond blue, as the clouds chase after each other overhead. Most of the time, however, the sunlight causes the lake to shimmer in hues of deep green, which lent it the nickname of Jade Lake."

Preceding pages: The giant crater of a volcano near Lake Turkana. Left: The waters of the lake provide sustenance for the local tribes.

The Turkana region, which was a sleepy hinterland for a long time, attracts increasingly large numbers of visitors, mainly because here, beyond the influences of civilization, a piece of original Africa has been preserved. However, the travelers are not lured here by the beauty of the landscape and the untouched wilderness alone, they are also drawn by its significant prehistoric finds.

The northern tip of Turkana Lake, which is about 300 kilometers long and 50 wide, is located in Ethiopia. Though several streams feed the lake there is not a single river flowing out of it. The increasing desertification of the surrounding area has intensified siltification and thus reduced the lake's size.

Safari in the North

There are several routes leading into the inhospitable northern reaches of the country, which is one of the most thinly populated regions of the world. Even today, an automobile trip into this area is an incomparable adventure. If you are extremely well equipped and sufficiently informed about the local living conditions, a safari to Lake Turkana is recommended by all means. Naturally, one might decide in favor of an organized tour, and with these have a choice from

179

many different variants. For example, a perfectly organized safari of six to eight participants can be made in relatively comfortable Land Rovers combined with overnight stays in pleasant lodges. Another option is to journey in a group of 10-20 people in remodeled trucks fixed up as busses, camping along the way. The price and your expectations will make the decision. Of course it is possible to fly to Turkana Lake, whereby one is spared the exciting, but fatiguing automobile journey there.

One of the reasons for the relatively late development of tourism in the north was a regulation by the colonial government which declared this province a "restricted area" and allowed access only to certain groups of outsiders, such as civil service officers and professional hunting associations.

Today it is possible to travel here without restriction, except that on the road between Isolio and Marsabit one must drive in convoys since there is a significant danger of being held up by bandits, named *Shifta* in the local vernacular. The *Shifta* are members of a Somalian tribe which lays claim to this area. It sends out guerillas to attack isolated settlements and rob individual vehicles.

It certainly is necessary to have a good deal of perseverance for a safari through this primitive, wild region, but the grandiose landscape and the wildlife are more than sufficient reward for all of the effort. One must by all means be certain to bring along enough food, water and gasoline, since the lodges in this area are spread out long distances from each other. For camping you will also need carefully chosen equipment. The best policy is to inquire in the various localities as to which problems could come up. Some absolute musts: A repair kit for flat tires, a selection of replacement parts for the vehicle, a car jack, a shovel and at least two sand ladders in case you should get stuck in a slough or sand-drift.

It is scarcely possible to plan the journey in one-day stages according to the kilometer distances on the map, since only slow progress over this craggy terrain is the usual order of the day. Depending on the weather, road conditions and the usefulness of the local travelling hints, covering a stretch of merely 80 kilometers can sometimes swallow a whole day. The indigenous people, most of whom are very friendly, often speak a bit of English and are eager to make contact with strangers. They are also more than ready to provide information on local conditions.

Since there is hardly any public means of transportation to speak of in this region, the natives often hitch-hike a portion of the route they are trying to cover. The men of the Samburu and Rendille tribes are often equipped with a short sword (*simi*) and a type of truncheon *(rungu)*, whereas the Turkana and Borana carry spears, the Merille and Gabbra mostly an old gun and a leather bullet belt around their waists. These weapons are preventative measures not only against bandits, but also against the lions which may be roving about. If you take a native along in the car, it is customary to offer him some water. Water is a precious commodity in the north.

Many Paths Lead to the Goal

One tour through northern Kenya runs from Lake Baringo, to the north along Lake Turkana's western shore up to the Sudanese frontier, then eastwards along the borders of Ethiopia and Somalia. Just as in the rest of Kenya, the larger roads pass through the respective district capitals, in this case **Lodwar, Maralal, Marsabit** and **Isiolo**.

A new (extremely difficult) asphalt road leads through **Kitale** and Lodwar to the middle of the western lakeshore. It takes at least five hours to cover the 400 kilometer stretch from Nairobi to Kitale.

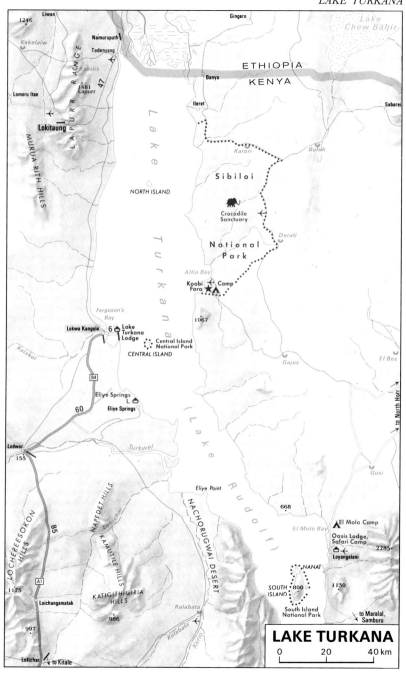

LAKE TURKANA

0   20   40 km

Another five hours is required for the fissured terrain from Kitale to Lake Turkana. The drive can take considerably longer. Optimally, the trip should be divided into two day-long stages.

The road leaving Kitale leads to the small town of **Lokichar**, which is located between two almost untouched wildlife reserves, **Nasalot** and **South Turkana**. There are no overnight accomodations in these parks. The plain becomes ever more sterile, and now and then dust-devils come whirling by. The rocky road descends into the hot environs of Lake Turkana and comes to an end in Lodmar, the marketplace and administrative center of the region.

The road from Isiolo via **Marsabit** goes over the Trans-East-African Highway. After passing Marsabit the route cuts across the **Chalbi Desert**. Mirages of distant trees and hills flutter over the parched, rock-hard clay soil, extending without the slightest acclivity, clear off to the horizon. **North Horr** is located right in the middle of this inhospitable desert. It consists of a couple of huts with corrugated iron roofs, a police post and a missionary school. Otherwise there's absolutely nothing here.

One of the most interesting trails leads from Maralal to Lake Turkana. It passes through a parched landscape with cattle, ostriches and zebras until reaching **Baragoi**, a picturesque town where many nomads meet and trade all sorts of necessities on a turbulent marketplace.

Beyond Baragoi, the road winds its way through a valley which is flanked on the right by the mountain **Koi Tokol** and to the left by the Kowop range. Here, in 1980, the Turkanas invaded the Samburu region. Heavy fighting between the two tribes resulted.

The **Horr Valley** is located past this region. The landscape on either side of the smooth sand trail only appears to be desolate and deserted: When making a brief stop, Samburu warriors will appear out of thin air to greet the strangers passing by. Now and then the track has to be cleared for the passage of the nomads' camel caravans. Sometimes that leaves an opportunity to do a little business, trading hand-made jewelry for ball point pens, for example. This road has a few other surprises up its sleeves: half-dried-out river beds which have to be crossed or pointed rocks which you really don't want to subject your tires to. Frequently, driving at walking speed is the only reasonable pace to continue the journey.

South Horr turns out to be an idyllic oasis with luxuriant vegetation. There is a foresters' administrative office, a church and some small hotels with mud floors, where the exhausted traveller can resuscitate with tea and doughnuts in Swahili style. Spectacular dances take place in the **Kudunga Valley Camp** (lodging in cottages available) past South Horr.

Now the trail winds through the fissured cliffs of the **Ol Doinyo Nyiro** and **Ol Doinyo Mara**, and once one has left the Horr Valley the landscape takes on dramatic forms: A seemingly endless plain littered with basalt globules slowly transforms into a moon-like landscape of black lumps. And then the Jade Lake suddenly appears. After hours of driving through black lava fields and desolate rock desert, the succulent green of the oasis at the lake seems like some sort of miracle.

LAKE TURKANA

Red soil extends to the lakeshore, which is hemmed with flamingos, pelicans, lapwings, ibexes, stilt-legged fowl, cranes and cormorants, and further in the background islands float on the blue-green water. The trail runs parallel to the shore to **Loyengalani** and the **Oasis Lodge**.

Right: The Rendille people have driven camel herds for centuries.

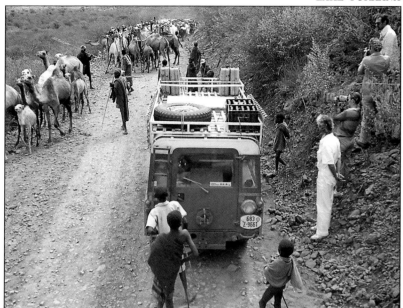

This alkaline lake is situated only 375 meters above sea level, and on its shores the temperature sometimes rises as high as 50 °C during the day. The storms that sweep across the lake at night have started many a traveller from their peaceful sleep.

In the vicinity of the lake, which has scarcely a human settlement, there are lions, zebras, gazelles and rhinoceroses as well as over 300 species of birds. The stock of crocodiles unfortunately has declined enormously in the last decades, primarily because of the Luo fishermen.

With only about 400 tribal members, the quiet, poor El Molo, who live on the shores of the lake, are probably the smallest of Kenya's ethnic groups. Of course, through marriage with the neighboring Samburus they could increase their numbers again, but, on the other hand, their language is in the throes of becoming extinct. In addition to the El Molos, the Rendille, Boran, Gabbra and the nomadic herdsmen of the Merille tribe live in this region.

The Rendille, who are relatives of the Somalians, live on the Marsabit side of the lake. Their legends recount how, many centuries ago, nine Somali warriors who were guarding their camels lost their way, and after days of wandering about arrived to the domain of the Samburus. Before the Samburu elders would allow the Somalis to take wives from their tribe, they had to give up their old customs and renounce Islam. The warriors agreed, and as a result of this connection with the women of the Samburu the Rendille tribe came into being.

Their men, women and children live in semi-permanent settlements in which only a few milk-camels are kept for food. In the search for good pasturage for their large herds of camels, the boys and young men of the tribe are in constant motion, while sheep and goats are kept by the girls.

Still today, just as in days gone by, the nomadic Rendille drive their herds across the thorny brush of the desert. However, recently constructed schools are intended

to prepare coming generations for the life of the modern age.

The Lake Turkana Lodge at **Ferguson's Bay** (western lakeshore) is an ideal base for travelers with a sense of adventure, as well as sport fishermen. For the most part, overland travelers park their vehicles on the mainland and then have themselves brought to the lodge by boat; travelers coming in by aircraft land on the new asphalt strip in Kalakol.

The lodge, which is situated in the midst of a small grove of palms, and consists of bungalows with bathrooms and verandas, conveys to visitors the feeling that they have temporarily left the 20th century and plunged into a timeless world, though they needn't forego modern comforts while they're at it.

A boat owned by the lodge transports sightseers in a roughly one-hour trip to the **Central Island** bird sanctuary, which is immersed in a cloud of pink flamingos.

Above: The El Molo people earn their livelihood as fishermen.

The paradisiacal **Flamingo Crater Lake** is their preferred breeding grounds, while the hippopotamui have cosied themselves into the second volcanic lake of the island. Nowhere else in the world are there as many hippopotamusses as at Lake Turkana, and entire hippoclans frequently pay visits to Ferguson's Bay in front of the lodge.

Fishermens' mouths start to water at the thought of the rich catch to be taken from Lake Turkana, which ranges from the huge, highly coveted cockup to the tilapia and tigerfish. It is possible to fish both on shore with a rod and spinning reel, or in a boat with dragline. The **Lake Turkana Lodge**, a member of the International Game Fish Association, has five boats for use by its guests.

Considering the wealth of fish in the lake, it is no wonder that the meals in the lodge consist primarily of an immense variety of fish dishes.

From the lodge there is also the possibility of viewing the volcano on the lake's southern shore by light aircraft. It's not exactly reassuring, however, to look down on the floor of a crater and see the wreck of a small plane, which was apparently wrenched out of the skies by the powerful winds in the Turkana area.

SIBILOI NATIONAL PARK

A road in extremely poor condition leads to the park from Loyangalani. To master it a four-wheel drive is absolutely essential. With an area of 1,570 square kilometers, the **Sibiloi National Park** extends one kilometer into the waters of Lake Turkana and includes the largest colony of crocodiles in the world, with over 12,000 specimens.

At the shores of Jade Lake it's not hard to get the feeling that you have somehow been transported back to Lake Nakuru because of the gigantic colony of flamingos living there. Despite its desolate appearance and the frequent harsh gusts that whip your face with heat, the Sibiloi has an astounding diversity of freely ranging wild animals, including the tiang, a sub-species of the topi-antelope.

Among the interesting sights in the Sibiloi National Park are the **Koobi Fora** prehistoric excavation sites. This is perhaps one of the most significant aspects of the Turkana region besides the beauty of the landscape and its picturesque tribes: It is probably the location of the much-discussed "cradle of humanity". Richard Leakey, the son of the renowned researcher-couple Louis and Mary Leakey, discovered the skull and bones of "homo habilis", which means skilled human, one developed enough to be able to devise and use tools, in other words. The remains of more than 80 people were found at Koobi Fora. Various footprints which have been studied with radiometric methods indicate an approximate age of between one and three million years. This area, which is almost abandoned today, is thus among the first known areas of human settlement.

LAKE TURKANA

LODWAR
Accommodation
Turkwel Lodge, PO Box 14, Lodwar.
Transportation
Buses run to Kitale, Kalokol (a small settlement on Lake Turkana) and to Lokichokio (near the Sudanese border – as border crossing here is not always possible). **Petrol**: Before continuing to Lake Turkana, make sure you've filled up your tank and spare can in Lodwar – you can't count on reliable petrol supplies further north.

LAKE TURKANA
Accommodation
Oasis Lodge, PO Box 56707, Nairobi. **Lake Turkana Lodge**, PO Box 34710, Nairobi. Both on the southeast shore of the lake.
Lake Turkana Fishing Lodge, PO Box 509, Kitale, and simple **bandas** at Eliye Springs.
Reserve your accommodation at these lodges well in advance. If the lodge is booked out, you can't rely on reaching the next one the same day. Accommodation on the northeastern shore is limited to camping only: **Alia Bay Sun Camp** and some simple self-catering camps.
Camping Tours
Safari Camp Service, PO Box 44801, Nairobi. **Best Camping Tours**, PO Box 40223, Nairobi. **Tip**: Because of strong nightly storms, camping at Lake Turkana is definitely a matter of taste.
Excursions
Central Island National Park, Elmolo Bay, the volcanic South Island, Sibiloi National Park with the prehistoric site Koobi Fora.

KALAKOL
Accommodation
BUDGET: **Skyways** and **Oyavo's**, comfort-lovers should settle for the lodges at the lake.

LOYANGALANI
Accommodation
Accommodation here is of the most basic nature – for comfort and amenities stay at the lodges and camps at Lake Turkana.

SOUTH HORR
Accommodation
At the beautifully situated **Kurungu Cabin Camp** or at the simpler camping site run by the Forest Department.
Excursions
Hikes in the nearby mountains with local guides or camel safaris in the surrounding countryside.

THE DIVERSITY OF WESTERN KENYA

KERICHO
KITALE
MOUNT ELGON
KAKAMEGA FOREST
LAKE VICTORIA
KISUMU

Western Kenya is still being, as it always has been, unjustifiably neglected by travellers. Granted, it doesn't have the huge animal reserves that are found in other parts of the country, but the variety of landscapes here more than compensates for that shortcoming.

Recently western Kenya has been visited by tribal violence. Hence, before travelling solo, you should inquire if it is safe, or whether it might be better to join a larger organized tour. Tremendous mountain ranges, tropical rain forests, secluded islands and dense virgin forests are all easily reached on well-developed roads. The outstanding points of interest in western Kenya include Lake Victoria, Mount Elgon, the Kakamega Forest and Saiwa Swamp National Parks and the tea cultivation region around Kericho.

KERICHO

When leaving Nakuru in a westerly direction, you come upon the little village of **Molo**. Molo lamb has earned itself quite a reputation in Kenya for quality, although it's rather doubtful whether it always comes from the vicinity of Molo.

Preceding pages: An orchid farm in western Kenya, flowers for export. Left: A mellifluous slope in the region north of Kitale.

Beyond the village, follow the road which branches off toward **Kericho**. Passing through a region of lovely hills and past the immense Mau forest conservation area, one reaches Kericho, the heart of Kenyan tea cultivation.

As far as the eye can see, the town is surrounded by fragrant, green tea plantations. The climate around Kericho, which is situated at an altitude of over 2000 meters, provides the ideal conditions for growing tea. Hardly a day passes without the necessary brief rain showers. The orderly, attractive little city can boast of being the center of the largest tea cultivation area in Africa. The renowned (and expensive) **Tea Hotel** has existed since 1952. It is owned by the British corporation Brooke Bond. Unfortunately, it often falls somewhat short of its reputation as an unusually fine hotel.

KITALE

Kitale, the gateway to Mount Elgon and a good starting point for safaris to Lake Turkana, is 380 kilometers from Nairobi. The town is located in an area featuring some of Kenya's most beautiful landscape.

Leaving Nakuru, the asphalted A 104 heads off to the northwest, ascends steeply into a part of Kenya dominated by

189

dairy farming, runs along the southern edge of the **Menengai Crater** and follows the ridgeline through the forest on **Mount Londiani**.

After it passes the **Mau Summit** the road climbs up the southern slopes of the Nandi Plateau, crosses the equator in the **Tinderet Forest**, and finally leads across the **Uasin Gishu Plateau** to the agricultural and industrial city of **Eldoret**. After 70 more kilometers you finally reach the city of Kitale.

Before entering Kitale the road is hemmed by huge blue gum and radiant flame trees. Just past the Kitale Club on the left is the **Western Kenya Museum** (originally named the Stoneham Museum), which is dedicated to Mount Elgon and the ethnic groups which inhabit this area.

The museum, opened in 1972, features as its first and foremost mainstay the collection of the deceased Lieutenent Colonel H.F. Stoneham, a farmer from the nearby **Cherangani Hills**. In addition to the numerous regional exhibition pieces it also houses a handicrafts shop. The museum also tends to a 750 meter-long nature trail that winds its way through the **Trans-Nzoia** rain forest, leading past springs and small, rocky river courses; passing by trees with garlands of climbing plants and lianas, dense underbrush, various species of mosses, orchids, lichens, ferns and wild bananas.

The path leaves the forest when it arrives at the museum's grounds, where a number of accurate replicas of huts display the different building methods used by the Nandi, Luo, Abaluhya, Sabaot, Pokot and Turkana cultures.

The museum also has a corral for snakes and turtles as well as a small **crocodile pond**. A remarkable fact about the crocodile pond is that it owes its existence to a case of poaching, in which the thieves attempted to smuggle crocodile eggs out of the country. However, the little beasts began to hatch right in the

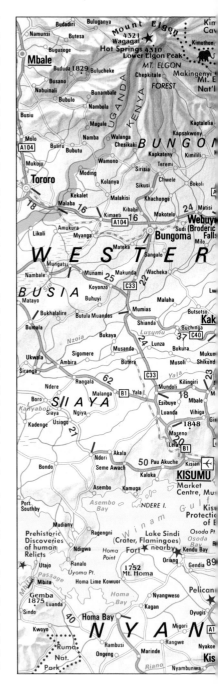

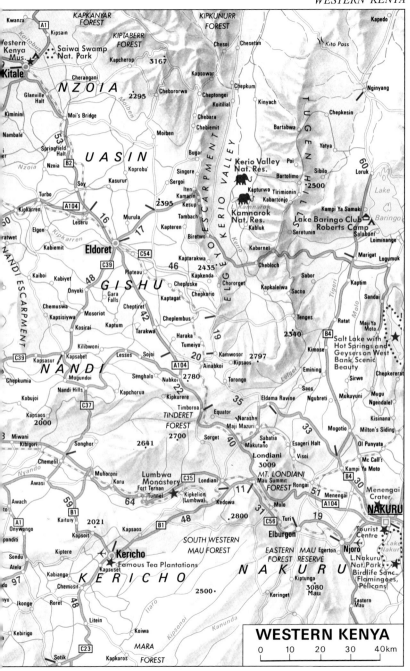

WESTERN KENYA

0   10   20   30   40km

midst of Nairobi. Two of the surviving crocodiles still can be seen here.

The museum also shows a fascinating film about how, in the course of thousands of years, the elephants have excavated caves reaching far into the mountain in their search for salt. Two or three hours should be planned at least for the museum.

The road now continues further on through the city and turns to the left onto Endebess Road, the main traffic artery to the **Mount Elgon National Park**.

Saiwa Swamp National Park

Only a few kilometers north of Kitale following the road to Lodwar, a turn-off to the right leads to the smallest of Kenya's national parks.

The **Saiwa Swamp National Park** is only 1.9 square kilometers in area. What

Above: Cranes picking their way through life in the Saiwa Swamp National Park. Right: Howdy, partner!

truly makes it special is that walking through the whole park is permitted. This swampy area was declared a national park in order to protect the sitatunga (swamp antelope), which is only found in this part of Kenya.

This species of antelope, which is threatened with extinction, lives half in the water and half on land. They are able to hide under water when in danger, and can be observed at best from one of the observation platforms in the trees at the edge of the swamp. Otherwise, it's a pleasure simply to walk through the untouched jungle of the park. You might come across the guenon or long-tailed monkey and the guereza or colobin monkey on a tour and discover a few of the numerous species of birds living here, such as the turako or a hooded crane in the trees or at the riverbanks.

Located several kilometers further up the road to the north is the village of **Kapenguria**, whose school is a national memorial. It was here that Jomo Kenyatta, who later became president of

Kenya, was sentenced to seven years' hard labor for his alleged role as leader of the Mau-Mau movement in a 1953 trial before the colonial government.

With a guide, one can visit the **Cherangani Hills'** breathtaking landscape. The Cherangani "Hills" reach altitudes of 3000 meters. This mountain chain, which is located to the northeast of Kitale, is overgrown with stone and scot's pines and eucalyptus trees.

MOUNT ELGON

The mountain for which the Mount Elgon National Park was named "sits" on the border with Uganda. On the Kenyan side, parts of the Trans-Nzoia district of the Rift Valley province are in its watershed, which extends in the southwest almost to **Bungoma**; to the northwest up to the **Elgeyo Marakwet Escarpment** at the edge of the Great Rift Valley towards Lake Turkana.

The 4321 meter **Mount Elgon**, an extinct volcano, is, in fact, the second-highest mountain in Kenya. There is still a portion of the flora and fauna preserved here from the times when the rain forests of central Africa extended from Zaire all the way to western Kenya. There are subspecies of elephant, horse and rhinoceros living in the Mount Elgon region which are found exclusively in this area.

Mysterious caves lead deep into the interior of Mount Elgon. To date at least 60 of them have been found. It is believed that they are the product of various kinds of erosion of the rock, which consists of a very broad range of materials. During the prehistoric volcanic eruptions, layers of fine, ashen mud were deposited, which formed the poorly drained surface of the agglomeration. These strata seem particularly well-suited to the formation of caves when they exert pressure on layers of softer tuff.

The numerous caves on the Kenyan side of Mount Elgon have not yet been

completely explored, since several of them – the Makingenyi Cave, for example – are so extensive that their sizes and depths can't even be accurately estimated. It is also difficult even to locate many of the caves since their entrances are often hidden with dense underbrush.

Among the local Kalenjin and Abaluhya tribes, rumours, sagas and legends are told about these caves of which so little is known. According to some of the stories, several of the caves are said to go all the way through the mountain to Uganda, and some people from the area supposedly know the path under the mountain and over the border.

Others believe to have evidence that the rocks in the mountain's interior are so porous and permeable that those who dare to penetrate too far into the mountain fall into huge abysses. Regardless of the degree of truth in all these tales, it is certain that a deep advance into the caves is impossible without oxygen masks, lamps and various spelunking equipment. They are so labyrinthine that it would

certainly appear to be anything but inept to follow the example of Theseus and fasten a rope near the entrance, which is then unraveled behind you as the exploration continues. It can then, of course, serve as the direction finder for the way back out.

The caves of Mount Elgon were already inhabited in ancient times. Depending on their size and accessibility they were also utilized for religious rites and ceremonies as well as places of worship. The larger, relatively inaccessible caves – to the extent that they haven't even been discovered and explored – were only occupied in the immediate vicinity of the entrance, where there is fresh air. Medium-sized, lower caves (as a rule taller than an average house) had enough fresh air to serve as human habitation, although they did have to offer proper protection from wild animals.

Above: Four-wheel drives are particularly vital when rain turns roads into swamps. Right: A cave in Mount Elgon.

Painted murals are a characteristic feature of other caves. These served as shrines in which sacrifices, rituals and various other religious activities took place. Nooks protected by rocks and exposed rock formations were used in the same manner.

On the basis of archeological studies of the caves (investigations of the floors, walls and ceilings) it is thought certain that they were already occupied by humans in the remote past. In more recent times as well, this theme was the subject of a study dealing with people who had established their domiciles in the caves.

In 1972 an old man, one of the last cave-dwellers on Mount Elgon, lived in a cave the size of a normal residence. It was divided into a fire area, a sleeping space, a goat stall and a stall for the other livestock. A fence of dried twigs at the cave's entrance defended against wild animals. There was also another gate which was kept closed at nights. The fire at the entrance burned day and night. The old man reported that his sons had indeed

built houses, however, every evening, his 36 grandchildren came back to his cave to sleep.

The Kimothon Cave, for example, once simultaneously served as both dwelling and a place of worship. It is located at 2400 meters altitude on the side of the mountain facing Kitale, which is only 40 kilometers away. The cave is reached by way of the Kimothon gate, one of the entrances to the Mount Elgon National Park, located four kilometers beyond the Saboti Center in **Endebess**.

Kimothon Cave

Kimothon Cave is divided by walls made of large stone blocks into three areas connected by narrow passageways, starting from the entrance and going backwards. Archeologists have determined that domesticated animals were kept in the exterior area, people lived in the middle spaces, and the depths of the cave, lacking oxygen, remained uninhabited. This lead to the conclusion that the Kimothon Cave was used in a manner similar to that of the caves which are still occupied in our time. Hundreds of thousands of years ago almost the same materials were utilized to build separating walls and fortifications.

The most significant feature of the Kimothon, however, is its stone shrine. It is known that its occupants didn't just live on the naked stone floor; in addition, the walls are richly decorated with murals. There is general agreement that the people who lived in the main cave used this space, which also served a protective function, as a shrine, the prehistoric equivalent of a church, mosque or temple.

In Mount Elgon there are, of course, still more caves and cliff shrines with murals quite nearby, however there is no evidence that they were ever inhabited in the distant past. They must have been sought out by visitors from other areas, just as today people visit churches in other towns.

The walls of the Kimothon Cave were originally covered with some 90 square

195

meters of murals. Their predominant colors were red and white. Several motifs are done exclusively in white, others were done only in red; but for the most part the murals are two-toned images which have been given several layers of paint.

The motifs of the cave murals include human forms and domesticated animals, such as the hornless cow (*bos brachyceros*) as well as everyday articles. Abstract drawings are relatively uncommon.

The **Chemasaria Rock Shelter** is also a shrine with white, red and yellow wall paintings. The painted surface area, however, is a great deal smaller than that in the Kimothon Cave. The style of the murals is also similar. There are three domestic animals, four human figures, a series of cult objects and a number of abstract motifs portrayed in the Chemasaria cliff shrine.

Above: The mysterious, foggy slope of Mount Elgon. Right: Lake Victoria, as it might have been centuries ago.

In the **Kakapeli Cave** the area of wall paintings is as large as in the Kimothon Cave, however, here abstract images are much more frequent. In addition to domestic animals, the free-roaming animals of the wilderness have been immortalized here, including turtles, rats and gazelles in hues of white, brown, yellow and black.

Mount Elgon, with its caves and cliff shrines, flora and fauna is still relatively unresearched, and although it is accessible to the public, a great deal must still be done to make it more attractive for tourists with interest in other cultures.

The Kenya Archaeological and Ethnological Research Agency has recognized the potential of this region very clearly. It is making efforts to ease accessibility to the caves and the shrines, as well as developing the mountain as a tourism area, while simultanously preserving the culture of this region for coming generations.

The **Mount Elgon Lodge** is located at the entrance to the national park. It offers

acceptable overnight accomodations and board (tourist-class fare). Numerous scientific expeditions can also be started from this point as well.

KAKAMEGA FOREST

The **Kakamega Forest** is located roughly 20 kilometers to the southeast of the city of Kakamega, north of Kisumu. This forest region is known to zoologists and botanists all over the world.

A piece of the rain forest which, approximately 400 years ago, stretched over the entire continent all the way to the Atlantic has indeed been preserved. Nowadays, vegetation comparable to this exists only in West Africa. The virgin tropical forest is home to many species of animals and plants which, as far as East Africa goes, exist only in this roughly 45 square kilometer area. Hundreds of species of birds live here, as well as numerous monkeys and fruit bats.

While taking a hike through this forest, which lies at an altitude of between 1520 and 1680 meters, it should be kept well in mind that there is one more reason for the fame of the Kakamega Forest: Nowhere else are there as many poisonous snakes, ranging from mambas to vipers and cobras.

Sleeping accomodations are available at the simple Forest Rest House, which, however, has only four double rooms. Prior reservations are positively advisable, especially for the weekends. The best starting point for a hike and to get to the Forest Rest House is the village of **Shinyalu**.

LAKE VICTORIA

The English explorer Speke, who, in 1875, was the first white man to gaze across the unbelievable dimensions of **Lake Victoria**, must have nearly lost his breath at the sight. He certainly lost little time giving it the majestic name that came to his mind, that of Victoria, his queen. During the ensuing 20 years the lake sank back into oblivion until the adventurous explorer Stanley decided to

scrutinize it more closely. The largest portion of the lake's area is located in Uganda and Tanzania, whose international borders run right through it.

The lake forms an almost perfectly geometrical square with sides of 350 kilometers each, except that in Kenya the **Winam Golf**, which is shaped like a gourd, cuts deeply into a volcanic equatorial tableland. Kisumu, the most important city of western Kenya, is located on the eastern corner of the gulf.

The Luo who are settled here also call themselves *Jonam*, the lake-people, and Winam, the name of the gulf means "head of the lake" in their language. The extraordinarily hospitable Luo give a hearty welcome to strangers who express a preference for the tilapia fish, or *ngege* in their tongue. The Luo are renowned as skilled boat builders and fishermen. Catching fish in the third-largest lake in

Above: Sundown is the time to make a catch in Lake Victoria. Right: Storks bring babies and eat frogs.

the world is not entirely without its dangers, however. There are frequent fierce tempests and thunderstorms. One consequence of the heavy rainfalls are the patches of lakeshore vegetation which are sometimes torn free and then move about the lake as floating islands.

KISUMU

The trip to Kisumu from Nairobi, a stretch of 350 kilometers, can be made quite comfortably overnight in a sleeping-car or in one hour by airplane on Kenya Airways. The good asphalt road from Nairobi through Nakuru, Molo and Kericho is quite fatiguing, though, since this primary transportation artery to Uganda is also travelled by convoys of heavy trucks.

The English dubbed the city Port Florence after the wife of a British railroad engineer who was involved in the construction of the Uganda Railroad. Today it is named **Kisumu**, and is Kenya's third-largest city. This sleepy town

was of far greater significance during the period of the East African Community between Kenya, Uganda and Tanzania than it is today.

Among the interesting sights here are a colorful fruit and vegetable market, a couple of churches, a temple and a museum which portrays the culture and way of life of the Luo.

The city has two good tourist hotels: The palace-like and fully air-conditioned **Imperial** and the impressive **Sunset** on the lakeshore, which provides box seats for watching the sunset over Lake Victoria in the evening. The **Hotel Royale** doesn't achieve the standards of the two first-mentioned hotels by a long shot. In addition to these, the city has several other hotels which are cosy and clean with a minimum of comforts.

Kisumu is a workers' city. Alongside a small casino where one can play blackjack and roulette there are also two good nightclubs, the **Flamingo** and **Octopus Bottoms Up**. As far as the remaining clubs go, that offer their services at all

hours of the day and night, you're better off giving them a wide berth.

Since western Kenya is still relatively undeveloped as concerns tourism, it's best to put together a tour according to your own taste. The boat cruise over the lake runs from Kisumu to **Kendu** and **Homa Bay**, then further to **Rusinga** and **Mfangano Islands**. One of the prehistoric excavation sites where Louis Leakey found a deposit of fossils millions of years old is located on Rusinga.

It is possible to interrupt one's journey in the fishing village of Homa Bay, staying for a night in the **Homa Bay Tourist Hotel** and then continuing on the ship the next day. The hotel is located only 500 meters away from the lake. Here, a rather out-of-the-ordinary "performance" takes place at night. The "Omena-city" which glows through the night, expands ever further as the fishermen light their lamps to lure the sardine-like omena into their nets. More and more boats arrive in the course of the night, as the glittering, floating "city of lights" continues to ex-

pand until the ayroral chorus of birdsong gives the signal for its dissolution.

Lake Simbi and the Ruma Park

One possibility for an autombile tour is a visit to the legend-shrouded volcanic **Lake Simbi**, located at the southern shore of Winam Gulf. A trip here can easily be combined with a drive through the **Ruma National Park** (the former Lambwe Valley Game Reserve). You should head out of Kisumu early in the morning, driving on the Kisii Road some 50 kilometers until reaching **Katito**, then continuing on the Katito-Pap Onditi-Kendu Bay Road. Lake Simbi, which is near **Kendu Bay**, plays a significant role in the local legends and is named *Simbi Nyaima* (Simbi the Inundator) by the indigenous peoples.

This region is the backdrop to an enormous number of legends which are still

Above: Two impalas – among the most graceful animals in the parks – cuddling.

being told today. It's worthwhile taking some time to listen to the stories of the tribal elders, some of whom actually resemble the legendary giant Gor Mahia from Luo country. The ancient stone forts at the **Kanyamwa Escarpment** (at Homa Bay-Mbita Road) were supposedly a part of the fortifications surrounding his home.

The Ruma National Park is a small forest area surrounded by grasslands. It is intended to preserve the rare sable antelope living in this remote region from extinction. There is no lodging available in this secluded park. Camping is allowed, but owing to the many tse-tse flies not advisable. A straight road is running through the Lambwe Valley to **Macalder**, a small village with an abandoned gold mine. The road continues to the town of **Migori**, about one hour's drive from the border on the main arterial road between Kenya and Tanzania. From there one can drive comfortably through the sugar-cane fields of Awendo and the banana plantations of Kisili back to Kisumi.

WESTERN KENYA

KERICHO
Accommodation

Tea Hotel, PO Box 75, Kericho. **Tas Lodge**, PO Box 164, Kericho. **Midwest Hotel**, PO Box 1175, Kericho.

Excursions

To the tea plantations, the Kiptariet Valley with the Chakaik Dam (there is a lovely Botanical Garden) or the wildly romantic Nandi Hills. (Kericho is one of the world's most important producers of tea). The streams southeast of Kericho, with their abundance of fish, are a must for passionate anglers. Further information in the Tea Hotel. Also trips down into the Kiptariet Valley.

ELDORET
Accommodation

Sirikwa Hotel, PO Box 3361, Nairobi. **Highlands Inn**, PO Box 2189.
Simple Accommodation in the **New Wagon Wheel**, PO Box 503 and the **New Lincoln**.

Transportation

Buses to Nairobi, Kisumu, Nakuru and Kitale. Train station with connections to Nairobi several times a week.

Excursion

To the impressive Kerio Valley, site of one of Kenya's more recent reserves.

KITALE
Accommodation

Bongo Hotel, PO Box 530, Kitale. Simple accommodation in the **New Kitale** and the **Executive Lodge.**

Transportation

Buses to Nairobi, Lodwar and Endebess.

Sightseeing

Western Kenya Museum, open daily from 9.30 a.m.–6 p.m.

Excursions

To the Saiwa Swamp National Park, the township of Kapenguria with the Jomo Kenyatta National Memorial, Cherangani Hills.

MOUNT ELGON
Accommodation

Mount Elgon Lodge, PO Box 42013, Nairobi. Various camping facilities, i.e. **Suam Fishing Camp**.

Border Crossing

From Kitale you can cross the border to Mbala in Uganda. Please bear in mind that the road on the Uganda side of the border is not passable during the rainy season.

KAKAMEGA
Accommodation

Golf Hotel, PO Box 42312, Nairobi. Simple accommodation is available at the **New Garden Guest House** and the **Kakamega Wayside House**.

Excursion

To the Kakamega Forest. Access: Buses from Eldoret to Kapsabet near the Kakamega Forest.

Transportation

Buses to Nairobi, Nakuru, Kisumu and Kisii.

KISUMU
Accommodation

Imperial, PO Box 1866, Kisumu, Tel: 40336. **New Kisumu Hotel**, PO Box 1690, Kisumu. **Sunset Hotel**, PO Box 215, Kisumu.

Ferries

To Kendu Bay and Homa Bay, daily except Thursday.

Sightseeing

Kisumu Museum, open from 9.30 a.m.–6 p.m.; **Jamia Mosque**.

Excursion

To the picturesque fishing village of Dunga.

Transportation

Buses run in all directions. There are daily train services and flights to Nairobi.

Border Crossing

To Uganda at the settlements Malaba and Busia. Buses from Nairobi and Kisumu stop here, and after a walk across the border into Uganda there are again good bus connections for travelling further into the country.

HOMA BAY
Accommodation

Homa Bay Tourist Hotel, PO Box 42013, Nairobi.

Excursions

Excursions to the volcanic hill Got Asego, Ruma National Park, Rusinga Island (prehistoric site), Mfangano Island. The Homa Bay Hotel organizes boat excursions.

Transportation

Matatus to Kisii and Kisumu. Ships to Kisumu.

KISII
Accommodation

Only simple hotels, i.e. the **Kisii Hotel**, Safe Lodge and the Mwalimu.

Transportation

Buses to Kericho, Nairobi, Homa Bay and Kisumu.

Excursions

To the Ruma National Park and the soapstone-carving village Tabaka.

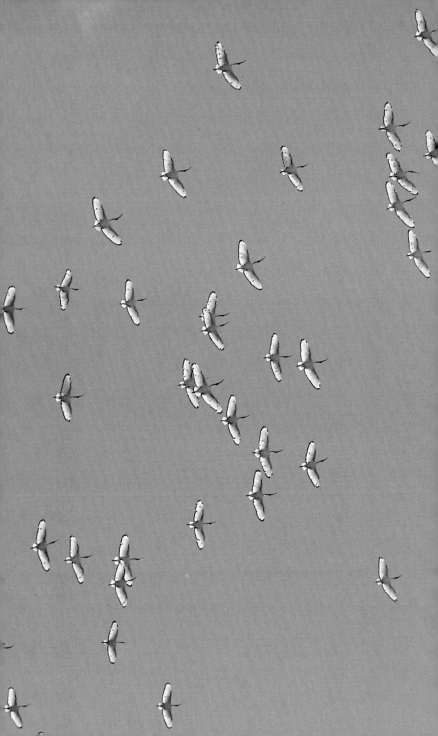

FLORA AND FAUNA

The chief attractions of Kenya are its fascinating natural beauty and the unique animal world, which includes a diversity of species scarcely to be found in any other country in the world. The various types of vegetation, ranging from open savannah to arid desert and on to fertile plains and lakes, provide wide variety of habitats for animals and plants.

Broad sandy beaches with coconut palms, river estuaries and vast banks of coral form the 1300 kilometer long coastal strip on the Indian Ocean. This fertile green swatch of land has ample precipitation and particularly high humidity, permitting mangos, lemons, oranges and tropical flowers to flourish, and provides a home for countless species of birds and insects.

Preceding pages: Ibices in flight. Gnus and vultures in the dusk. Above: The grass steppes of the Masai Mara, a barren country – but not for wildlife.

Not very far behind the coast, the succulent green changes into arid bushland and savannah. Briars, umbrella acacias, and baobabs are also able to withstand the long dry periods. From the savannahs, the land rises as you proceed northwest up to the snow-covered peaks of Mount Kenya (5199 meters), the Aberdares and Mount Kilamanjaro (5895 meters), which is located in Tanzania. At the different altitude levels on the mountain slopes, evergreen rain forests alternate with moors and scree. The tropical rain forest, behung with lianas and ferns, recalls the stories of Tarzan.

The adjacent Great Rift Valley of East Africa constitutes a geological phenomenon. Millions of years ago, the earth's crust broke open along a length of 6000 kilometers, extending from Mozambique to the Dead Sea, leaving behind a fissure 700 meters deep which is as much as 300 kilometers wide. From Kenya's northern reaches down into the southern part of the country, a series of lakes is located in this plain: Turkana, Baringo, Bogoria,

Nakuru, Naivasha and Magadi, some alkaline and others freshwater, but all of them genuine bird paradises.

The former White Highlands, the farmland on which the European settlers once made their homes, is used intensively for agriculture and densely settled. The primary crops cultivated there are coffee, tea, vegetables, flowers and sisal.

Lake Victoria is the second-largest fresh-water lake in the world, with small islands, papyrus swamps and a huge stock of fish. Its shores border on Kenya, Uganda and Tanzania. Due to evaporation from the lake there is plentiful precipitation in its vicinity.

A particularly deserted region of Kenya is located north of Lake Victoria, the massif around Mount Elgon. This former volcano's slopes are overgrown with bamboo jungle and moorlands.

The visitor to the north of Kenya will have a chance to become familiar with fascinating semi-desert and desert areas. Hot winds sweep over the land around Lake Turkana, rendering survival possible for only a few plant species. The lake's volcanic islands are the nesting grounds for many species of birds. The region of Kenya most hostile to life is the Chalbi Desert to the east of the lake. Only after the rare heavy rainfalls do the most gorgeous flowers briefly bloom there.

Even if wild animals are found all over Kenya, the national parks and reserves are nevertheless the most abundant for the observation of wildlife. There are nature handbooks which can help the visitor identify the various animals. Here is only a list of the most well-known:

The Most Important Animal Species

Buffaloes are herd animals and broadly distributed in the steppes and forests. Among big-game hunters, the bulls living in isolation were once considered the most dangerous of all wild animals.

Dikdiks prefer dense brushlands. This smallest of antelope grows to a height of only 40 cm and looks like a hare with its zig-zagging gait.

Elephants, the largest land mammals, live for the most part in forests or savannahs. Elephants raise their young in familial units. The pachyderms are peaceful vegetarians.

Elend antelope or *Cape elk* are widely disseminated in the steppes. This gregarious creature has helical horns and dewlaps on its throat.

Flamingos are found in undescribably huge groups at the lakes in the Great Rift Valley. They feed on plants and animals in shallow water.

Hippopotamui can easily be found in all rivers and lakes which flow through grasslands. The snorts they make when emerging can often be heard before they are even visible. They are frequently seen dosing lazily on the shores in mornings and evenings.

Cheetahs inhabit the open steppes and savannahs of Kenya. This beautiful, long-legged cat is the fastest runner of all mammals, able to reach speeds of up to 80 kilometers per hour. They live alone or in small families.

Gerenuks propagate in arid brushlands. They are also called giraffe gazelles because of their white necks. This species is unmistakable when it stands on its hind legs to munch on the leaves of bushes.

Giraffes prefer to graze on savannahs and open forests with acacia trees. The Maasai giraffe found south of the Tana River is the most common species in Kenya. The smaller reticulated giraffe is found in the north.

Gnus live in herds on the steppes and open grasslands. They can be best observed during their annual migration in the Masai Mara.

Grant's gazelle is commonly found in open brushlands as well as grasslands. It is somewhat larger than its closest relative, the Thomson's gazelle, without the black stripes on its flanks.

Hyenas appear almost everywhere. The two most familiar varieties are the spotted and the striped. Even though their food consists primarily of carrion, they also hunt smaller mammals.

Impalas live in acacia savannahs and brushlands. When fleeing, this antelope can make leaps of up to ten meters.

Kongon, also called the *Coke's hartebeest*, lives in the steppes to the south of the Tana in open grassland.

Crocodiles are at home in most of the Kenyan rivers. They are most often seen dosing on sand banks along the rivers. These dangerous beasts grow to as much as six meters in length.

Kudus live in dense forests and brushland, and are therefore difficult to see. They are classified into the greater (160 cm) and the lesser kudu (100 cm). Both are striped and have helical horns.

Leopards live in all types of landscape, although they especially like forests,

Above: Lions drinking at a waterhole. Right: Giraffes enjoying low food.

thickets and caves. This nocturnal creature is quite difficult to find. Because of its magnificent fur they have been heavily hunted. Leopards are loners; they often drag their prey into the trees.

Lions are broadly distributed through savannahs, bush and open forests. The king of beasts is the only feline which lives in groups called prides. During the day they spend most of their time sleeping under bushes and trees.

Mungos appear in Kenya in various species. Several of these are easily tamed and live at lodges or camps. These little beasts are very entertaining. When danger arises they warn each other with loud whistles and chirps.

Rhinoceroses live in Kenya in savannahs, moors and forests. The rhino is recently among the most gravely threatened of all Africa's animals species. There are two varieties, the black rhinoceros and the white or wide-mouthed rhino. The latter in Kenya can only be found in the Meru National Park, where it has been imported a couple of years ago.

The *Oryx*, also known as *gemsbock* or *spike-buck*, prefers dry brushlands. The *Eritrean* and *tuft-eared* oryx occur in Kenya. The former is grey and lives to the north of the Tana River; the latter is dark brown and has ears with protruding tufts of hair.

Baboons are particularly common in rivers flowing through tropical grasslands and lava fields. They live in large families and are extraordinarily aggressive. They can even kill unguarded young gazelles with their sharp canine teeth.

Secretary birds appear primarily in the savannahs. They are easily recognized by the feathers projecting from the backs of their heads and their affected gait.

Ostriches are found on the steppes and in grasslands. Despite their feathers they are unable to fly, they can run at speeds of 70 kilometers per hour. At one time, ostrich eggs and feathers were coveted hunting trophies.

Thomson's gazelles are close relatives of the Grant gazelle and are widely found through the savannah and grassland.

Topis or *bustard hartebeests* live in the open savannahs. These large antelopes, with coloration ranging from blue-black to brown, occur in West Kenya. They are often spotted on a small rise in the earth standing up and carefully observing the surrounding area.

Wart-hogs are happiest when living near water on the savannahs. The gray wart-hog is unmistakable when it takes to flight with its tail held vertically. They live in small familial groups.

The *water-buck*, also called the *koba* or *bohor reedbuck*, a powerful species of antelope, has a shaggy grey-brown coat and lives in clear forests and stony hills.

Zebras are found in open steppes and grasslands. There are two sub-species: Burchell zebras have broad stripes and live primarily in southern Kenya. They can be seen, along with herds of gnus, in the animal migrations into the Masai Mara. The rarer Grevy zebra has narrower stripes which end on their flanks above the belly. Grevy zebras are found mainly in Meru and Samburu.

A DYING PARADISE?

The importance of preserving wild animals in their own habitats couldn't have been more fittingly described than it was by Professor Wallace Stignor of Stanford University: "Something will have gone out of us as a people if we let the remaining wilderness be destroyed; if we permit the last vergin forests to be turned into comic books and plastic cigarette cases; if we drive the the few remaining members of wild species into zoos or to extinction; if we pollute the last clear air and dirty the last clean streams and push our parved roads through the last of the silence so that never again will people be free in their own country from the noise, the exhaust, the stink of human and automotive waste, so that never again can we have the chance to see ourselves single, seperate, and individual in the world, part

Above: Tranquil buffalo in the Masai Mara.
Right: Watching for poachers, Kenya's most vicious enemy.

of the environment of trees, rocks and soil, brother to the other animals, part of the natural world and competent to belong in it. We simply need that wild country available to us, even if we never do more than drive to its edge and look in, for it can be a means of reassuring ourselves of our sanity as creatures, as part of the geography of hope."

Observing wild animals living in freedom is the high-point for most people on a trip to Kenya. Even the shortest of visits lends the "human zoo" a new dimension: Rhinoceroses and elephants might attack, giraffes, zebras, buffaloes and other animals ogle humans inquisitively or ignore them entirely. After all, it is the animals who are at home here. In contrast, the human is only a visitor in his own cage, the automobile.

For the majority of tourists who have experienced nature in this manner an entirely new feeling begins to settle in, a feeling that such a world is more natural and simply better. After arriving back home everything seems painfully empty.

Perhaps then the question might be dropped, for once, as to what actually happened to the stock of wild animals in Europe and North America.

This danger also looms in Kenya. Around the turn of the century, the railroad builders "ran over" thousands of wild animals in what is now the industrial area surrounding Nairobi. It only took 90 years to reduce huge stocks of wild animals almost to extinction, as happened to the Cape lion, for example. These tragic mass-slaughters are justified by such inexcusable reasons as the large business surrounding leopard pelts for coats or elephant tusks for jewelry. The ridiculous rumor that the horn of the rhinoceros has aphrodisiacal effects, resulted in a flourishing trade in them.

The reasons farmers and ranchers take action against free-ranging animals might perhaps, to a degree, be justified, since the animals sometimes really trample the farmers' crops or infect herds with cattle-plague, ticks and fever illnesses.

Of course, the future of animal and nature protection rests ultimately in all of our hands. A direct connection exists between the preservation of wild animals and Kenya's economic survival. Particularly, as tourism is the equal of coffee cultivation as a sector of the economy able to generate hard currency.

Wildlife Conservation

. The first wildlife conservation reserves were established as early as the forties. The Nairobi National Park was opened in 1946, soon to be followed by the Tsavo and the Masai Mara National Reserve. To date the number of conservation areas has grown to 50, comprising 7 percent of Kenya's total land area.

One significant step toward the preservation of wildlife was the 1976 passage of the Wildlife Conservation and Management Act, which was followed by a hunting prohibition in May, 1977.

Before this time, permits were issued for the limited shooting of particular animal species. However, the armed hunters

211

occasionally became poachers or exceeded their permitted quotas.

Along with the hunting prohibition came a ban on the sale and possession of hunting trophies. Right up to the night before the prohibition went into effect, ivory, horn, claws and skins were offered for sale in hunting trophy shops all over the country, and it was an open secret that trophies which had obviously been bagged by poachers were being traded in a completely official manner.

After the imposition of the hunting prohibition it became clear that poachers represented the greatest threat to Kenya's free-ranging wild animals. The problem was accentuated by the fact that many ethnic groups, particularly the Somalis and the Borans, consider hunting the honorable duty of a future warrior.

On occasion, the business of entertaining Kenya's tourists has an impact on the preservation of the stock of wild animals as well. In areas which were especially attractive for tourists, artificial watering holes were installed, particularly in the neighborhoods of the lodges. During droughts, which, of course, didn't spare the national parks, masses of animal streamed to the artificial holes to drink. The resulting overcrowding was accompanied by the propagation of diseases and death of large numbers of animals.

The destruction of trees by elephants represents a special problem. Overpopulation of these beasts is a serious danger to trees and bushes, and by extension to the ecological balance as a whole. There is an unusual phenomenon at work here: The shortage of large wild animals outside of the parks is compensated within them by a glut of the very same species. The original idea of preserving an area of land in ecological balance with intact wildlife has begun to appear increasingly doubtful.

One further bone of contention is the collision of various agricultural interests.

Above: This abandoned elephant is being raised in David Sheldrick's animal orphanage near Nairobi.

The national parks lay claim to large areas of pasture land, while on the other hand the extensive stocks of wildlife cause damage to the adjacent, intensively cultivated croplands. This is the case on the slopes of the Aberdares and Mount Kenya as well as in the area of Laikipia. These regions have repeatedly been devastated by roving herds of elephants, and for quite a while now the incensed farmers have been threatening to simply poison the animals.

The population of Kenya, which is increasing sharply each year, exerts considerable pressure on cultivated lands. Disregarding the threat posed by wild animals upon the harvests entirely, the reduced pasturage areas at agriculture's disposal arouses envy within the communities neighboring the national parks, whose constantly growing populations need more land. Ethnic groups like the Maasai in the Mara Reserve have repeatedly forced their way into the reserve because of the farm and pasture lands on hand there. The government is attempting to set up tea cultivation zones around the alpine forest areas to help secure both the livelihood of the population and the preservation of the forests.

Animal lovers can help contribute to the preservation of wild animals through the payment of entrance fees for the national parks as well as membership in the East African Wildlife Society.

History and Some Accounts

The first laws for the protection of free-ranging wild animals were enacted by a special department of the government, whose director was a gamekeeper. An independent ministry wasn't formed until after 1920.

At that time the white settlers coming to the country were looked upon as the greatest threat to wildlife. It was believed that their use of huge areas for agriculture, the methods of which contrasted so starkly with those of the indigenous population, would push free-ranging animals off to the most remote wildernesses. A minority held the view that a large stock of animals in the area of Nairobi would be able to survive. In 1912, assistant gamekeeper Martin Seth-Smith made a list of which animals were to be found within a 16-kilometer radius of Nairobi. He was convinced that the majority of species would soon die out and that his notes would become little more than an historical document. Concerning the rhinoceros he briefly entered: "The rhinoceros appears today in very limited numbers." Since 1904 their number sank rapidly, until by 1914 there were probably none left. However, in the beginning of the sixties this species was reintroduced in the Nairobi National Park. Since that time things have developed well. As a result, and contrary to the expectations of Martin Seth-Smith, there are still rhinoceroses within a 16-kilometer radius of Nairobi 80 years later.

Things went similarly with the buffalo. Quoting Martin Seth-Smith: "Buffalo were sometimes sighted in small numbers in the Kikuyu Forest on the Ngong side of the railroad tracks. These are probably fringe groups of the herds in the Ngong Hills, although it is certainly conceivable that a couple of old bulls live in this forest continously."

The buffalo disappeared in the years following 1912, and for a long period they could only be found in the Ngong Hills. The buffalo was settled in the Nairobi National Park again in 1963. This species is also more numerous nowadays than it was at the time of Seth-Smith's records.

In the chronicle's year 1912, only a handful of people lived in Nairobi. Today the city has more than two million inhabitants. Seth-Smith's prognosis was well founded at the time, although the facts of history have disproved it. The wildlife conservation plan is working.

Without neglecting other aspects of wildlife conservation, the most concentrated efforts have consistently been for the preservation of the most seriously threatened species, some examples being the Rothschild giraffe and the elephant. The government has begun a comprehensive campaign to save the black rhinoceros, which has been hunted by poachers so pitilessly that the stock still in existence in all of Kenya wouldn't even meet North Yemen's demand for their horns for one year. The white rhinoceros, which is the second-largest land mammal (behind the elephant), was just barely saved from extinction and is now present in larger numbers in the Nakuru National Park. Today (1995) there are only 3000 of each species left, although even in 1970, the black rhinoceroses

Above: How many leopards are hanging on the backs of the upper crust? Right: Rhinos – their horn is alleged to make credulous men more potent.

alone numbered 65,000. The majority of them lives in Kenya, Namibia, South Africa and Zimbabwe.

Last-chance Rescue for the Rhinoceros

During the first half of this century Kenya's rhinoceros population was hunted by people greedy for a trophy. The reason for the sudden eradication of one of Africa's most impressive animals is the strong demand for its horn. It consists of keratin, the horny material of which fingernails and hair are composed as well. In the Far East it is utilized primarily for its alleged aphrodisiacal and febrifugal effects; in North Yemen for the production of costly dagger handles.

One consequence of the hunting prohibition, imposed in 1977, was a dramatic increase in poaching of wild animals in general, which lead to the accelerated killing of rhinoceros. After the kill, their voluminous bodies wind up in the garbage, of course; only their single horns are marketed or exported.

In 1985 the government authorized the Kenya Rhino Rescue Project. Within a period of five years, the "Save the Rhino Project" was to take measures to save the great beast from extinction.

The project included the establishment of four special rhinoceros reserves and surveillance units in national parks. The measures to prevent poaching were intensified throughout the country and the rhinoceros herds registered. In order to protect them and find suitable breeding specimens, the animals who were living dispersed about the countryside were gathered together and put in the safer reservations. Concerned tourists to Kenya made generous contributions. In the majority of tourist-class hotels there are donation boxes at the reception desks on which all animal lovers are encouraged to make a contribution of money to the "Save the Rhino Fund".

First to be established was the Nakuru National Park Rhino Sanctuary. It is some 74 kilometers long, covering an area of 140 square kilometers and is equipped with a five-thousand-volt electrified fence powered by solar energy. This single measure has been so successful that since the erection of the fence not one single rhinoceros has been stolen. The example of the Nakuru National Park demonstrates that the rhinos in the conservation areas are truly safe. One more small sanctuary under government control for the protection of the rhinoceros was established in the Tsavo National Park. There are already plans in the works to enlarge it.

The wildlife conservation movement in Kenya is based on the engagement and commitments of individual persons. This is particularly true of the African Fund for Endangered Wildlife (AFEW), which was first brought to life specifically for the rescue of the Rothschild giraffe. Many years ago, the founders, Jock and Betty Leslie-Melville, acquired a young

giraffe which they named Daisy. When she was successfully bred the idea came up to save more members of her species.

The fruits of the intensive efforts being devoted to the protection of nature and its fauna are enjoyed first and foremost by visitors to the national parks. You should behave accordingly. The regulations in the parks, which are open from 6 A.M. to 6 P.M., are to be observed without fail. In the majority of conservation areas, leaving the roads or trails is forbidden, and there are speed limits as well. Motor vehicles may only be left at designated observation and picnic places. It must never be forgotten that the peacefully browsing elephants and rather droll lions are wild animals who have the right, without human disturbance, to proceed with the activities of their daily lives. Driving up too close and loud cries of delight through open automobile windows or roofs are often perceived by the animals as threats. For example, mother cheetahs are sometimes so frightened by safari vehicles that they leave their cubs.

215

RICHARD LEAKEY

The name Leakey has become inextricably associated with the archeological excavation of Kenya's prehistoric sites. Dr. Richard Leakey also became Kenya's Minister of Nature Conservation in a rather unusual manner.

Dr. Leakey is the son of the deceased Dr. Louis Seymour Bazett Leakey and Dr. Mary Leakey, a Kenyan couple of European extraction, both of whom enjoyed tremendous success as archeologists in Kenya. Since the thirties, they had been searching for prehistoric man. Richard Leakey was born in Nairobi in 1944, and became interested in the work of his parents at quite an early age. His father's expeditions brought the young Richard to Tanzania, where the skeleton of an early human was found in the Olduvai Gorge; it was later named *homo habilis* (handy man), and represents one of the most important links in the chain of human evolution.

With a stipend from the National Geographic Society, Richard began with excavations of his own on the eastern shore of Lake Turkana. Earlier expeditions had disclosed the possibility of fantastic fossil finds in the area. The first hominid was already uncovered a mere three weeks after the beginning of the digs. The decisive find occured in 1972, however, with the discovery of an approximately 2.2 million year-old skull, proving the existence of *homo habilis* first suggested by Louis Leakey. The discovery of *homo erectus* a few years later finally sealed the issue of where the cradle of mankind was to be found. Leakey's career took an abrupt turn when, at the end of the eighties, elephants and rhinoceroses were being slaughtered by large bands of poachers, the Ministry of Tourism and Nature Conservation made

Right: Dr. Richard Leakey, at one time Kenya's Minister for wildlife protection.

the results of an elephant census public. Leakey denounced this report as a glossing over of the facts and criticized the ministry tolerating the annihilation of these wild animals. To the surprise of many, the incumbent minister was dismissed and Richard Leakey was appointed to his post. President Daniel Arap Moi let it be known that the color of a Kenyan's skin made no difference to him; that what was important was only the safeguarding of the national interest by each individual. The game trophies posed something of an embarrassment because the government had accumulated millions of dollars worth of tusks, horns and skins over the years. If the trophies were to be released onto the market, the government would be making a profit out of the killing of animals.

In a widely publicized and unique decision, president Moi decided that all the loot must be burnt and in two ceremonies in Nairobi National park witnessed by the world. He personally set fire to the accumulated stocks which were burned to ashes. The renewed government commitment to wildlife conservation has strengthened Leakey's hand in ending the slaughter and there are encouraging signs that the poachers are nearly defeated.

With the help of the government, Leakey strengthened the security personnel in the parks. The poachers were put on the run virtually overnight. Machine guns, ammunition and hunting trophies were confiscated by wildlife managers.

There are some positive indications of a victory over the poachers. Richard Leakey is directing his entire enthusiasm towards making Kenya's nature conservation organization into an efficient and viable unit. He has been urging the general public the world over to give financial and ideological support to efforts for the protection of endangered species. But owing to alleged corruption scandals in the Ministry of Wildlife, he stepped down from his post in 1994.

UNDERWATER WONDERLAND

Among the greatest attractions Kenya's coasts have to offer are the wonderlands of tropical fishes, the lovely coral banks, the starfish, turtles and clams. Nature has protected Kenya's coast with a reef which extends along almost its entire length. Between the coral reef and the beach you can explore the landscape of the sea without danger. Just a little ways below the surface, one already enters a world of colors and forms without compare.

In the conservation areas nothing can be harpooned by fishermen or taken home by souvenir hunters for a remembrance. The underwater environment is meant to be preserved as a unique paradise, to be seen and photographed only.

Malindi Watumu Marine Reserve: When the tides are out, it is possible to go hiking for kilometers in the coral reefs here. The coral gardens in the southern section of the Malindi Marine Park are a unique opportunity to become familiar with the diversified, fascinating species of coral. A special attraction of the Watamu Marine Park are the three underwater caves at the mouth of Mida Creek.

Kiunga National Marine Reserve: The Kiunga Reserve is situated almost on the Somalian frontier. Many marine birds have their breeding grounds in this isolated, often ignored area. The breeding season is during the months from July to October. In particular, the tortoises living here and several especially rare species of coral are protected in this reserve. The small coral islands belonging to the reserve are especially attractive; they are best reached by boat from the village of Kiunga.

The **Kisite Marine National Park** and the adjacent **Mpunguti Marine Reservation** are located on the south coast. It is only possible to get to the enchanting coral gardens and expansive mangrove swamps by taking a boat from Shimoni. The marine park's centerpieces are the little Wasini Islands, which are immediately before Shimoni and Kisiti.

DIVING

Kenya has some of the most beautiful diving areas in the world. The clear warm water of the Indian Ocean and the breathtaking world beneath its surface draw ever larger numbers of diving fans from around the world to the coast of East Africa. Diving courses can be arranged right in Kenya or booked through specialized travel organizations or large diving schools at home. The most convenient, naturally, is to choose a hotel which has its own diving base. A lot of time can be saved by doing so.

Of course, the view with diving glasses just under the water's surface is a fascinating glimpse into another world. The fantastic colors of the fish and plants and the grotesque figures of the coral gardens can be admired in this manner, or, even more comfortably, through the floor of a glass-bottom boat. It is a completely different experience, however, to dive into the depths, swim among the fish and go for a walk along the ocean floor.

Diving schools have meanwhile been established at many hotels along the coast. They frequently have the most up-to-date of high standards equipment on hand. It is possible to rent all the necessary equipment there from snorkeling tubes and diving masks to compressed air flask and fins.

Despite the high water temperature, you shouldn't ever go without a diving-suit. In the greater depths it can get rather cold, and furthermore the suit is always a good protection against spiny corals and jelly-fish.

The best time of year for a diving excursion is from October to March. Afterwards the winds and waves are stronger, causing more turbulence on the sea-floor and therefore reduced visibility. Especially riding on a boat when the winds are

Right: Kenya's beauty also extends to the bottom of its territorial waters.

heavier is not something for everybody. Even if you may not be sea-sick when actually diving, it's not very pleasant to start out the dive when you're not feeling in best of shapes.

Those who have already had diving experience are nonetheless well advised to take along a diving teacher who is familiar with the local conditions. A certificate showing that you already have the necessary skills for a diving excursion is also required in Kenya. The diving centers in Kenya recognize the following certifications: British Sub-Aqua Club, NAUI, Padi and CMAS or a CMAS equivalent. In other words, always bring along the diving card and the training book.

If you have chosen Kenya to become acquainted with diving for the first time, then a physical examination, especially at an ear doctor, should be done before leaving home. This should certify that one is also fit for underwater adventures.

The first attempts at diving usually take place in the safety of a swimming pool. Merely after these exercises and several class-hours of theory does a trip into the underwater world of the sea show up on the curriculum. Even though it may seem exaggerated to undertake so much preparation for a diving trip, it is certainly necessary. Rising up too fast from greater depths, for example, has brought some unskilled divers into mortal danger. The sign-language which is learned during the theoretical class hours is an important means of subsurface communication. In addition, the changing of the oxygen bottles must be sufficiently practiced for a possible emergency.

The successful participation in such a course is, finally, always rewarded with an internationally recognized certificate which you can use on your next trip.

Any dive, particularly for the inexperienced, is more fatiguing than one might think. It's a good idea not to plan too much else on the same day and make room for a good rest after the outing.

Once a person has had a glimpse into the fascinating world under the waves they will probably be captivated forever. The experience of being completely dependent upon each other underwater in a group of divers is another exciting part of the adventure.

Diving can be learned at almost any age. Children, however, should have at least reached the age at which they can understand the theoretical instruction and are also able to cope with difficulties.

What is the upper age limit? It is not fixed, and depends, naturally enough, on the personal disposition and constitution of the individual. The renowned photographer Leni Riefenstahl still wanted, at over 70 years of age, to learn diving in Kenya. She cheated on her registration form concerning her age, making herself more than ten years younger.

Her enchantment with her first diving experience and the many-hued splendor of the underwater world was so great that she became an enthusiastic underwater photographer. The numerous fascinating shots which resulted can be seen in several books.

Those wishing to busy themselves as underwater photographers in Kenya will find plentiful rewarding subjects, for example the colorful angelfish or the butterfly-fish. The slow-swimming lion fish is especially spectacular with its red, white and black stripes and long feather-like fins. Be careful of toughing them, however, the dorsal (backbone) fins contain a very painful poison.

There are few dangerous residents on Kenya's reefs, but one should definitely watch out for the poisonous stone-fish. This member of the scorpion-fish family has poison bladders under each of its dorsal fins. He lays motionless on sandy or rocky ground awaiting his prey.

The majority of other sea creatures you come across during an underwater tour are that much more harmless in comparison: the parrot-fish or the thorny starfish, the hermit crab, mussels, or the sea-turtles, which should not be disturbed for reasons of animal protection.

FISHING
– Marine Safaris –

With its great diversity of beaked and predatory fish (such as dolphins), Kenya has the best prerequisites anywhere in Africa for deep-sea fishing.

Shimoni is a paradise for the deep-sea fisherman. This is where the well-heeled white business people from Kenya's highlands come to spend their vacations fishing on the high seas. One can also rent boats at many water-sport centers between Lamu and Shimoni. They are for the most part well equipped and have experienced crews.

Heading out on one of the last great adventures, you are accompanied by experienced high-seas fishermen who are also ready to teach the newcomer all the important points. The season is from November to March; outside these times

Above: An alpine tour to Mount Kenya.
Right: Good condition is essential when climbing Mount Kenya.

only the sea-worthy (not susceptible to sea-sickness) should dare participate in a deep-seas fishing safari. Between October and April, although particularly in May, June and July, the waves outside of the reefs get so high that even some experienced old salts have had to sacrifice their breakfasts to the fish.

The cruise toward the open sea begins in the morning hours. One can never be sure what the day will bring, whether it be the biggest catch of the season or merely a couple of bonitos, one of which might even wind up being snatched away by a shark chasing after the ship, leaving the overjoyed fisherman with no more than a gnawed skeleton on his hook.

The big catches are a duel between fisherman and fish. You never know if the line will hold up when you've got your hook into a sailfish or marlin weighing several hundred pounds. Strapped onto the "battle-seat" the fisherman tries his or her best to keep the catch from getting away. This demands not only strength, but skill and endurance as well. It can often take several hours before the victor is decided: Will the fish dive back into the depths of the Indian Ocean, or can he be hauled on board?

Not every high-seas outing is crowned with the success of having made a possible record catch. If, however, one is among the happy few it will be an experience to remember for a long time.

There are, in particular, good fishing grounds in Malindi, Africa's best spot for sail-fish, and in the Pemba Channel, which is famed for its schools of striped marlins, yellowfin tuna-fish and shark.

Deep-sea fishing is not at all a cheap thrill. A well equipped boat for four people with crew costs about US$ 300 per day. Those with more modest angling aspirations than high seas fishing, however, can fulfill them in the streams and lakes of the Kenyan highlands at reasonable prices. And, the prospects for success are excellent as well.

Fish-filled Lakes and Streams

There are many trout streams at altitudes above 2200 meters for which the fees would be very expensive in Europe. In contrast, a fishing license is quite cheap in Kenya (only 100 Kenyan shillings annually).

The trout was introduced from Europe at the beginning of the century and seems perfectly happy with the cold brooks of the Aberdares and Mount Kenya.

Most of the trouts served in the restaurants of Nairobi are bred at a trout farm on Mount Kenya. One of the best fishing spots is in Ngobi, site of one of Kenya's commercial fish farms.

Good fishing grounds are also found in the lakes of the Rift Vally, of which several have fresh water, while others are alkaline. The most popular fishing "pond" is Lake Naivasha, which is good for black river-perch and tilapias.

On the other hand, the great cockup (*lates niloticus*) is a far bigger challenge. They are found in Lakes Victoria and Turkana, sometimes weigh more than 200 kilo and are very tasty. Lake Victoria, by the way, has the greatest stock of fish of any body of water in East Africa. A day trip to go fishing there can be arranged for visitors in Masai Mara.

Commercial Fishing

Fishing is not a factor of significance in the Kenyan economy. The tilapia, popular in virtually every restaurant, is caught primarily in Lake Victoria.

Of course, plentiful fish and other sea-creatures are caught on the coast. Due to the shortage of suitable boats, however, deep-sea fishing scarcely plays a role.

Commercial fishing is the biggest business at Lake Turkana. After a famine in northern Kenya in the 1960s, many Turkana families were resettled near the lake to give them a new means of subsistence. Equipped with modern boats, they can support themselves by fishing. The catch is either dried or frozen and transported south for sale in the cities.

221

MOUNTAIN ADVENTURES

Most people hearing about travel to Kenya think of swimming vacation on the Indian Ocean, safaris in the many animal reserves, of tropical heat, savannahs, deserts and jungles, but not of towering mountain ranges, snow-covered peaks, steep precipices and extensive mountain climbing.

Mount Kilimanjaro, one of the peaks which indeed lures alpine enthusiasts from all around the world, has its summit in Tanzania, of course, though its foothills extend into Kenya. So, whether you set your sights for an alpine tour on Kenya's loftiest peak, Mount Kenya, the Aberdares range or Mount Kilimanjaro, you will be delighted in each case by the untouched nature, the overwhelming vegetation and the fascinating animal world.

Above: An alpine tour to Mount Kenya.
Right: Good condition is essential when climbing Mount Kenya.

Mount Kenya and the Aberdares

The Mount Kenya National Park extends over an area of 492 square kilometers. The highest peaks tower up at altitudes of over 5000 meters. Africa's second-highest mountain, which is located at the equator, is an attraction for climbers. Its slopes rise up from farmlands through dense forest, bamboo jungle and moors interspersed with valleys.

In 1887, Count Samuel Teleki and his companion, Ludwig von Hohnel, climbed up to 915 meters short of the summit. Twelve years later, an Englishman, Halford Mackinder, reached the top in 1899. From that time on this ascent has been very popular. Today there are many broad as well as several smaller hiking paths to the summit. All laws of the national parks are applicable on the mountain. Visitors must register at the gates for either a day-excursion or overnight stay. Unaccompanied hikers are only allowed to enter the park for day outings, which must be concluded by four in the afternoon. For longer stays, one must travel in groups of at least two.

The Naru Moru River Hunting Lodge is the starting point for most mountain climbers. The Teleki Lodge, a subsidiary, is the highest lodge in all of Africa. Several trails for motor vehicles wind their way up the mountain's forested slopes. The Sirimon Route climbs up to 3930 meters in altitude; the Tiwari ends at 4160 meters. From the Naru Moru Gate the route continues through swamplands to Mackinder's Camp, the starting point for the second day's hike, which brings you on up to Point Lenana and back. No special knowledge of mountain climbing is required therefore, though good physical condition is necessary.

The **Aberdares Park** is best suited for hiking tours of several days. Because of the danger posed by lions, camping is not recommended. There are, however, cabins for overnight lodging. It's best to take along a guide who is familiar with the locality. The "Mountain Club of Kenya" in Nairobi organizes alpine tours.

Mount Kilimanjaro

With its two peaks, Gillman's Point (5683 m) and Uhuru Peak (5895 m), Kilimanjaro is the highest mountain in Africa. The ascent of Gillman's Point is possible for any mountain hiker with endurance. Getting accustomed to the rarified atmosphere is the only real difficulty. For this reason, dividing the ascent into several one-day stages for the sake of acclimatization is a must.

The majority of people taking alpine tours either take along a mountain guide and porters, or connect up with a group. Nights are spent in cabins on the mountain. On the most popular route, one reaches the Mandara cabins on the first day by way of a gently ascending path leading first through plantations and then a dense rain forest. On the second day there are 1000 meters of altitude to over-

come. The landscape changes into impressive high-mountain vegetation with lobelias and senecia. The next day at the Horombo cabins is devoted to altitude adjustment; not until the following day do you put the next 1000 meters' altitude behind you, up to the Kibo cabins. This night ends at two in the morning, so that the bleary-eyed hiker can start out as early as possible for the final stage, up to Gillman's Point, which takes as long as five hours. Only a few undertake the two hours' additional march up to the highest summit, the Uhuru Peak.

Furthermore, there are excellent mountain climbing opportunities on Kilimanjaro, with degrees of difficulty ranging from II to VII. The necessary equipment should be brought along. It is, of course, possible to rent it, but the gear is (usually) in poor condition. Mountain-climbing boots, rain gear and a sleeping bag suffice for hiking excursions. Alpine safaris can be booked in Mombasa and Nairobi at various travel agencies, as well as at home through specialized organizers.

SPORTS, SPORTS, SPORTS

Whether soccer or golf, diving or sailing, track and field or boxing, the palette of sports in Kenya is broad indeed. Some kinds of sports are practiced primarily by vacationers; others have, in contrary, a broader following among Kenya's population. Kenyan runners have made a name for themselves as high-performance athletes over the world.

The Ball is Round...

...at least most of the time. Of course, it sometimes happens that in the poorer quarters people playing "kick-ball" have to make do with a tin can or somthing of the sort. Association football (*soccer* in the U.S.) is undoubtedly the most popular sport in Kenya. Whether at schools or on village plazas, young people find a place

Above: Kenyan boxers are a dangerously skillful collection of sportsmen. Right: Relaxing after the Mombasa marathon.

to indulge in their favorite sport. Enthusiasm for it was given an extra boost with Cameroon's success at the 1990 world soccer championship. In Kenya, just as everywhere else in black Africa, phenomenal forward Roger Milla became a new hero. Kenya's elimination was totally forgotten – in the qualifying rounds it took last place.

For rather good soccer at a national level there are both the AFC Leopards and the Gor Mahia from Kisumu, which have been at the forefront of the national league for several years now.

For thousands of soccer fans in the country there is nothing more exciting or suspense-packed than a game between the two rivals. It's no surprise that they are also accompanied by some major brawls now and then.

Individually or on the Team

Kenya's by far greatest pride are three famous professional boxers: Robert Wangila Napunyi, who after having won

a gold medal (the first for an African) in the bantam-weight category at the Seoul Summer Olympics is now boxing professionally in the USA; Chris Sande, the winner of the bronze medal in the same games, and Steve Muema. Kenya has claimed victory four years in a row now in the East and Central Africa Boxing Championship.

Kenya participated in the Commonwealth Games for the first time in 1966. On the same occasion in 1974, Kenya's boxers won their first medals, one gold and three bronze.

During the fifties, a sport new to Kenya grew in importance: hockey. At first it was only played by the Sikhs and Goans. Kenya didn't become a serious competitor on the international level until the early seventies. With the installation of artificial turf in the City Park Stadium, this sport is experiencing a new upsurge. On the strength of it, the team from Kenya won the gold medal in the 1987 All-African Games in Nairobi. Other widespread sports include rugby, cricket

and volleyball, which is especially popular in schools and colleges and also offered at many companies. The womens' team from the Kenya Post and Telecommunications became champion in 1990 and represented Africa in the 1991 world championship in Japan.

The golf courses are still reserved for the high-income upper class and tourists. In the world of golfing, Kenya is highly regarded for its splendidly situated golf courses. Day-visitors are welcome at most of the golfing clubs.

The Miracle Runners

Kenya has always claimed that its athletes are its best ambassadors. It is known around the world for its outstanding track-and-field athletes. With every justification, the saga of the Kenyan miracle runners has now already lasted for several decades. Kenya had already distinguished itself in track-and-field events when it was still a British colony. The country's first international medals were

225

claimed by Anere Anentia in the 10,000 meter run and Borotjo Rotich in the 400 meter sprint, both at the 1958 British Empire and Commonwealth Games held in Cardiff, Wales.

Kenya's national anthem was first played at the Olympic Games in Tokyo in 1964. After this starting shot, Kenya soon continued with its athletic career at the All- African Games in Brazaville, Congo (now Zaire). Altogether, Kenya won eight gold medals, ten silvers and seven bronze.

Kenya's legendary track-and-field athlete, Kipchoge Keino, broke the world record in the 3000 and 5000 meter runs. He received the USA's Helms award as best track-and-field athlete in Africa.

Kenya took the world's breath away at the 1968 Mexico Olympic Games. It won, all totalled, three gold, four silver and two bronze medals. Only 18 track

Above: If driving is a sport, then the Safari Rally is a marathon. Right: Kenyan youths preparing for the Safari Rally.

athletes participated in the games. Nonetheless, they were second behind the USA. At that time, some critics claimed that the spectacular victories were due only to the fact that the stadium in Mexico was located at the same altitude as the training camps in Kenya. The truth was clearly demonstrated, however, in the 1972 games in Munich. It rained medals there: Kipchoge Keino received a silver and a gold, there was a silver for Benjamin Jipcho, gold in the relay competition as well as two bronzes.

Finally, when Kenya participated in the 1988 Seoul Summer Olympics, it proceeded to win seven medals, five of them in track-and-field.

The victorious era of the Kenyan runners is certainly far from over. They won numerous medals at the track-and-field world championship in 1993 in the long-distance and mid-range events. However, Kenya is not home to world-class runners alone. The bulk of competitive marathon runners also has an audience there.

The Mombasa Marathon

The Mombasa Marathon is 42 kilometers in length. It was established in 1985 by the Severin Sea Lodge, which is under German management. The marathon begins and ends in the neighborhood of the Sunline sports complex.

Since its founding, it has become the second most important race in Africa south of the Sahara, and has achieved a steady place on the international marathon calendar.

At the 1990 marathon there were more than 5000 participants at the starting line, coming from Switzerland, Germany, Holland, France, Great Britain, Australia and the USA, in addition to teams from the Seychelles, Somalia, Ethiopia, Tanzania, Uganda and Ruanda. Runners from the Far East will also participate in the near future. The marathon always takes place in July.

The Safari Rally

Almost forty years ago it was held for the first time, then as the coronation safari in honor Great Britain's Queen Elizabeth II's ascension to the throne. Today it is one of the most renowned motor rallys in the entire world – the Safari Rally through Kenya.

It is a race of superlatives: the hardest test for motor and drivers and the most exciting race of all the rallys in the world. The majority of present-day participants claim that arriving at the goal is more rewarding in and of itself than winning is in some other rallys.

Maybe they are right. The Safari Rally leads the driver over the roughest roads in Kenya, through wild bush-savannah, up and down precipitous slopes and through flooded river-beds. It is more than 4000 kilometers long.

The 1953 Rally was just short of 2000 kilometers in length and passed over three different routes. The drivers could decide whether they wanted to start out in Nairobi, Kenya, Morogor in Tanzania or Kampala, Uganda. At the end, all of the cars came together for their run at the goal in Nairobi.

The event was described as an informal matter at the time. The participants arrived about 15 minutes before the start of the race. None of them had thought ahead of time to take a look at their respective circuits. Route descriptions were not distributed. The first heros of the Safari Rally were certainly not spared the adversities which plague today's drivers. The mud and rugged country allowed only 16 of the original 61 cars through to the finish line in Nairobi.

In 1955 the committee decided to permit only one starting point for the future: Nairobi. Another sensational innovation: A female crew reached the finish-line and received the Lady Macmillan Cup.

The Rally was entered into the Rally Calendar and set for Easter, the rainy (!) season of the year. Today the drivers fight more with the Kenyan roads than they do for the honors themselves.

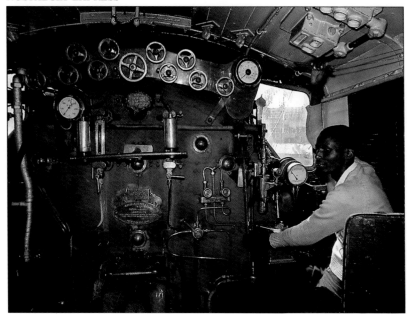

THE NOSTALGIA EXPRESS

Who doesn't remember the famous scene in the film *Out of Africa* when Dennis Finch (Robert Redford) stopped the train midway along its route to load his quarry onto it and thereby come to meet the lovely Baroness Blixen?

Of course big game hunters don't appear along this route anymore, but otherwise not much has changed. To this day, the legendary Nostalgia Express still rumbles back and forth through the deserted wilderness between Mombasa and Nairobi, the capital city, a trip of almost 500 kilometers and it can still happen that a herd of elephants may force the train to a stop. Of course, the cars of the pioneer days have been standing in the Railroad Museum in Nairobi for a long while, nonetheless the first-class passengers still travel in plush railroad cars from the thirties.

Above: All aboard the Nostalgia Express, which follows the tracks of the old railway.

In 1886 the British decided to connect Mombasa and Uganda by rail. It was no simple undertaking. The tracks of the "iron rhinoceros" had to be laid not only through an undeveloped wilderness, they also had to overcome the steep slope of the Great Rift Valley. The British brought 32,000 Indian laborers to the country to bring their large-scale construction plans to reality. In the process many of the latter lost their lives. They were either snatched away by epidemics or fell victim to surprise attacks from rebellious natives. Among the stories which can still make anyone shudder is the man-eaters' of Tsavo. In the course of ten months, 28 Indians and at least the same number of Africans are supposed to have been eaten by lions.

After its completion, the railroad contributed substantially to the development of Kenya's interior highlands. Where it had previously taken months to reach Lake Victoria, the travel time from Mombasa to Kisumu now took only six days. Life on the train is no longer quite as exciting as it was in the pioneer days. Among travellers to Kenya today, the most popular stretch is that between Mombasa and Nairobi.

When travelling first class it's not with persons unknown. The names of fellow travellers, the car and compartment numbers stand hand written on a large announcement board at the Nairobi railroad station.

"First class" on the Kenya Railway still means class: Each compartment has two single bunks with individual reading lamps, a closet, a wash-basin and a fan. Each set of two compartments are connected with a sliding door which can be opened or closed at need.

At 7 P.M. on the dot, the stationmaster allows the train to depart. The conductor blows his whistle, the train lurches and heaves a bit, and quickly gains speed after leaving the station. Along the tracks, children stand waving in dawn light.

The crisply uniformed steward provides courteous service in the comfortable compartments and distributes reservations for any of the various dining rounds. If you decide in favor of the first round you will enjoy the advantages of a clean table and the availability of all selections, however, on the down side it can happen that the waiter may snatch away a half-full plate so that the next round of guests can be seated.

As the tropical night sets in outside, the xylophone-playing conductor calls the first round of diners to a five-course evening meal in the wood-paneled dining car. Fans waft cool air down from the ceiling and the mahogany tables, covered with white cloths arranged for two to four persons, await the guests.

The head waiter guides each passenger to table, which is laid with silver. There is soup with home-baked rye or white bread, fish, and a selection of main dishes with rice or vegetables, a dessert and tea or coffee. All of this is cooked on a tiny gas range in the dining car's galley. One should definitely not miss taking a peek into the tiny kitchen.

Drinks are served in the compartments until 11 o'clock, after which the bar closes. However, the steward won't be mad if the passengers bring their own whiskey instead, and is pleased to provide glasses for a small tip.

During the evening meal the steward will have already arranged the beds. The gentle clatter of the train on the tracks rocks you off to sleep.

Chimes awaken the passengers shortly after the break of day. It's worth getting up early during this journey, not only in that one can then still enjoy something of the landscape passing by, but also because of the breakfast. Those not among the first to be seated will be jostling in the cue later on. It requires a certain power of assertion to get the eggs of your English breakfast the way you want them. The waiters find it more practical to slap whatever they have at hand down in front of the guests.

Although there are always uniformed railroad police on the train, the warning signs should never be ignored. Leave neither money nor items of value in the compartments!

Two passenger trains per day travel the Mombasa-Nairobi stretch (and back). In order to secure a compartment, one should book early enough in advance. There are three classes: In the first, the trip costs less than US$ 19, half of that in second, and less than $ 5 in third. The latter should be avoided by all means. A five-course dinner costs about $ 5, chilled European wine approximately $ 27 per bottle.

The trains depart simultaneously from both Mombasa and Nairobi. A slow train leaves at 5 P.M. and arrives at 8 o'clock the next morning. The faster train, leaving at 7 P.M., stops only in Voi and arrives at 8.30 A.M. The earlier train has the advantage that you can still admire the landscape before night falls.

A CULINARY TOUR

In all of Africa, Kenya can boast of having the most diversified cuisine. Nairobi has more than one hundred restaurants ranging from shabby street-stands selling skewers of roasted meat and corn-on-the-cob, on up to those elegant, expensive establishments offering such delicacies as lobster and caviar. In Mombasa, Malindi and along the coast there is something for everyone's taste and pocketbook as well.

For the most part, foreign guests will first become familiar with hotel cuisine. It is adjusted to an international clientele, tasty and generous for the most part, but offering little in the way of the exotic. Tropical fruits and seafood on the lunch buffet are frequently the only concessions made to the fact that one is in a country on the Indian Ocean. Despite the

Above: Kenya's restaurants provide for every type of taste bud. Right: Indigenous cuisine is a must.

oversupply of oranges, lemons, papayas and pineapples, the fruit juices offered are seldom freshly pressed.

Many hotels have à la carte restaurants with Italian, French and sometimes Indian cuisine as well. One praiseworthy and quite edible legacy from the period of British colonialism is the Sunday afternoon curry offered in some hotels, mostly in the country's interior: Chicken, lamb or beef fried together with Indian spices and served with rice, chutneys and finely-chopped mangos, tomatoes, onions and pineapple or whatever else the cook happens to come up with.

The Kenyan national dish is *ugali*, a porridge of maize enriched with vegetables or meat, millet, beans, yams, cassavas, bananas and sweet potatoes. A type of cheap cabbage, called *sukuma wiki* by the natives, is also very popular. The name means "getting through the week". Another popular dish is *irio*. It is made of vegetables including peas and squashes and cooked in a clay pot.

In those African restaurants which have made adjustments for tourists, the food is often served up with a side-dish of folklore. So, those wanting to kill two flies – dining and entertainment – with one swing of the swatter, will be in the right place at these establishments.

The Indian and Arabic influence on Kenya's simpler cuisine is unmistakable, especially along the coast. Samosas, crisp filled pockets of dough, and chapatis, an Indian flat-bread, can be bought on every street-corner. Among meat dishes, beef, chicken, goat and lamb predominate.

On the coast too, the seafood and fish are especially recommended. The prices are reasonable when compared with international standards. There are several specialty restaurants which prepare some truly outstanding dishes. Among the seafoods, highest honors go to the king crab, kilifi oysters, malindisole and smoked tuna or sailfish. Fish are also caught in the lakes and rivers in the interior. Hence,

perch and trout are frequently on the menus in the camps and lodges.

In foreign cuisine, Indian restaurants are especially popular. They serve very different dishes, depending on the owner's origin. South Indian food is mostly vegetarian, Mughlai cuisine spicy, Singh curry somewhat hotter, and Ismaili and Goa curry very hot. The list is endless. Indian restaurants often have their own specialties. Several are renowned for their chicken tika, others offer excellent prawn masala. In particular, the wide selection of fried and baked appetizers with sauces ranging from hellishly hot to mildly sweet are not to be missed.

The number of Italian spots significally increased during the last few years. Their use of a pinch of the exotic in the preparation of noodle, meat and fish dishes yields some very interesting results. The dubious blessing of the American fast-food joint hasn't passed Kenya by, either. Whether hamburger, chicken or french fries, it can be found in Nairobi as well as in Mombasa.

There is a large selection on the drink lists at bars, restaurants and hotels. The Kenyan beers Tusker, White Cup and Premium enjoy great popularity among the natives and vacationers alike. The prices of both beer and soft drinks are determined by the state, and correspondingly low, even in the exclusive restaurants. Only the most hard boiled throats would try their luck with *pombe,* the domestic beer brewed from maize, millet or bananas.

For the most part, wines are imported from Italy and France. Wine is also produced at Lake Naivasha; it is perfectly drinkable, althought the same can't always be said of the palm wine.

The sugar-cane spirits "Kenya Cane" is rather cheap but above the quality of pure rotgut, as is the coffee liqueur "Kenya Gold".

At any rate, the same truth applies to food and drink the world 'round: "Without trying you'll never make a culinary discovery!" And there are certainly enough possibilities for that in Kenya.

THEATER AND MUSIC

The music of Kenya has both traditional and modern forms. Each tribe has its own musical instrument. Drumming of the sort found in West Africa, however, is practically unknown in Kenya, except among the Embu, Meru and Wakamba. Kenya's traditional instrument always was the lyre. It appears in different versions; the Abaluhya, for example, use the *litungu* for dancing, the Luo use the *nyatiti* and the Gusii the *obukano*. The instrument specific to the Teso in West Kenya was the *adende*, while stringed instruments such as the *amadinda*, the *siriri* and the *marimba* were in general circulation. The *abu*, a wind instrument, traditionally was used by the Luo for ceremonies and signalling. The Kikuyu and several nilotic tribes use variations of these instruments.

Above: Pantomime and limbo dancing for the benefit of the tourists. Right: Kenyan singer in the Safari Beach Hotel.

In neo-traditional music, individuals or small groups play traditional African rhythms with guitars and with various improvised instruments. Among the better-known interpreters of this music are Daudi Kabaka, Fadhili William and John Nzenze. In addition, there are other musicians who draw strongly on "outside" influences. They cultivate the following styles: Jazz (high-life), *kwela* (spirituals) and *benga*, which is a melting of many musical directions.

In the related genre of dance, the highly animated and acrobatic performances of the Wakamba have become very well-known meanwhile in addition to the war dances of the Kipsigis and the Embu, the erotic dance rituals of the Giriama and the womens' dances of the Gusii. Most of these are usually accompanied by instruments, although the Maasai and related Nilotic tribes employ only rattles and the like. The Luo wear full-blown costumes for their dances; the Maasai, on the other hand, wear simple, ornamented swatches of cloth.

For all important events, including marriages, births and initiation rites, the accompanying emotions are translated in a very intense manner into music and dance. Traditionally, poetry, which was not put down in writing, has also been handed down through song. During the battles for independence, song also served the function of informing and mobilizing people.

Theater was also used to spread information about the battles of independence. In 1951, the colonial government decided to establish a national cultural center which was supposed to provide all of Kenya's inhabitants with entertainment and culture without regard to their race and land of origin. The performances were of a scientific and educational nature. Following independence, Kenya's culture has managed to recover only gradually from these restrictive measures. Its theatrical life was limited primarily to Mombasa and Nairobi with occasional performances in other cities. In the meantime, cultural activities springing primarily from young people have also been popping up in smaller towns. Theater troups have been established in each of Kenya's provinces. After they have performed their pieces in the provinces the players move on to Nairobi in search of big-time success.

Being the capital city, Nairobi has Kenya's most interesting theater scene. As has always been the case, the majority of pieces are foreign productions; on top of that, the only acting school in Kenya is managed by Americans.

Be that as it may, several indications suggest a better development of Kenya's theaters. The **Mombasa Little Theater Club** has been in existence for decades. Once a folkloristic dance locale, it has developed into a theater troup which performs not only the best in African plays, but British comedies as well.

Three years ago the **East African Players** troup was founded. This is an

amateur group which appears primarily in Nairobi, and it already has, indeed, great successes to show for itself. The **Phoenix Players** are the only professional theater company which is based in Nairobi.

The **Mbalamwezi Players** and the **Saraskasi Players** predominantly perform African works, both in Nairobi. Among the pieces in their repertoires are *The Gods are Not at Fault* by Ola Rotimi and *The Trial of Brother Jero* by Nigerian Nobel prize-winner Woyle Soyinka.

Although the popularity of theater is on the increase in Kenya, much more must still be done in support of it. Many talented young actors have financial difficulties in completing their training. There is no public acting school, and the governmental allocations for the Kenya Cultural Center are very small.

Street theater is especially popular in Nairobi. Acrobats and actors perform mostly during lunch breaks or on the weekends. Their earnings depend on the audience alone.

A DAY WITH GEORGE ADAMSON

George Adamson, born in Etwah, India on September 20, 1906, was known to Kenyan natives as "Bwana Simba", and became a legend in his own time. He travelled to Kenya in 1924 to seek his fortune. After several adventures, among them as a gold digger, he landed temporary work as an assistant gamekeeper in 1938. On Christmas, 1942, he made the acquaintance of his future wife Friederike Victoria, a native of Czechoslovakia. They married in 1944. She was later to become known simply as Joy Adamson.

In 1956, George Adamson was forced to shoot a lion attacking him. One of the animal's three cubs became world-famous as the lioness Elsa in the film *Born Free*. She had been raised by George and Joy Adamson. Assisted by Elsa, in her

Above: George Adamson (1906-1989), a legend in his own time. Right: The Adamsons devoted their lives to lions.

own particular way, the couple began raising orphaned lions and preparing them for life in the wilds. In 1963, Adamson quit his gamekeeper's post in order to devote his life to his lions. From 1971 onward, he lived in Kora, whereas Joy moved to Shaba to concern herself with leopards. In 1980, she was murdered by a servant, an event that cast a long shadow over the rest of George Adamson's life. He thereafter more or less retired from all public activity in his "kampi ya simba" in Kora.

Kora lies about 150 kilometers east of Mount Kenya, in an area of arid bushlands. It is one of the most beautiful areas of Kenya, but by the same token one of its most desolate. The terrain is virtually impassable, and only has appeal for connoisseurs of wilderness. The camp lies in the shadow of Kora Rock, about six kilometers from Kora's airstrip.

When we visited him in 1989, George Adamson seemed to be in fine physical condition. The camp itself consisted of 12 huts, with the largest one serving as

the central point. That is where George Adamson received the guests who had made such a long and difficult journey to visit him. The walls were covered with photographic memorials. Modern life had sickered into his everyday activities: He remained in contact with the outside world by means of a CB radio, and a generator produced electricity to run a refrigerator, where he kept the vital serums in the case of snake bites. The camp's bar consisted of a small, locked case containing a few bottles of Gin and Whiskey.

Adamson's three lions greeted us in a quiet and trusting fashion. The one-year-old cubs, whom Adamson still wanted to tend to for another year, disappeared slowly into the wilds. Using a megaphone and a special language devised by him, Adamson called the still tufted beasts back to the camp. The 83-year-old man walked over to his animals; the lions playfully sought body contact with him.

Shortly before midday, Adamson's worker returned from an inspection with guests through the reserve. George listened to the report they gave. In the meantime, his cook Hamisi Farah prepared a lunch on the open fire. We all sat down around the set table. George's other pets, too (hornbills, mandrakes). The camp's daily schedule also included feeding animals. This process took place in an enclosure bordering on the camp's fence. One lion caused some excitement when it clambered through a hole into the residential area of the camp. But Adamson's presence ensured no panic. His helpers drove the lion back into the enclosure.

The most important problem was getting food for the animals. The Somalis supplied him with camels; but to avoid becoming dependent on them, he kept a number of goats in the camp. When we left George standing at the entrance of his camp, he looked strong and healthy. On August 20, 1989, he was shot by poachers. A salvo was fired at his burial on September 2 in kampi ya Simba. He lies beside his brother Terence, who died in April 1986, and his favorite lion *Boy*.

235

RELIGIONS

The inhabitants of central Kenya are primarily Christians or adherents of animistic sects; in contrast, the coastal region and the North Eastern Province are Islamic. The same also applies to Kenyans of Arabic heritage and to the majority of Asians.

They all succumbed to the influence of the Arabs, who began to settle the coasts in the 9th century. It wasn't until considerably later, in the 19th century, that the islamization wave reached the country's interior. There, however, Christian missionaries had already thoroughly performed their duties. As a result, Islam never achieved the dominance in those regions that it has on the coasts.

Most of the African Moslems settled on the coast are orthodox Sunnites. The Asian population is classed more among the Shiites.

Above: Kenya's religious landscape is as varied as its people and landscape itself.

Moslems are also predominant among the Somalian tribes. Roughly 5000 Kenyans are members of the Ismailian sect of Moslems. They are a diminutive group, although they exert great influence which is mainly due to the activities of the Agha Khan Foundation. Their leader is the Imam of the Ismailians, His Highness Karim Agha Khan IV, direct descendant of the Prophet Mohammed. The Agha Khan Foundation has built a lot of schools, hospitals and homes.

The influence of Islam is especially strong in the Lamu Archipelago. Not only is the prohibition against alcohol strictly observed there (even though there are bars and hotels which serve alcoholic drinks), clothing also follows Islamic conceptions. Outside their homes, women wear the traditional *bui-bui*. The men on Lamu, at least the older ones, wrap themselves in ankle-length garments, the so-called *kanzu*. A small cap, the *kofia*, is popular as headwear.

Lamu is also rather famous for the most important Islamic festival on the entire East African coast: the *Maulidi al-Nebi,* the celebrations on the birthday of the Prophet.

Christians, Moslems, Hindus, Sikhs and members of various nature religions coexist in Kenya without any discriminations or conflicts worth mentioning. Their individual histories have resulted in an uneven distribution of the groups across the country, with varying concentration between the coast and the inland region.

Altogether, the biggest part of the Kenyan population is either member of one of the Christian religions or of the numerous nature religions. The Christian religion achieved its importance primarily through the indefatigable work of its countless missionaries. Schools as well as hospitals have repeatedly been founded and financed by several orders. In more remote areas, around Lake Turkana for example, the only opportunity for children to get an education is at one of the missionary institutions like the North Horr missionary station. The nomadic families frequently leave their offspring in the care of the missionaries for several months. Quite frequently one of the children is so successful that he or she later attends a continuation school in one of the larger towns.

Even when Sunday church attendance is quite consistently planned into a Kenyan Christian's life, indeed, the beliefs of the forefathers are still of paramount significance.

The ancestral religions of Kenya's various ethnic groups differ in their modes of expression, but their fundamental elements are actually very similar. For the most part, the basic notion is a belief in one god who, as the highest being, created everything. This god is accompanied by a great number of good and evil demons and spirits which have to be humored with sacrifices and amulets.

Nature also plays a major role in most of these belief systems. Trees or mountains are frequently holy places which may only be set foot upon at particular times and by certain people.

The most important role, however, is played by the ancestors. Contact is made with them in the presence of various mediums; they are then asked for support and help. The mediums can be either medicine men or one of the eldest of a family. The goodwill and favor of the ancestors is among the most important sources of help in life.

On the other hand, people also require protection against the hatred and envy of their enemies. Anyone who had supposedly brought misfortune to friends or neighbors could quickly become denounced as a witch or magician. He or she would be accused of using "black magic". Protection from its effects can be had by fetishes obtained from the medicine man, a person of great importance in the village communities. He is traditionally a healer who applies his knowledge of medicinal herbs, roots and plants for the well being of the community at large. He shouldn't be seen as some crazy magician, rather as a doctor and priest in one person.

Perhaps the reports dealing with nature religions always sound a bit as though their practitioners are naive stone-age people.

If considered a bit more closely, however, there are similar rites and rituals, which through force of habit seem entirely normal to us, to be found in religions and life-styles which we perceive to be progressive.

Superstition is also no stranger to the people of Europe and America. In addition, healing arts which are not solely based on allopathic medicine are gaining increasing numbers of adherents in the West. Individuals can decide only for themselves what they perceive as belief or superstition. At any rate, tolerance toward other religions is something which can be learned in Kenya.

DEVELOPING KENYA

In comparison to other African nations, Kenya is considered quite progressive. Its social and economic problems are nonetheless tremendous. Some reasons for this can be seen in the effects of colonization, in mass unemployment, in a four percent population growth rate and, finally, in recurring periods of drought.

Still today, about three quarters of Kenyans live outside of the cities, but only one quarter of the nation's land is actually arable. The most important agricultural products are coffee, tea, fruit, vegetables and flowers. Cattle and sheep breeding also play a significant role. Only the big farms can run a profitable operation, but they remain an exception on the economic landscape. A major land reform was enacted after independence, giving African farmers and breeders land

Above: The high population growth rate is Kenya's most pressing issue. Right: Employment is concentrated in the cities.

to work on, but the parcels soon proved to be too small to even supply their new owners with food. Any profits reinvested in more modern agricultural techniques have only produced positive results with bumper crops.

All hopes have been repeatedly put on irrigation projects such as those on the Kerio and Turkwell Rivers. But the agricultural programs and the government both promised more than they could deliver, although these have met with only partial success. The costs of most such projects are immense, the long-term success is generally doubtful.

The greatest threat facing Kenya is population growth, which far outspaces the growth in the agricultural sector. Since independence the nation's population has more than doubled. Already at present, half of the population is under 15 years of age. They all require nourishment, schooling and employment. To date the illiteracy rate is still running at 50 percent. Of course, many are unable to afford school fees. The policy of tuition-

free grammar school may prevail, at least, but learning materials and the school uniforms must be paid for. This is impossible for poor families with many children.

The poor outlook for the future in the countryside drives many people to the cities, where unemployment is the only thing awaiting them. The chasm between Kenya's social classes is vast. There is a small upper stratum which can afford anything it wants standing opposite the roughly 50 percent living at or below the poverty level.

In the near future, job creation will be among the tasks of highest priority to the Kenyan government. New branches of the economy must be developed in order to make Kenyan products competitive on the world market and bring urgently needed hard currency to the country.

Crime and prostitution are flourishing, particularly in Nairobi, the capital city, as well as the port city of Mombasa. Tourism is also partially at fault for this fact. It certainly sparks future hopes and expec-

tations which can't be fulfilled. The cameras and jewelry of vacationers make them appear immeasurably wealthy to the natives. For the sake of acquiring such status symbols, the step into crime is often not a big one. The most important industrial sectors are cement, sisal and soda production as well as textiles and the manufacture of fertilizers. Most of the major industrial operations belong, to a large degree, to foreign companies. Traditionally, Kenya's largest trading partner has been Great Britain, followed by Germany and the USA.

Tourism in Kenya has experienced an enormous upswing, especially in the 1980s. As a result, many new jobs have indeed been created, but the largest profits of the tourism business remain in foreign lands, since the majority of trips have already been paid for in the vacationer's home country. Most hotel employees live separated from their wives and children for the greater part of the year because there is no employment available near their homes. The highly-

239

touted tourism branch of the economy doesn't yield benefits alone, even though it is important as a source of foreign exchange and generator of employment. It is also a fragile industry: The 1973 oil crisis, the political turbulence of 1982, the war in Somalia and the Gulf War all had drastic consequences on the income from tourism.

The multiplicity of difficult problems facing Kenya is not being met with inactivity. Both on its own and with the help of foreign support, efforts are being made to improve the economic and social status of the country and its peoples through a variety of projects. In doing so, measures for the protection of the environment are just as important as the implementation of family planning programs and irrigation projects. In these efforts, individual initiatives have been just as successful as those of foundations.

To Plant a Tree

Kenyas most pressing environmental problem today lies in desertification. There were once huge forested regions in Kenya. The expansion of agriculture and the demand for timber caused the stands to decrease from over 30% of Kenya's land area to only 3% within 50 years. Wood is still the most important source of energy for the poorer population. Logged areas of forest often turn into semi-deserts. Stopping soil erosion resulting from deforestation was the concern of the university Professor Wangari Maathai. She founded the **Green Belt Movement** reforestation project. In one government-supported campaign, each Kenyan was called upon to plant a tree and afterwards see to its watering.

Through efforts on their farm in the Meru hill-country, Minister Kanake and his family have also been working to in-

crease tree cultivation for quite some time. Lengthy studies of a number of growing methods have made them into exemplary agriculturists. They raise seedlings in tree-schools, which they then either plant among their various other agricultural products or sell to other farmers for their plots. Their green oasis is convincing proof of their success.

A model example of successful reforestation has been achieved by René Haller of Switzerland. Africa's largest cement factory, where coral limestone is mined, is located to the north of Mombasa. A desolate rocky desert is all that remains after the mining. Haller started his project 20 years ago. To date he has planted roughly one million casuaries, the only tree species which could survive in the nutrient-poor "soil". The millipedes he then introduced transform the fallen needles into a layer of humus, which in turn provides sustenance for additional plant varieties. But this wasn't enough. Haller settled a number of animal species in his green paradise to keep the ecological system in balance. From hippopotamui to crocodiles and fish, cattle and sheep, all profits they yield are to be used for financing the project.

Numerous development projects, for example owe their existence to the Agha Khan Foundation, the aid organization of the Ismailian Moslems. The organization finances several important health programs in Kenya. Among these is the construction of wells in remote villages and the provision of first aid training for their inhabitants, as well as carefully directed family planning efforts. Helping others to help themselves is the guiding principle of the Agha Khan Foundation. Among the Ismailians great value is placed on education, thus the foundation has established numerous schools and kindergartens. These are open not only to the members of their own religious community, but also to all other population groups as well.

Right: 75 percent of Kenyans live in often far-flung rural communities.

PREPARATIONS

Kenya is a cosmopolitan, English-speaking country on the equator in East Africa. Nairobi, the capital, is a modern city with a well developed infrastructure. Its sizable international airport is flown to regularly by some 40 international airlines in addition to Kenya Airways, the national airline. The second-largest city in the country, Mombasa, is located on the coast. It also possesses an international airport with good connections to Nairobi and the rest of the world.

Climate
Kenya has a variety of climatic zones. Because of the immense altitude differences, ranging from 0 meters on the coast to the high mountains at over 5000 meters, there are great deviations of temperature and humidity between the various regions of the country. The coastal region is hotter and moister than the highlands; the desert region in the north is a very dry, hot area in which sometimes even the rainy season fails to appear.

For these reasons there is no particular travel season for Kenya. There are two rainy seasons: The long rains are normally in April and May; the shorter ones in October and November. The months of June, July and August are cooler, January and February warmer.

Luggage / Clothing
Kenya is a casual country. Jackets, ties and evening dress are required only in the most expensive hotels and restaurants. It's a good idea to avoid very bright colors when on safaris in the wildlife reserves. Made-to-order safari clothing can be finished quite rapidly. Long pants for men and women and plenty of shirts are all that are needed for a safari besides a light sweater for the cool evenings. In the coastal areas, it's best to wear thin cotton clothing and something casual in the evenings. Keep in mind that the coastal regions are inhabited almost exclusively by Moslems. Swimming in the nude is forbidden. When taking a walk along the beach and in the city, women should wear shawls or scarves over their shoulders and arms in order to avoid unpleasant incidents.

Equipment
Photo gear and binoculars, especially to observe animals and birds.

Toilet Articles
Suntan oil and sun protectants are available in any of the better drugstores, although they are rather expensive. It's better to bring your own things from home. The same goes for shampoo, lotion, shaving cream and tampons.

Passports
All incoming travellers must have a valid passport. If you are on a through-flight or have booked a return flight, it is possible to get a visitors' permit upon your arrival. This pass is normally valid for three months, although it can be prolonged for another three months at the Department of Immigration. Work permits can only be obtained at the main Immigration Office, and this can take a good while.

Visa
A visa is required of all visitors with the exception of passport holders from the British Commonwealth and other countries which have special agreements with Kenya.

Exceptions are Australia, Nigeria, Sri Lanka and South Africa: Visas are also required for citizens of these countries, although they can be obtained upon arrival. This is, however, a lengthy and wearisome business. It's a better idea to take care of it ahead of time. Visa are available from the Kenyan embassies in a traveller's home country.

Currency Regulations

The Kenyan shilling (KSh) is divided into 100 cents. There are 500, 200, 100, 50, 20 and ten shilling notes. Coins range in value from five and one shilling to 50, 10 and 5 cents. In general it could be said that the high inflation rate in Kenya alters the exchange rates rather to the benefit of the foreign visitor.

The stringent currency regulations that had travellers fill out lengthy forms detailing all the money they were carrying with them, have been abolished. Still, Kenyan shillings can neither be imported nor exported. Small amounts, what you might need to buy a drink or a snack at the airport are allowed. Inquire at the customs or with your tour company to find out the actual permitted export or import amount. The customs official might try and talk you out of the sum exceeding the legal amount. When changing shillings back into your home currency, make sure you get a receipt from an official changing booth.

Destruction or damage of kenyan shillings is punishable by law.

Customs

Personal property, photographic equipment and film can be brought in duty-free. The import of 200 cigarettes, 50 cigars, one liter of alcohol and 250 milliliters of perfume are allowed. Items such as radios, cameras, video, stereo equipment can be brought in duty-free if they have been entered into your passport and are taken back out upon leaving the country.

Guns may only be brought in with permission from the Central Firearms Bureau, PO Box 30263, Nairobi.

Health

Yellow fever vaccination is no longer required, but is recommended. On demand, travellers from countries with cholera danger must show a certificate of recent immunization.

Malaria: Malaria prophylaxis is always important. Malaria is among the greatest health risks in Kenya. It is transmitted by mosquito bites. Up to the present day there is no vaccine; the only preventatives are certain medications (examples are Lariam and Resochin) which must be taken during the stay in Kenya. They all have more or less strong side-effects and must be taken exactly according to the instructions. Malaria is a serious fever illness and can also wind up being deadly if it is not promptly recognized and treated. If you should get a fever in Kenya or various other suspicious complaints should arise, it is absolutely necessary to seek out a doctor and indicate to him/her that you have been in the tropics. A blood test can ascertain whether a person is infected or not.

Even the intake of prophylactic medications is not a sure protection. Mosquito repellents for application to the skin and sleeping under a mosquito net are by all means recommended as additional measures. In the twilight, the time when most mosquito bites occur, long pants and long-sleeved shirts should be worn as minimum protection.

Aids: Aids is an additional danger, although it can be avoided. The epidemic is widespread in East Africa, and it is reasonable to operate on the assumption that the preponderance of Kenya's prostitutes are infected. If you should be so unfortunate as to fall ill during your vacation or have an accident, it can be assumed that the majority of blood products have been tested for the virus. The particularly cautious may want to bring along a supply of single-use syringes and surgical gloves.

Bilharzia: The majority of Kenya's inland bodies of water are contaminated with bilharzia and are therefore unsuitable for swimming. The bilharzia parasite is even able to penetrate into the body through undamaged skin and migrate into organs such as the liver, where they can cause very serious damage. Treatment is possible, but extremely lengthy. The main problem is that for the most part the disease is not properly diagnosed. The symptoms include tiredness, diarrhea and itching.

TRAVELLING TO KENYA

There are daily flights to Nairobi's Jomo Kenyatta International Airport starting from London; there are two or three flights a week from other cities. PamAm flies from America via Europe and has connection with the Lufthansa flights in Frankfurt. There are also regularly scheduled flights from the Gulf Region (Near East), India and the Far East, as well as from other African countries.

Airlines with international flights to and from Kenya:

Aeroflot Soviet Airlines, Tel: Nairobi 20746. **Air Cananda**, Tel: Nairobi 20746. **Air Djibouti**, Tel: Nairobi 335325. **Air France**, Tel: Nairobi 333301. **Air India**, Tel: Nairobi 334788. **Air Madagascar**, Tel: Nairobi 26494. **Air Malawi**, Tel: Nairobi 340212. **Air Mauritius**, Tel: Nairobi 29166. **Air Tanzania**, Tel: Nairobi 336244. **Air Zaire**, Tel: Nairobi 25625. **Air Zimbabwe**, Tel: Nairobi 20106. **Alitalia**, Tel: Nairobi 337439. **British Airways**, Tel: Nairobi 3344440. **Cameroon Airlines**, Tel: Nairobi 337788. **Egypt Air**, Tel: Nairobi 27683. **El Al Israel Airlines**, Tel: Nairobi 338560. **Ethiopian Airlines**, Tel: Nairobi 26631. **Iberia Airlines**, Tel: Nairobi 331648. **Japan Airlines**, Tel: Nairobi 333277. **Kenya Airways**, Tel: Nairobi 29291, Mombasa 237192. **KLM**, Tel: Nairobi 332673. **Lufthansa**, Tel: Nairobi 226271. **Nigeria Airways**, Tel: Nairobi 336536. **Olympic Airways**, Tel: Nairobi 338027. **Pakistan Airways**, Tel: Nairobi 333900. **Pan Am**, Tel: Nairobi 23581. **Royal Swazi Airlines**, Tel: Nairobi 339303. **Sabena Belgian Airlines**, Tel: Nairobi 333248, Mombasa 21995. **Saudia Arabia Airlines**, Tel: Nairobi

331456. **Scandinavian Airlines**, Tel: Nairobi 338060, Mombasa 313623. **Somali Airlines**, Tel: Nairobi 335409. **Sudan Airways**, Tel: Nairobi 25129. **Swiss Air**, Tel: Nairobi 331012. **TWA**, Tel: Nairobi 20265. **Uganda Airlines**, Tel: Nairobi 21354. **Varig Brazilian Airlines**, Tel: Nairobi 3378097. **Zambia Airways**, Tel: Nairobi 29908.

TRAVELLING IN KENYA

By Air

Kenya Airways flies regularly from Nairobi to Mombasa, Malindi and Kisumu. Charter associations at the Wilson Airport offer regular flights to Lamu, Diani Beach, Amboseli, Masai Mara, Nyeri and Lake Turkana.

Before take-off on all domestic flights a fee of 50 shillings is collected. When departing Kenya, a tax of roughly US$ 18 must be paid.

By Bus

The city busses are usually overcrowded, especially during peak hours. In addition, it's not always a simple matter to find out where the bus is actually going. Long-distance busses between Mombasa and Nairobi always travel by night. They are all not particularly luxurious, but, as a consolation, they are very cheap.

By Car

The better-known car rental agencies in Mombasa and Nairobi offer a wide spectrum of vehicles, ranging from beat-up four-wheel-drives for wilderness safaris to air-conditioned limousines with chauffeur for the city. It should be added that it's not easy to find any rentals without mileage limitations.

The customary international rental agencies such as Hertz, Avis and Europcar maintain branches here as well, especially in Nairobi and Mombasa. In addition there is quite a number of domestic car rental companies. The prices of the international outfits are higher than those of the local firms, but the cars are also frequently in better shape. Overall, the price levels for rental cars are rather high.

If staying in Nairobi, along the coast or in other better-developed areas of the country, a normal passenger car will do the job. On the other hand, when on a safari in one of the national parks or in the northern part of the country, an all-terrain vehicle with four-wheel drive will be necessary.

By Taxi

There are many so-called taxis which are not especially reliable. One is better off sticking with the approved "Kenatco Taxis" as well as the "English Taxis" in Nairobi. The remaining taxis can easily be recognized by the yellow lines on their sides. The fares should definitely be settled before you start the trip in order to avoid heated discussions upon arrival at the destination.

Matatus are a Kenyan peculiarity. They are a sort of cross between the public bus and the taxi, consisting mostly of remodeled Land-Rovers with six to eight seats. Usually they haul about thirty people, offering neither seating nor safety equipment. Riding on a *matatu* should be attempted only by very courageous or poor-one's life is at stake in several ways. Usually overloaded, *matatus* are not in particularly good repair, always in a hurry and therefore adventurously driven. The majority of traffic accidents in Kenya involve *matatus*.

By Train

Riding the train in a first- or second-class sleeping car is an inexpensive and comfortable way to explore Kenya.

Trains leave daily for Mombasa and Kisumu. The trip is really agreeable, especially as it is, including a five-course meal, sleeping accomodations and breakfast. There are also third-class cars, which are, however, mostly over-filled and not very comfortable.

PRACTICAL TIPS

Business Hours

The hours of businesses vary from city to city. The majority, however, open at 8 or 8.30 a.m. The lunch-break is between 12.30 and 2 p.m.; offices close at 4.30 or 5.00 p.m.. Stores are open longer, in the larger shopping centers even to 8.30 p.m.

Credit Cards

The majority of hotels accept such major credit cards as *Diners'*, *Visa* and *American Express*. If this is the case there will be a sign clearly indicating so at the hotel's entrance. It is possible to get cash with credit cards in banks or at American express offices, although the amount permitted is quite low.

Electricity

The electricity network in all of the larger cities corresponds to the British norms, in other words 220-240 volts. The smaller hotels and guest-houses have their own generators. For most European equipment a plug adaptor is necessary; for North American units a transformer as well. These are available in electrical stores in the travellers' home countries.

Fax

For some time, most larger hotels offer a telefax-service to their guests. Frequently offices and copy-shops also have fax machines; most prices are calculated per page. Peculiarly enough, the fax lines usually work better than those for regular telephone service.

Flying Doctors

It is better in the country's interior to become a member of the Flying Doctor Service, in case an evacuation by aircraft should become necessary. The membership fee for a year is 300 shillings.

Holidays

There are eleven legal holidays in Kenya:

January 1st: *New Year*
March/April: *Good Friday* and *Easter Monday*
May 1st: *Labor Day*
June 1st: *Madaraka Day*
October 10th: *Moi Day*
October 20th: *Kenyatta Day*
December 12th: *Jamhuri* (Independance Day)
December 25th/26th: First and second days of Christmas
Variable: *Idd ul Fitr* (End of Ramadan)

Personal Safety / Crime

There are plenty of rumors about the dangers of Africa with regards to crime, however, the problem is no more serious here than anywhere else.

Naturally, such crimes as robbery and muggings, break-in, pickpocketing and so forth do happen here, too, but certainly no more often than in New York or London.

With a bit of healthy care and precaution nothing should happen to you.

Don't walk alone on the streets at night. If you walk through the city, stay on well-illuminated streets or take a taxi.

Conceal goods such as photographic equipment, money, etc, and don't leave anything of value lying around in the car or your hotel room. Most people leave their expensive jewelry at home anyway. If you have nonetheless brought something along, it should be deposited in the hotel's safe.

Avoid secluded beaches, shady bars and alluring offers for especially cheap tours of the city.

Pharmacies

Pharmacies in the big cities are well stocked and equipped.

However, medications which have already been prescribed should be brought along.

Photography

Few tourists come to Kenya without photography equipment. Several things should be kept in mind.

Respect the powers that be: Photographing the president or other prominent people is not permitted. This also applies to police officers and the army.

Do not photograph anyone without their consent. In the countryside, one frequently sees people in their traditional garb as they drive their herds of cattle or goats.

They know that they are a popular photographic subject for tourists and, accordingly, expect some payment. Be friendly when dealing with them about the price of your photographs.

Film can be obtained in cities and hotels, but it's expensive. Therefore, it's really better to pack along a sufficient amount of it from home. Film can be developed quickly in Nairobi and Mombasa, and for a reasonable price good prints can be made as well.

Telephone

Kenya is connected to the international telephone network. It's possible to dial directly to countries around the world. The prefix for Kenya is 254, the city-code for Nairobi 2; 11 for Mombasa.

The codes for other cities can be called from telephone books or directory-assistance.

Tipping

Service is already included in the price at the majority of restaurants. In the others, a good rule-of-thumb is about 10%. Porters should not be given more than 10-20 shillings. Most tourists also tip taxi drivers and city tour-guides. Gifts like clothing, shoes, cosmetics and books are always welcome.

Weights and Measures

Weights and measures correspond to international standards.

ADDRESSES

Clubs

There are many sports clubs of which tourists can become temporary members. **Nairobi Club**, Tel: 336996, offers cricket, tennis, squash, bowling, hockey and a swimming pool. **Impala Club**, Nairobi, Tel: 568573, offers rugby, hockey, cricket, tennis, squash, soccer and a swimming pool. **Karen Golf Club**, Nairobi, Tel: 882802. **Muthaiga Golf Club**, Nairobi, Tel: 762414. **Royal Nairobi Golf Club**, Nairobi, Tel: 725769. **Nairobi Sailing Club**, Tel: 501250. **Mombasa Yacht Club**, Tel: 313350. **Kenya Sub Aqua Club**, Nairobi, Tel: 501250. **The Mountain Club of Kenya**, Nairobi, Tel: 501747. **The Jockey Club of Kenya**, Nairobi, Tel: 566109.

Societies

Nairobi Photographic Society, Tel: 337129. **The East African Wildlife Society**, PO Box 20110, Nairobi, Tel: 337422. **The East African Natural History Society**, PO Box 40658, Nairobi, Tel: 742132.

Embassies / Consulates

There are embassies from over 100 foreign7 countries in Kenya. Most of these also maintain a consulate in Mombasa. A complete list of addresses can be found in the magazine *What's On* as well as the telephone directory. The most important are:

Australia: Nairobi, Tel: 749955. **Austria**: Nairobi, Tel: 228281; Mombasa, Tel: 313386. **Belgium**: Nairobi, Tel: 23879; Mombasa, Tel: 741564. **Brazil**: Nairobi, Tel: 337722. **China**: Nairobi, Tel: 722559. **Denmark**: Nairobi, Tel: 331088; Mombasa, Tel: 316051. **Finland**: Nairobi, Tel: 336717; Mombasa, Tel: 316051. **France**: Nairobi, Tel: 339973; Mombasa, Tel: 21008. **Germany**: Nairobi, Tel: 712527; Mombasa,

Tel: 21273. **Great Britain**: Nairobi, Tel: 335944; Mombasa, Tel: 25913. **Greece**: Nairobi, Tel: 225331; Mombasa, Tel: 315478. **India**: Nairobi, Tel: 222566; Mombasa, Tel: 311051. **Italy**: Nairobi, Tel: 227545; Mombasa, Tel: 26948. **Japan**: Nairobi, Tel: 332955. **Netherlands**: Nairobi, Tel: 227111; Mombasa, Tel: 311043. **Nigeria**: Nairobi, Tel: 224681. **Norway**: Nairobi, Tel: 337121; Mombasa, Tel: 313386. **Portugal**: Nairobi, Tel: 338990. **Saudi Arabia**: Nairobi, Tel: 229501. **Spain**: Nairobi, Tel: 335712; Mombasa, Tel: 335712. **Sweden**: Nairobi, Tel: 229042; Mombasa, Tel: 20501. **Switzerland**: Nairobi, Tel: 227736; Mombasa, Tel: 316684. **USA**: Nairobi, Tel: 334141; Mombasa, Tel: 315101.

Travel Agencies

There are many travel agencies with tour offerings for both natives and tourists. Travellers have frequently not booked their safaris yet and, after spending a few days in their hotels, decide to undertake a little excursion on their own. The better travel agencies can be helpful in this planning.

In no case should you try to save a little money by making dubious arrangements with someone-or-other met in a café. Also, make certain that the travel agent has a real office with telephone lines, and has good knowledge of the country and the travel possibilities within it.

The largest travel agencies are:

Archer's Tour and Travel, Nairobi, Tel: 331825

Bruce Travel Ltd., Nairobi, Tel. 26794.

Bunson Travel Service, Nairobi, Tel: 337604; Mombasa, Tel. 311331.

Diners World Travel, Nairobi, Tel: 337604; Mombasa, Tel: 24587.

Express Travel, Nairobi, Tel: 334722; Mombasa, Tel: 312461.

Flamingo Travel, Nairobi, Tel: 331360.

Let's Go Travel, Nairobi, Tel: 340332. offices in Nairobi.

LANGUAGE

The official languages of Kenya are English and Swahili. English is understood almost everywhere, however, a couple of words of Swahili can be quite useful, and the natives are eager to teach their language to interested people. The Swahili language has its roots on the East African coast. It is understood by everyone here. It originates from Bantu and possesses many foreign words, particularly from Arabic. The missionaries loved this simple language and transferred it into the Latin alphabet. Swahili is pronounced exactly as it is written. Here is a list of several useful sentences and expressions:

Hello . . . . *jambo*
How are you (doing)? . . *habari yako?*
I'm fine . . . . *mzuri*
Thank you . . . . *asante*
Thank you very much . . *asante sana*
Good-bye . . . . *kwaheri*
Food . . . . *chakula*
Coffee . . . . *kahawa*
Tea . . . . *thai*
Hot (or warm) . . . . *moto*
Cold . . . . *baridi*
Beer . . . . *pombe/tembo*
Bread . . . . *mkate*
Meat . . . . *nyama*
Fruit . . . . *matunda*
Vegetables . . . . *mboga*
Fish . . . . *samaki*
Butter . . . . *siagi*
Sugar . . . . *sukari*
Salt . . . . *chumvi*
Now . . . . *sasa*
Today . . . . *leo*
Tomorrow . . . . *kesho*
Fast . . . . *haraka*
Slow . . . . *pole pole*
Where? . . . . *wapi?*
Why? . . . . *kwanin?*
What? . . . . *nini?*
Who? . . . . *nani?*
Yes . . . . *ndio*

No . . . . *hapana*
How Much? . . . . *ngapi?*
Eat . . . . *kukula*
Drink . . . . *kukunywa*
Sleep . . . . *kulala*
Walk . . . . *kuanda*
Stop . . . . *kusimama*
Buy . . . . *kununua*
Sell . . . . *l Kuuza*
Shop/store . . . . *duka*
One . . . . *moja*
Two . . . . *mbili*
Three . . . . *tatu*
Four . . . . *ine*
Five . . . . *tano*
Six . . . . *sita*
Seven . . . . *saba*
Eight . . . . *nane*
Nine . . . . *tisa*
Ten . . . . *kumi*
Eleven . . . . *kumi na moja*
Twenty . . . . *ishirni*
Thirty . . . . *thelatini*
Forty . . . . *arobani*
Fifty . . . . *hamsini*
Sixty . . . . *sitini*
Seventy . . . . *sabini*
Eighty . . . . *themanini*
Ninety . . . . *tisani*
One hundred . . . . . . *mia moja*
One thousand . . . . . *elfu moja*
Morning . . . . *saubuhi*
Evening . . . . *jioni*
Daytime . . . . *mashana*
Night . . . . *usiku*
Monday . . . . *jumutatu*
Tuesday . . . . *jumanne*
Wednesday . . . . . . *jumatano*
Thursday . . . . . . *alhamisi*
Friday . . . . *jumaa*
Saturday . . . . *jumamosi*
Sunday . . . . *jumapili*

Common signs:

Hatari . . . . . caution!/pay attention!
Hakunja nija . . . . do not enter
Mbwa Mkali . . . beware of the dog!
Hakuna kazi . . . . . fully occupied

AUTHORS

Angela Anchieng works in the Ministry of Information and Broadcasting. She was co-author of *Nairobi, Ngong Hills, Gikomba, Tsavo National Park Taita Hills, Lake Jipe* and *Lake Chala*.

Zdenka Bondzio, from Cologne has been traveling to Kenya for ten years. She wrote *A day with George Adamson*.

Michie Gitau is a graduate of the University of Nairobi. He wrote *Masai Mara Game Reserve, Lake Jade, A Dying Paradise?, Richard Leakey* and *Mountain Adventures*.

Eric Hanna is director of a Nairobi advertising agency. He was author and co-author of *The South Coast, Malindi* and *Lamu Archipelago*.

Jean Hartley is a freelance editor and writer in Nairobi. She was author and co-author of *Underwater Wonderland, Diving, Deep Sea Fishing* and *The Coast*.

Brigitte Henninges is a freelance writer and photographer in Munich. For more than 15 years she has been traveling to Kenya. She contributed as author, co-author and editor to the entire book.

Clive Mutiso is an advertising agency director and freelance writer in Nairobi. He was author and co-author of *Lake Naivasha, Lake Elmenteita and Lake Nakuru, Lake Bogoria, Lake Baringo, Thika and Vicinity* and *Sports*.

Clement Obare is a professional educationalist who has served as Provincial Education Officer in several regions of Kenya. He was author of *Kakamega Forest, Lake Victoria* and *Kisumu*.

Prof. Osaga Odak is one of Kenya's leading anthropologists. He teaches at the University of Nairobi. He was author and co-author of *Kenya's People, Kericho, Kitale, A Culinary Tour, Theater and Music* and *Developing Kenya*.

Philip Okwaro is a freelance writer and photographer. For several years he was a game park ranger. He was co-author of *Amboseli National Park*.

Mourine Wambugu is a librarian and freelance writer in Nairobi. She was co-author of *Around Mount Kenya, The Aberdares, Mount Kenya National Park, Meru National Park* and *Samburu, Maralal and Marsabit*.

Rupert Watson is a lawyer and freelance writer. He was author and co-author of *Lake Magadi and Olorgesailie, Nairobi National Park* and *Lakes of the Great Rift Valley*.

PHOTOGRAPHERS

Explore the World

NELLES MAPS

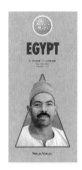

AVAILABLE TITLES

Afghanistan 1 : 1,5 M
Australia 1 : 4 M
Bangkok - *Greater Bangkok,*
Bangkok City 1 : 75 Th / 1 : 15 Th
Burma - *Myanmar* 1 : 1,5 M
Caribbean Islands 1 *Bermuda,*
Bahamas, Greater Antilles
1 : 2,5 M
Caribbean Islands 2 *Lesser Antilles*
1 : 2,5 M
Central America 1 : 1,75 M
Crete - Kreta 1 : 200 Th
China 1 - *Northeastern* 1 : 1,5 M
China 2 - *Northern* 1 : 1,5 M
China 3 - *Central* 1 : 1,5 M
China 4 - *Southern* 1 : 1,5 M
Egypt 1 : 2,5 M / 1 : 750 Th
Hawaiian Islands
1 : 330 Th / 1 : 125 Th
Hawaiian Islands 1 *Kauai* 1 : 125 Th
Hawaiian Islands 2 *Honolulu*
- Oahu 1 : 125 Th
Hawaiian Islands 3 *Maui - Molokai*
- Lanai 1 : 125 Th
Hawaiian Islands 4 *Hawaii, The*
Big Island 1 : 330 Th / 1 : 125 Th
Himalaya 1 : 1,5 M
Hong Kong 1 : 22,5 Th
Indian Subcontinent 1 : 4 M

India 1 - *Northern* 1 : 1,5 M
India 2 - *Western* 1 : 1,5 M
India 3 - *Eastern* 1 : 1,5 M
India 4 - *Southern* 1 : 1,5 M
India 5 - *Northeastern - Bangladesh*
1 : 1,5 M
Indonesia 1 : 4 M
Indonesia 1 *Sumatra* 1 : 1,5 M
Indonesia 2 *Java + Nusa*
Tenggara
1 : 1,5 M
Indonesia 3 *Bali* 1 : 180 Th
Indonesia 4 *Kalimantan* 1 : 1,5 M
Indonesia 5 *Java + Bali* 1 : 650 Th
Indonesia 6 *Sulawesi* 1 : 1,5 M
Indonesia 7 *Irian Jaya + Maluku*
1 : 1,5 M
Jakarta 1 : 22,5 Th
Japan 1 : 1,5 M
Kenya 1 : 1,1 M
Korea 1 : 1,5 M
Malaysia 1 : 1,5 M
West Malaysia 1 : 650 Th
Manila 1 : 17,5 Th
Mexico 1 : 2,5 M
Nepal 1 : 500 Th / 1 : 1,5 M
Trekking Map *Khumbu Himal /*
Solu Khumbu 1 : 75 Th
New Zealand 1 : 1,25 M
Pakistan 1 : 1,5 M
Philippines 1 : 1,5 M

Singapore 1 : 22,5 Th
Southeast Asia 1 : 4 M
Sri Lanka 1 : 450 Th
Tanzania - *Rwanda, Burundi*
1 : 1,5 M
Thailand 1 : 1,5 M
Taiwan 1 : 400 Th
Vietnam, Laos, Cambodia
1 : 1,5 M

FORTHCOMING

Colombia - *Ecuador* 1 : 2,5 M
Trekking Map *Kathmandu Valley /*
Helambu, Langtang 1 : 75 Th
Venezuela - *Guyana, Suriname,*
French Guiana 1 : 2,5 M

Nelles Maps in european top quality!
Relief mapping, kilometer charts and tourist attractions.
Allways up-to-date!

Explore the World

NELLES GUIDE

AVAILABLE TITLES

Australia
Bali / Lombok
Berlin and Potsdam
Brittany
California
 Las Vegas, Reno,
 Baja California
Cambodia / Laos
Canada
 Ontario, Québec,
 Atlantic Provinces
Caribbean
 The Greater Antilles,
 Bermuda, Bahamas
Caribbean
 The Lesser Antilles
China
Crete
Cyprus
Egypt
Florida
Greece - *The Mainland*
Hawaii
Hungary
India
 Northern, Northeastern
 and Central India

India
 Southern India
Indonesia
 Sumatra, Java, Bali,
 Lombok, Sulawesi
Ireland
Kenya
Malaysia
Mexico
Morocco
Moscow / St Petersburg
Munich
 Excursions to Castels,
 Lakes & Mountains
Nepal
New York - *City and State*
New Zealand
Paris
Philippines
Prague / Czech Republic
Provence
Rome
South Africa
Spain - *North*
Spain
 Mediterranean Coast,
 Southern Spain,
 Balearic Islands
Thailand

Turkey
Tuscany
U.S.A.
 The East, Midwest and
 South
U.S.A.
 The West, Rockies and
 Texas
Vietnam

FORTHCOMING

Corsica
Israel - with Excursions
 to Jordan
London, England and Wales
Portugal
Sri Lanka

Nelles Guides – authorative, informed and informative.
Always up-to-date, extensivley illustrated, and with first-rate relief maps.
256 pages, appr. 150 color photos, appr. 25 maps
UK £ 8.95   USA US$ 14.95   AUS $A 21.95